THE ARTIST-OPERAS OF PFITZNER, KRENEK AND HINDEMITH

The Artist-Operas of Pfitzner, Krenek and Hindemith

Politics and the Ideology of the Artist

CLAIRE TAYLOR-JAY

ASHGATE

Published by
Ashgate Publishing Limited
Gower House
Croft Road
Aldershot
Hampshire GU11 3HR
England

Ashgate Publishing Company
Suite 420
101 Cherry Street
Burlington, VT 05401-4405
USA

Ashgate website: http://www.ashgate.com

British Library Cataloguing in Publication Data
Taylor-Jay, Claire
  The artist-operas of Pfitzner, Krenek and Hindemith :
  politics and the ideology of the artist
  1. Pfitzner, Hans, 1863-1949. Palestrina 2. Krenek, Ernst,
  1900-1992. Jonny spielt auf 3. Hindemith, Paul, 1895-1963.
  Mathis der Maler 4. Opera 5. Art and society
  I. Title
  782.1

Library of Congress Cataloging-in-Publication Data
Taylor-Jay, Claire.
    The artist-operas of Pfitzner, Krenek and Hindemith : politics and the ideology
    of the artist / Claire Taylor-Jay.
        p. cm.
    Includes bibliographical references (p.) and index.
    ISBN 0-7546-0578-7 (alk. paper)
        1. Opera–Political aspects–Germany. 2. Opera–Social aspects–Germany. 3.
    Opera–Germany–20th century. 4. Pfitzner, Hans Erich, 1869-1949. Palestrina. 5.
    Krenek, Ernst, 1900-1992. Jonny spielt auf. 6. Hindemith, Paul, 1895-1963. Mathis
    der Maler (Opera) 7. Art and society–Germany–History–20th century. I. Title.

ML3918.O64T39 2003
782.1'092'243–dc21
                                                                    2003041875

ISBN 0 7546 0578 7

Printed and bound in Great Britain by MPG Books Ltd, Bodmin, Cornwall

Contents

List of Music Examples, Tables and Illustrations

Music Examples

Tables

Illustrations

Acknowledgements

I am very grateful to all those who have helped in bringing this book to fruition. It has grown out of my doctoral thesis, and thanks are particularly due to those who commented and advised me at that stage: those who gave hints, and read either chapters or the whole dissertation are Julie Brown, Nicholas Cook, John Deathridge, Erik Levi, Anthony Pople, and Claudia Maurer Zenck. Subsequently, I have benefited from the thoughts of Kevin S. Amidon, Stephen Downes, Peter Franklin, Bennett Zon, and the anonymous readers at Ashgate. For help with tracking down particular pieces of information, I would like to thank David Farneth, James Garrett, and Robert Vilain; and the staff at Ashgate, particularly Rachel Lynch, for editorial guidance.

For funding three years of my doctoral study, I am grateful to the University of Southampton; subsequently, the Deutsche Akademische Austauschdienst and the University of Surrey Roehampton have made research trips to Germany possible. I would like to thank the staff at the Paul Hindemith Institut, Frankfurt am Main, particularly Susanne Schaal-Gotthardt, for their help in providing source materials.

I thank my friends and family who have shown their encouragement, particularly my parents Pat and Bob Jay, and Gerda and Wolfgang Gresser. Finally, for his help and support over the course of the writing and preparation of this book, I am grateful above all to Clemens Gresser.

1 Introduction

According to the nineteenth-century cliché, the creative artist is a mortal on a higher level of existence, ignored and unappreciated by the world around him, deeply feeling and suffering. While reality has rarely been so straightforward, the ideology of the isolated genius has persisted; artists have positioned themselves in relation to this myth ever since it became current. In the early twentieth century, though, with the advent of new technologies and a changing relationship between art and its audience, the idea of what an artist should be, and his or her place within society, began to be re-evaluated. This book investigates re-assessments of the artist ideal which took place in Germany in the first decades of the twentieth century, through examining three 'artist-operas', or, to use the original German nomenclature, *Künstleropern*: Hans Pfitzner's *Palestrina* (completed 1915), Ernst Krenek's *Jonny spielt auf* (1926) and Paul Hindemith's *Mathis der Maler* (1935).[1] Through placing an artist as the central character (composers in the case of the Pfitzner and Krenek operas, a painter in Hindemith's), these *Künstleropern* construct a particular relationship between the character and his social environment; the composers of these works thus contributed to the contemporary debate about the artist and society, and interrogated ideas of what it means to be an artist.

The Relationship of Artist and Society: Historical Perspectives

The idea that an artist would (and perhaps should) be isolated from society appeared in the early nineteenth century, with the rise of Romanticism. Until the end of the eighteenth century, composers were, on the whole, in a secure position regarding their income and their audience, as they were in the service of a patron; Haydn's employment as the court composer at

---

[1] The majority, although not all, of the works in this genre are in German, and may also be seen as an offshoot of the early Romantic German literary genre of *Künstlerroman*, or artist-novel; I will therefore often use the German name in preference to the less widely-found English one.

Esterháza is a typical example. With the decline of such patronage at the end of the eighteenth century, however, brought about chiefly by the evaporation of aristocratic fortunes, composers needed to look for new ways to earn a living. Composers of the Romantic era, like other artists, were now dependent upon their fellow citizens for the means to live, and had to sell their music through concerts and publishers. Many composers embraced this lifestyle, writing 'light' works for the popular market. Simultaneously, though, others deemed that to be a true artist, one must scorn this 'prostitution' of one's superior talents. The belief in the artist as a higher being, above the mundane concerns of the world, was fostered in the late eighteenth century by, for instance, Goethe and Schiller, and embraced by such individuals as Beethoven and Wagner.

For the followers of the Romantic aesthetic, art's purpose was to lead the listener towards the transcendental, and music, in particular, could offer a glimpse of an eternal, ideal reality. However, the Romantic artist believed that few could understand the mystical vision which he was trying to communicate; hence the artist, with apparent reluctance, turns inwards towards his own subjectivity, searching for Utopia, perhaps joined by a select band of faithful disciples. Utopia always remains tantalisingly out of reach, though, and the artist is therefore tormented by unfulfilled longing. The world outside, offering only a cold, monotonous reality and unable or unwilling to understand the artist, is rejected. Rather than embracing his solitude gladly, the artist sees it as an inevitable predicament, given the society in which he finds himself.[2] This is the clichéd description of the artist which has found its way into the popular imagination: the artist pursuing his own dreams and inspiration, whilst living with little money, in poor surroundings, perhaps also plagued by an unrequited love. The Romantic philosophers helped to create this ideal of artistic isolation: Hegel, for instance, argued for the necessity of autonomous art, which carried with it the requirement for a specific, separate 'artistic' way of life for the creator, while Schlegel wrote that the artist's way of life 'should be fundamentally different from that of other people'.[3] The theme of the isolated, tormented

---

[2] See Edward F. Kravitt, 'Romanticism Today', *Musical Quarterly* 76/1 (Spring 1992), 93.

[3] Hegel quoted in Bernhard Schubert, *Der Künstler als Handwerker: zur Literaturgeschichte einer romantischen Utopie* (Königstein: Athenäum Verlag, 1986), 22; Schlegel, 'Ideen', no.146, quoted in ibid. (All translations are my own unless specified otherwise.) On the idea of the artist's loneliness in the nineteenth century, also see Ulrike

individual became a commonplace of Romantic art, encompassing such figures as Goethe's Werther, the hero of Schubert's *Winterreise*, and Wagner's Flying Dutchman. These characters, although not creators, betray a sensitivity to their position in the world which was readily carried over into the ideal of the artist. This concept of the artist itself found expression in works such as Berlioz's *Symphonie Fantastique*, as well as in many *Künstleropern*.

Such a picture of artistic individuals, however, does not tell the complete story, and its ubiquity is to a large extent dependent upon the subsequent writing of history. While the cliché certainly had some currency during the nineteenth century, most artists had more interaction with the real world than this image gives them credit for. Many composers, by necessity or by choice, continued to take part in society, working as teachers, conductors or performers.[4] The artist-myth did persist for some, though, as an ideal: even if composers participated in society out of economic necessity, they may still have felt uncomfortable in it, and aspired to live apart from the world. For some nineteenth-century composers, the belief that music was an art which expressed a higher reality was coupled with a wish to educate a broad audience to the virtues of the art. However, the pedestal on which art, and particularly music, had come to be placed meant that the wish for a wider audience on the part of these composers was on very particular terms. For example, Wagner possessed a messianic vision of a society centred around art, a view which can hardly be compared to the populism of a composer of light opera, although both, in some way, wished to reach a large audience. Unlike his populist contemporary, Wagner's ideal audience was one which revered not only the artist but also art itself, as a manifestation of a higher truth, rather than treating it as mere entertainment. In fact, he viewed anyone who intentionally wrote for the public as engaging in 'a lower form of activity'.[5] Wagner believed that a rebirth of society and of art would only be possible through social revolution. As he wrote in such tracts as 'Art and Revolution' and 'The Artwork

---

Kienzle, *Das Trauma hinter dem Traum: Franz Schrekers Oper 'Der ferne Klang' und die Wiener Moderne* (Schliengen: Edition Argus, 1998), 272.

[4] See John Rink, 'The Profession of Music', in Jim Samson (ed.), *The Cambridge History of Nineteenth-Century Music*, (Cambridge: Cambridge University Press, 2002), 65.

[5] Leon Botstein, *Music and its Public: Habits of Listening and the Crisis of Musical Modernism in Vienna, 1870–1914* (Ph.D. diss., University of Harvard, 1985), 32.

of the Future', art had become a privilege of the wealthy; if capitalist, industrial society were abolished, then the people would be able to listen to music in a suitably respectful way once more.[6] For Wagner, art after the Revolution would become a communal experience, binding the people together, and bringing true spiritual values back into society.[7]

Other nineteenth-century composers paralleled Wagner in their wish to educate the populace while simultaneously maintaining a superior position for music itself and hinting that art could never be comprehended by many. Berlioz's self-organised concerts, for example, were generally staged to appeal to a wide audience, something in the manner of extravaganzas; however, he also helped to cultivate the Romantic myth, with his belief that the great composer is inevitably misunderstood and neglected, having to defend himself against philistines.[8] Berlioz was distrustful of the public, writing of its 'brutishness..., its lack of understanding in matters of imagination and the heart, its love of brilliant platitudes, the baseness of all its melodic and rhythmic instincts'.[9] Liszt, in a similar way to Wagner, saw the artist as a kind of high priest, bringing the religion of art to the people. In his manifesto 'Zur Stellung der Künstler' ('On the Position of the Artist'), he argued for the establishment of music schools and libraries, and for cheap editions of great music, and criticised what he saw as poor teaching and criticism.[10] In contrast, though, in his preface to the 'Album d'un voya-

---

[6] See Martin Gregor-Dellin, *Richard Wagner: His Life, His Work, His Century*, trans. J. Maxwell Brownjohn (London: Collins, 1983), 153, 188, 192 and 217.

[7] Ibid., 215–17, and Henry Raynor, *Music and Society since 1815* (London: Barrie and Jenkins, 1976), 33. Nineteenth-century writers, particularly of the *Junges Deutschland* school, held a similar philosophy, believing in the importance of social revolution in order to bring about an improved place for art (Herbert Marcuse, 'Der deutsche Künstlerroman', in *Schriften*, Vol.1 (Frankfurt a.M.: Suhrkamp Verlag, 1978), 182). According to Botstein, Wagner simultaneously believed in the difficulties an artist faced in finding understanding from the world around him, and saw 'a dialectic of necessary opposition between the public and art' (*Music and its Public*, 32).

[8] Raynor, *Music and Society since 1815*, 23.

[9] Berlioz, *Evenings in the Orchestra*, trans. Charles E. Roche (New York and London: Alfred A. Knopf, 1929), 158. Also see William Weber, 'Wagner, Wagnerism, and Musical Idealism', in David C. Large and William Weber (eds), *Wagnerism in European Culture and Politics* (Ithaca and London: Cornell University Press, 1984), 44.

[10] Alfred Einstein, *Music in the Romantic Era* (London: J.M. Dent and Sons Ltd., 1947),

geur, Années de Pèlerinage' (Book 1 (1842)), he demonstrated his view that art is not for the whole people but for a select few, writing: 'I address myself rather to the individual than the crowd, hoping not for success but for the patience of those few who believe that art has a destiny other than that of whiling away a few empty hours, those who ask of her something more than the mindless distraction of fleeting amusement'.[11]

In the nineteenth century, then, art could occupy a variety of positions in relation to society: it could be revered for its quasi-religious significance, or used solely for the purposes of entertainment; it could be allowed to rest on its higher plane undisturbed, or attempts might be made to bring about a broader understanding of its wonders. At the same time as many artists cultivated a rarefied devotion to art, they could also appreciate the realities of the world around them: economic growth which had provided financial support for the arts, as well as the expansion of education and the benefits of modern technology.[12] Moreover, as Leon Botstein points out, composers were less often ignored than the Romantic aesthetic suggested; even if a composer met with resistance to his or her works at first, it was a relatively short amount of time, within a few decades, before this opinion changed.[13] At the same time as nineteenth-century artists felt themselves misunderstood by the public, this same public wished to venerate the geniuses of both the past and the present.

The creation of the Romantic myth of the isolated artist, and the positions composers took towards their society at this time, were rooted both in aesthetics and in a variety of sociological phenomena which took place during the century. These socio-economic factors, which arose during the course of the nineteenth century and which helped to foster the apparent

---

347. Also see 31.

[11] Quoted in Peter Le Huray and James Day (eds), *Music and Aesthetics in the Eighteenth and Early-Nineteenth Centuries* (Abridged Edition. Cambridge: Cambridge University Press, 1988), 365. Also on Liszt, see John Williamson, 'Progress, Modernity and the Concept of an Avant-Garde', in Samson (ed.), *The Cambridge History of Nineteenth-Century Music, passim.*

[12] Rey M. Longyear, *Nineteenth-century Romanticism in Music* (Englewood Cliffs, NJ: Prentice Hall, 1988), 11.

[13] Botstein, *Music and its Public*, 26 ff. Also see Jim Samson, 'Music and Society', in Jim Samson (ed.), *The Late Romantic Era: From the mid-19th Century to World War I* (London: Macmillan, 1991), 40 ff.

split between composer and audience, have been outlined by Botstein, who discusses how musical life became more institutionalised during the nineteenth century, with the establishment of civic organisations designed to hold concerts and to provide an educational opportunity for the public.[14] As a result, the concert became more significant in the relationship between public and art music than had previously been the case, and the audience for such concerts grew both in size and in the range of social classes attending; public performance also became increasingly professionalised and commercialised.[15] Taste in music was shaped by two further factors: the ubiquity of the piano in music education and as the predominant means of music-making in the home, with a corresponding standardisation of repertoire; and the increase in writing about music by professionals, which became 'essential and crucial avenues for the acquisition and maintenance of musical taste for the music lover and concertgoer'.[16]

Rather than having a positive effect for 'progressive' composers, though, Botstein writes that the consequence of these changes during the nineteenth century was the 'museumization of classical music' – the canonisation of an established repertoire with which the public felt familiar, and through which they felt part of an educated and sophisticated class.[17] Amateurs came to have 'a special sense of competence', because they played the same repertoire as they heard in professional concerts, in arrangements and simplifications.[18] The conjunction of amateurism with expanding numbers of public concerts meant that classical music 'developed a wider-ranging public whose sense of expertise was non-trivial and hard-earned... . That one "understood" music as an art revealed some special achievement'.[19] As a result, Botstein argues, any composer who wrote music which challenged these expectations was likely to find himself or herself marginalised. The public 'did not take lightly any attempt to snub it

---

[14] Botstein, *Music and its Public*, 8 and 81–2. Although Botstein's study is centred specifically on Vienna, his work nevertheless holds good for the musical climate of Europe in this era more generally. Also on the growth of urbanisation and its effects on music, see Longyear, *Nineteenth-century Romanticism in Music*, 3 and 333–4.

[15] Botstein, *Music and its Public*, 9–10.

[16] Ibid., 10.

[17] Ibid.

[18] Ibid., 84.

[19] Ibid.

or to challenge its hard-earned and special self-image as musically know-ledgeable and highly cultured. ...It was sensitive to insult and took evident umbrage at a young composer's seeming unwillingness to speak a musical language with which it was familiar and which it associated with the tradi-tion of great classical music'.[20] By the late nineteenth century, therefore, composers potentially found themselves in a position of increasing isola-tion, particularly if they wished to reach beyond the conventions of musical style; this situation both reinforced and contributed to the image of the lonely Romantic artist.

Artist and Society in the Early Twentieth Century

After the formulation and widespread acceptance of an aesthetic viewpoint during the nineteenth century which gave a privileged position to 'Art', and where artists called their relationship to the world increasingly into ques-tion, the period around the *fin-de-siècle* gave rise to cultural and sociologi-cal phenomena which seemed to add new urgency to the issue of an artist's interaction with society. In the decades around and following World War I, composers in Germany took various positions regarding the Romantic ideal of the artist, from outright rejection by those composers happy to be popu-lar, to an even more extreme extension of the myth amongst the modernists. The split between popular and 'art' musics, which had begun to take place during the previous century, continued, and was exacerbated by the pro-found changes in musical life, and in society more generally, which took place at this time. Simultaneously, many early twentieth-century artists followed the logic of the nineteenth-century ideal, and deliberately pursued their own solitary aims. Disdain for the audience in these circles became more explicit, and composers such as Schoenberg expressed the view that it was up to the audience to follow the artist's path, rather than vice versa.

Other cultural factors contributed to how artists saw their place in the world, as an unprecedented change in the structure of Western society took place. What Marshall Berman calls the 'maelstrom' of modern existence was set in motion through technological advances and increased industri-alisation, which let to demographic upheaval, rapid ubranisation and the

---

[20] Ibid., 86. Also see Katharine Ellis, 'The Structures of Musical Life', in Samson (ed.), *The Cambridge History of Nineteenth-Century Music*, 350.

destruction of old environments.[21] The structure of everyday life altered, with an increase in the tempo of existence, the generation of an increasingly capitalistic and corporate economy, and the advent of systems of mass communication. In addition to these material changes, previous intellectual paradigms were challenged, and replaced, from the latter part of the nineteenth century, with such innovations as those of Darwin, what Nietzsche called the 'death of God', and the shift in ideas about individual identity provoked by Freud.[22] While some of these phenomena had their roots in the nineteenth century, others were specific to the early twentieth century or an even more closely definable period such as the 1920s. Contributing to the sense of upheaval were specific political events, such as World War I, and, in Germany, the 1918 revolution and subsequent founding of the Weimar Republic. Wilfried van der Will writes of the twenties that 'nowhere had the modernization process occurred with such haste as in Germany. In the space of two generations industrialization, urbanization and mass society, the anonymity of mechanized warfare, the overthrow of the monarchy, the establishment of republican democracy, the advent of ideological pluralism, and the rationalization of large parts of the economy had all followed in rapid succession. ...If Germany had initially lagged behind in all the major developments which brought about modernity, it made up for lost ground through the intensity of the process of catching up'.[23]

These rapid changes in society naturally had an effect on the individuals who lived through them. Some people could accept the shifts which were taking place with excitement and enthusiasm, but for many this was a time of dangerous uncertainty and crisis, and even those who were less hostile than others to modern innovation could still feel unsettled by the pace of

---

[21] Berman, *All That is Solid Melts Into Air: The Experience of Modernity* (New York: Simon and Schuster, 1982), 16.

[22] Ibid., 21; Christopher Butler, *Early Modernism: Literature, Music, and Painting in Europe, 1900–1916* (Oxford: Clarendon Press, 1994), 89; Jacques Le Rider, *Modernity and Crises of Identity: Culture and Society in Fin-de-Siècle Vienna*, trans. Rosemary Morris (Cambridge: Polity Press, 1993), 31. Jim Samson says that Freud's achievement 'was magnificently expressive of the universal change in interpretative perspective which accompanied modernity' ('Music and Society', 44).

[23] van der Will, 'Culture and the Organization of National Socialist Ideology 1933 to 1945', in Rob Burns (ed.), *German Cultural Studies: An Introduction* (Oxford: Oxford University Press, 1995), 105.

change around them. The early twentieth-century response to the contemporary alterations in society has been summed up by many later historians as one of crisis and alienation, in which modernity was frequently seen as dangerous to moral and spiritual well-being. Detlev Peukert, for instance, points to this traumatic experience of modern life in his book, *The Weimar Republic: The Crisis of Classical Modernity*, while van der Will comments that the process of modernisation 'exacted a profound psychological price and inflicted on German society traumatic experiences in a crisis where everything that was modern appeared only to spell political and social division, alienation, and proletarianization'.[24] The sweeping changes in society had an effect on the social position of composers and musicians, which was accompanied by a shift within the language of music itself. In combination, these two factors added to a sense amongst many composers that they needed to redefine their place in the world.

The perception of a crisis in musical life in Germany in the years around and after World War I is shown in the frequent discussions at this time about the problematic relationship between musicians and audiences. Egon Wellesz traced the contemporary predicament back to the years preceding the war, expressing in 1922 his belief that the situation had arisen as the result of earlier trends: 'What we are experiencing today, what divides our time, our feelings, our experience from that of earlier epochs is the crisis of the individual. Romanticism cultivated it, and the time at the turn of the century led it to its highest intensification; we see its fruit, the fruit of this excess, in the spiritual and material devastation which we experience everywhere'.[25] Max Hofmüller, discussing opera, attributed the same problem to the emergence of numerous musical styles: 'The diversity of styles had to lead to a levelling. ...the most important appearances of inner illness (*inneren Krankheitserscheinungen*) are to be found in the splintering of styles. It brings opera into danger of losing its strongest and most beautiful power: to awaken the listener's experience of his soul'.[26] Josef Dasatiel

---

[24] Peukert, *The Weimar Republic: The Crisis of Classical Modernity*, trans. Richard Deveson (London: Penguin, 1991); van der Will, 'Culture and the Organization of National Socialist Ideology', 105.

[25] Wellesz, 'Der Musiker und diese Zeit', *Anbruch* 4/1–2 (1922). 3. Also see Susan Cook, *Opera for a New Republic: The* Zeitopern *of Krenek, Weill and Hindemith* (Ann Arbor: UMI Research Press, 1988), 3 and 9–10.

[26] Hofmüller, 'Opernkrise und Stilpflege', *Anbruch* 9/1–2 (1927). 30. Also on contempo-

pointed out that the wish by composers to go to 'extremes', which had begun at the turn of the century, had helped to give rise to an economic crisis in the music industry as a whole. Composers demanded larger and more expensive orchestras, which resulted in higher ticket/prices that could not be afforded by the middle classes, and the costs of the event were therefore not covered.[27]

Other economic and cultural factors came into play after World War I which further changed the cultural environment for composers. The effects of the 1918 revolution in Germany and the hyperinflationary period of the early twenties altered the audience for art music, bringing about what was called the *Umschichtung* of society, the rearrangement of the constitution of social classes. Michael Walter comments that the middle-class public were less able to afford to go to concerts and opera during the inflationary period, and were effectively 'dispossessed'.[28] A contemporary writer, Paul A. Pisk, commented that this process of *Umschichtung* had begun in the last third of the previous century, but had become ever stronger, and was 'particularly hastened' during the war and the inflation. 'The middle class, the art-consuming majority (*Masse*) at that time, has since then disintegrated, a course of events which was brought about by the history of the economy'.[29] The 'devastation', as Wellesz termed it, was described by Kurt Weill, who said that concert life in big cities was 'useless, unworkable...[it] has had its day'; the music industry 'has become unprofitable', and virtuosos 'appear every evening before empty halls'.[30] Parallel views were expressed about the situation of opera. Hugo Leichtentritt said that the severe financial situation following the war 'endangers the prosperity of

---

rary debates about opera, see Kevin Scott Amidon, *'Nirgends brennen wir genauer': Institution, Experiment, and Crisis in the German* Zeitoper, *1924–31* (University of Princeton: Ph.D. dissertation, 2001), 5 ff.

[27] Dr. Jos. A. Dasatiel [sic], 'Die musikalischen Krisen der Gegenwart', *Anbruch* 3/17–18 (1921), 304–5.

[28] Walter, *Hitler in der Oper: Deutsches Musikleben 1919–1945* (Stuttgart and Weimar: Verlag J.B. Metzler, 1995), 106–7.

[29] Pisk, 'Das neue Publikum', *Anbruch* 9/1–2 (1927), 94.

[30] Weill, 'Fort vom Durchschnitt! Zur Krise der musikalischen Interpretation' *(Berliner Börsen-Courier*, 29th August 1925), in Stephen Hinton and Jürgen Schebera (eds), *Musik und Theater: Gesammelte Schriften* (Berlin: Henschelverlag Kunst und Gesellschaft, 1990), 22.

opera to a degree which must disturb all true friends of dramatic music. ...German opera is now threatening to die off slowly'.[31] Similarly, Hofmüller commented that 'the economic conditions and the reorganisation of the classes (*Umschichtung*) in our society after the war brought about our critical condition in opera'.[32]

A number of other significant developments in musical life at this time helped to reshape the landscape within which composers worked. One of the most significant of these during the years leading up to World War II was the apparently irresistible rise of popular music. This was significantly affected by the impact of new technology, and made a considerable impression on composers' perceptions of their roles. Especially in the years following World War I, technological advances had immediate and tangible consequences. Gottfried Wagner writes that 'the thrillingly quick technical developments at this time opened up new paths; simultaneously, *the* problem of this century became ever clearer with it: the confrontation of the artist with the mass in the context of industrial society. The development of mass media...forced one to confront this phenomenon'.[33] Recording was the most well-established of the new technologies: while the very first recording dated back as far as 1857, the modern recording industry was established in 1877, when Edison invented the phonograph. Commercial recordings were available from 1888, and the gramophone gradually became more and more popular, with many homes possessing one by the early 1920s.[34] Improvements in technology, especially the change from acoustic to electric recording in 1923, made the recording process easier and more lifelike, resulting in cheaper, better quality recordings.[35] Recording redefined the musical environment and the audience for music, and

---

[31] Leichtentritt, 'Die deutsche Opernbühne und der künstlerische Nachwuchs', *Anbruch* 8/5 (1926), 217 and 220. Also see Michael Walter, *Hitler in der Oper*, 101 ff.

[32] Hofmüller, 'Opernkrise und Stilpflege', 30. Also see Grosch, *Die Musik der Neuen Sachlichkeit* (Stuttgart and Weimar: Verlag J.B. Metzler, 1999), 6, and Amidon, *'Nirgends brennen wir genauer'*, *passim*.

[33] Wagner, *Weill und Brecht: Das musikalische Zeittheater* (Munich: Kindler Verlag, 1977), 25.

[34] 'Sound Recording', in Stanley Sadie (ed.), *The New Grove Dictionary of Music and Musicians* (London: Macmillan, 1980), Vol.17. Also 'Gramophone' in ibid., Vol.7.

[35] Christopher Hailey, *Franz Schreker, 1878–1934: A Cultural Biography* (Cambridge: Cambridge University Press, 1993), 229.

therefore had an impact on the perceived position of the composer within society. They were likely to be of popular music in order to appeal to a mass audience, precisely the people from whom the contemporary composer felt isolated; alternatively, they would be recordings of 'classics', thereby exacerbating the problem of a 'museumised' established repertoire. Recording also changed the psychological relationship to music, which now became an 'object' to be possessed, rather than an event.[36]

Other technologies contributed to this changing landscape. Radio was a more recent phenomenon than recording, dating from Marconi's experiments in 1896. The first public broadcasting stations were not established until several decades later: the BBC was the first station in Europe, in 1922, with Germany following in 1923 (the first Berlin station) and 1924 (in other German cities).[37] Christopher Hailey writes that radio was 'the most far-reaching post-war development' in technology, and that its 'enormous potential – as well as significant limitations – had a profound impact upon the relationship between musicians and audiences'.[38] Another important technological development was film. Both silent film and the later arrival of sound film (in 1927) impacted on the professional musician: both kinds of film required music in some form, thereby potentially offering employment. However, at the same time, the cut-rate ticket prices available to cinema-goers meant that this new form of entertainment was in direct competition with older traditions, such as the opera and the concert, and had the added attraction of its novelty.[39] The new technologies meant that the future for musicians was less certain: a piece of music need only be recorded once, and then existed independently of the performer. This threatened the

---

[36] See Michael Chanan, *Repeated Takes: A Short History of Recording and its Effects on Music* (London: Verso, 1995).

[37] 'Broadcasting', in Sadie (ed.), *The New Grove Dictionary of Music and Musicians*, Vol.3. For statistics about radio in Germany, see Peukert, *The Weimar Republic*, 171 and Hailey, *Franz Schreker*, 230.

[38] Hailey, 'Rethinking Sound: Music and Radio in Weimar Germany', in Bryan Gilliam (ed.), *Music and Performance during the Weimar Republic* (Cambridge Studies in Performance Practice 3. Cambridge: Cambridge University Press, 1994), 13.

[39] Bryan Gilliam, 'Stage and Screen: Kurt Weill and Operatic Reform in the 1920s', in Gilliam (ed.), *Music and Performance during the Weimar Republic*, 1.

livelihood of musicians, who feared that they might now be expendable, at the same time as it offered practical opportunities.[40]

New technology was seen to exacerbate the problems brought about by the difficult economic situation. Weill, for instance, points not only to changes in material conditions, the impoverishment of people interested in music and a surplus of artistic performances, but also to the radio, 'which lures the masses through its convenience, cheapness, and through the appeal of the new'.[41] Leichtentritt made a parallel observation: 'German theatres suffer not only because of the economic depression; the *Umschichtung* of the public, the impoverishment of the educated middle class, the taste of the broader circle of the people which has become raw, [and] the concurrence of cinema and radio, help to pull the ground away from under the operatic stage'.[42] Critics were eager to discuss the implications of the new technology, and many saw it as a threat to the existing musical order. Alfred Baresel, for instance, said that the danger of technology and broadcasting for 'real' art was not grounded in the specific characteristics of the technology itself, but in a 'striving for comfort' on the part of the public.[43] One of the most well-known detractors from technology was the philosopher T.W. Adorno, who had a similar view to Baresel, reviling what he would later call the 'culture industry' which, he believed, indoctrinated the populace and required it to assert no intellectual effort.[44] Arnold Schoenberg too expressed reservations about the new technological advances: in 1930, he declared 'Quite certainly the radio is a foe! – and so are the gramophone and soundfilm. ...opposition is a hopeless prospect'. Schoenberg objected to the radio because it 'accustoms the ear to an unspeakable coarse tone', and resulted in a 'boundless surfeit of music', which 'will lead to a state where all music has been consumed, worn out'.[45]

---

[40] For more on the impact of radio, recording and film on performing musicians, see Joel Sachs, 'Some Aspects of Musical Politics in pre-Nazi Germany', *Perspectives of New Music* 9/1 (Fall–Winter 1970), 94.

[41] Weill, 'Fort vom Durchschnitt!', 22. However, Weill also believed that radio offered interesting new opportunities to composers.

[42] Leichtentritt, 'Die deutsche Opernbühne', 220. Also see Walter, *Hitler in der Oper*, 108.

[43] Baresel, 'Kunst, Technik und Publikum', *Anbruch* 8/2 (1926), 61.

[44] See Adorno, *Philosophy of Modern Music* (London: Sheed and Ward, 1973), 10.

[45] Arnold Schoenberg, *Style and Idea: Selected Writings of Arnold Schoenberg*, ed. Leonard Stein, trans. Leo Black (London: Faber and Faber, 1975), 147.

Others, though, were more positive. Leichtentritt saw new technology as playing an important role in the dissemination of music: 'What the individual can no longer play himself at home will be played by professional artists to the hundreds of thousands, who can absorb it comfortably at their leisure at home'. Artists were therefore presented with an opportunity: it must be 'a concern of interested circles to ensure that an intelligent choice of works' is presented, so that 'repeated hearing of important works at appropriate intervals' is made possible. This would in time produce 'repercussions for our desolate concert life. In the long run, radio and gramophone are only a substitute for a real performance', so as a result, the 'now well-prepared amateurs', who have become familiar with a work through frequent hearings at home, will 'gladly go to hear it in the concert hall'.[46] Many saw technology as an opportunity; even Schoenberg, despite his frequent misgivings, could see its uses. In 1930, he wrote to the *Intendant* of Berlin Radio that it would be 'a very good idea' to have a series of broadcasts 'with the title *Propaganda* for New Music', with 'elucidatory talks' as well as performances, which would 'help to create a basis of understanding'.[47] In the same year, he wrote his *Begleitungsmusik zu einer Lichtspielszene*, a short accompaniment to an imaginary film.

Other composers wrote specifically for new technology, for instance, Weill, Hindemith and Franz Schreker; it was also given a place in many operas of the era, such as the radio in Krenek's *Jonny spielt auf* and the gramophone in Weill's *Der Zar lässt sich photographieren*. Schreker's experiments are discussed by Hailey in his essay 'Rethinking Sound: Music and Radio in Weimar Germany'. Hailey demonstrates how the limitations of the radio medium at this time – its weak projection of bass lines and the way in which some instruments became indistinguishable in timbre from others – affected the musical style of the works Schreker wrote as radio commissions.[48] In 1927, Hindemith helped to institute a department to work with radio at the Hochschule für Musik in Berlin, where he was a pro-

---

[46] Leichtentritt, 'Konzertierende Künstler und zeitgenössische Musik', *Anbruch* 8/6 (1926), 279.

[47] Schoenberg, *Letters*, ed. Erwin Stein, trans. Eithne Wilkins and Ernst Kaiser (London: Faber and Faber, 1964), 137 (Feb.–March 1930). Schoenberg's emphasis. Also see Grosch, *Die Musik der Neuen Sachlichkeit*, 11–12, 43 and 187.

[48] Hailey, 'Rethinking Sound', *passim*.

fessor, and also wrote film music and music for mechanical instruments.[49] Weill was particularly interested in new technology, and wrote for the radio magazine *Der deutsche Rundfunk* between January 1925 and May 1929.[50] He frequently expressed a positive opinion about technology: an interview with Weill in 1927 reported that the composer believed that 'today, all young creative musicians must engage with the question of how film music is created', while in 1926 he commented that the radio has become 'one of the most important factors of modern public life'.[51] Weill said that he could understand why both creative and performing musicians could see radio as a threat, but countered that radio has an important place in the reorganisation of musical life, taking music out of the exclusive world of the well-off, and bringing it to the majority of people who have been 'musically dispossessed'.[52]

Whether the reaction to it was one of enthusiastic embrace or categorical rejection, technology had a considerable impact on composers' standing towards society during the 1920s, and helped to redefine their relationship to their audiences. Another important cultural development which took place at this time, and through which some composers similarly reoriented themselves towards particular audiences, was the attempt made by political movements during the early decades of the century to bring music to the 'people'. Of primary importance here are the 'Music Movements' of the Socialist and Communist parties, in both Germany and Austria, which had begun during the 1890s. These movements boasted a large membership; for instance, the Socialist Party's *Deutscher Arbeiter-Sängerbund* (German Workers' Singers' League), founded in 1908, became one of biggest organisations of its kind in world in the 1920s, reaching a membership of

---

[49] Cook, *Opera for a New Republic*, 21. Also on 'mechanical music', see Grosch, *Die Musik der neuen Sachlichkeit*, 49 ff., and on radio music, ibid., 181 ff.

[50] Stephen Hinton and Jürgen Schebera, 'Editorische Vorbemerkung', in Weill, *Musik und Theater*, 163–5. Also see Amidon, *'Nirgends brennen wir genauer'*, 173.

[51] Weill, 'Musikalische Illustration oder Filmmusik?' (*Film-Kurier*, 13th October 1927), *Musik und Theater*, 297; 'Der Rundfunk und die Umschichtung des Musiklebens' (*Der deutsche Rundfunk*, 13th June 1926), *Musik und Theater*, 221.

[52] Ibid., 223. In an earlier article about the radio, he wrote that it has brought about a revitalisation of musical life ('Die Stellung des Rundfunks innerhalb des Musiklebens' *(Der deutsche Rundfunk*, 21st June 1925), *Musik und Theater*, 191).

440,000 in 1928.[53] The aims of the Social Democratic Party (*Sozialdemo-kratische Partei Deutschlands*, or SPD) and the Communists in instituting these organisations diverged. Somewhat in a spirit of paternal benevolence, the SPD organised musical activities, such as orchestras and especially choirs, in working-class districts in an effort to educate the ordinary people about classical music. Their repertoire consisted chiefly of art-music of the seventeenth to nineteenth centuries.[54] R. John Specht writes that 'the fundamental principle underlying efforts to organize the proletariat was one of "highmindedness mingled with social puritanism". There was a belief that, if the worker was sober, well read, and "cultured", he would come to understand the undesirable position of his own class within the empire and would certainly then join the struggle for a socialist society'.[55] The conductors of these SPD-affiliated groups were sometimes renowned musicians: both Schoenberg and Webern, for instance, conducted workers' choruses for a time.[56] With their belief in the value of educating the popu-

---

[53] Pamela M. Potter, *Most German of the Arts: Musicology and Society from the Weimar Republic to the End of Hitler's Reich* (New Haven and London: Yale University Press, 1998), 5; Jost Hermand and Frank Trommler, *Die Kultur der Weimarer Republik* (Munich: Nymphenburger Verlagshandlung, 1978), 124 and 342. Parallel cultural groups, such as the *Arbeiter-Theater-Bund* (Workers' Theatre League), were even larger, the latter boasting 600,000 members. Similar activities included *Buchgemeinschaften* ('book communities'), and an *Arbeiter-Radio-Klub* (Workers' Radio Club), as well as numerous sporting societies (ibid., 124).

[54] Hermand and Trommler say, for instance, that an extensive part of the repertoire of the *Arbeiter-Sängerbund* was 'bourgeois men's chorus music (*bürgerliche Männergesangs-vereinmusik*) of the nineteenth century' (ibid., 342). Also see Potter, *Most German of the Arts*, 6; Eckhard John, *Musikbolschewismus: Die Politisierung der Musik in Deutschland 1918–1938* (Stuttgart and Weimar: Verlag J.B. Metzler, 1994), 304–5; and David B. Dennis, *Beethoven in German Politics, 1870–1989* (New Haven and London: Yale University Press, 1996), 57.

[55] Specht, 'Schoenberg Among the Workers: Choral Conducting in pre-1900 Vienna', *Journal of the Arnold Schoenberg Institute* 10/1 (1987), 29.

[56] Schoenberg conducted men's choruses in the towns of Stockerau, Meidling and Mödling, and wrote at least one song for them, 'Aus den "Flüchtlingssonetten vom Jahr 1849" von Ludwig Pfau', in 1897; see Albrecht Dümling, '"Im Zeichen der Erkenntnis der sozialen Verhältnisse": Der junge Schönberg und die Arbeitersängerbewegung in Österreich', *Österreichische Musikzeitschrift* 36/2 (Feb. 1981), 71. Webern conducted the Schubert-bund (1921–2), the Vienna Workers' Symphony Concerts (1922–34), the Mödling Male

lace about the virtues of art, these socialist movements may be seen as an attempt to put into practice the philosophies of Wagner and Liszt, regarding the artist's function to serve as an art-priest who administers to the public.

The activities organised under the aegis of the Communist Party, in contrast to those of the SPD, took a more obviously political line from the early years of the Weimar Republic, for instance with their agit-prop theatre productions.[57] The Communists were often critical of SPD organisations such as the *Arbeiter-Sängerbund*, seeing them as pandering to the taste of the bourgeoisie instead of agitating for real political reform. Writing in 1931, Hanns Eisler described the repertoire of the Social Democratic movement and dismissed its ideological implications: 'The reformist musical activity of the Social Democrats is only the cheap noise-making (*Abklatsch*) of the bourgeois middle class. They are for concert music and for [Fritz] Jöde and for Stravinsky and for Richard Strauss. They are, generally, for everything'.[58] Of the *Arbeiter-Sängerbund*, he said that the organisation 'stands under the leadership of reformism and the petty-bourgeoisie. ...Their political art (*Tendenzkunst*) is petty-bourgeois, red-tinted music-material. Their position is more reactionary than progressive'.[59]

As well as these musical ensembles associated with left-wing political parties, similar organisations existed which were affiliated with radical right-wing politics, despite being similar in their musical practices. The *Wandervogel* and the *Bündische Jugend* are instances of such right-wing groups explicitly aimed at children and young people, which, like their socialist and communist counterparts, used communal music-making to disseminate a political ideology, this time a nationalist one. They therefore placed particular emphasis on folk music, and nominally rejected most 'art' music, which was seen as inaccessible to ordinary people. (Despite this, classical music of the eighteenth and nineteenth centuries was played in

---

Chorus (1921–6) and the Vienna Workers' Chorus (1923–34) (Paul Griffiths, 'Webern', in *The New Grove: Second Viennese School* (London: Macmillan, 1980), 90). For Schoenberg's later attitude to his time conducting these choirs, see *Style and Idea*, 505–6.

[57] Hermand and Trommler, *Die Kultur der Weimarer Republik*, 125.

[58] Quoted in ibid., 342. Jöde was one of the leading members of the Youth Music Movement.

[59] Ibid.

practice.)[60] Such organisations were later to become incorporated into the National Socialist movement. Other amateur organisations also flourished at this time which had no direct involvement with political parties, but which nevertheless betrayed clear ideological standpoints. The *Deutscher Sängerbund*, for example, unlike its counterpart the *Deutscher Arbeiter-Sängerbund*, was nominally independent of political organisations, but nevertheless saw itself as fostering a German identity through music. Its charter of 1927 stated its goal as 'the proliferation and refinement of German male choral singing and the promotion of German feeling. ...Through the unifying power of German song [the organization] hopes to preserve and enhance the German national consciousness and a feeling of solidarity among German tribes'.[61] The *Deutscher Sängerbund* had a membership far exceeding that of its socialist rival; in 1929 it possessed at least 1.3 million members, spread throughout 13,000 choirs.

If the socialist music movement followed the lead of nineteenth-century composers by seeking to educate the people through art, another important aspect of the nineteenth-century aesthetic was also to have its implications carried further. The Romantic cult of Art as Religion became of prime importance to the generation of modernists, and it is here where the belief in the necessity of the artist's separation from society became confirmed. These composers had a highly ambivalent, and often hostile, relationship to their potential audiences, and, following the nineteenth-century lead, saw popularity as antithetical to true artistry. In his discussion of nineteenth-century 'Wagnerism', William Weber suggests that the roots of this characteristically modernist position lay in the Wagnerians' assertion of the controversial and progressive nature of modern music, which to them was a positive indication of quality.[62] The Wagnerian movement split into those who, following Wagner's own philosophy, wished to expand the audience for concerts, and those who were devoted to supporting the newest music, unconcerned with whether or not an audience existed for it. Weber argues that this latter trend became stronger as the century came to a close, so that by the 1890s, avant-garde composers were likely to reject the public, and

---

[60] Potter, *Most German of the Arts*, 7–9.

[61] Quoted in ibid., 5.

[62] William Weber, 'Wagner, Wagnerism, and Musical Idealism', in David C. Large and William Weber (eds), *Wagnerism in European Culture and Politics* (Ithaca and London: Cornell University Press, 1984), 63.

began to define their role as separate, both in the musical and the social spheres. This Romantic 'idealist' trend metamorphosed into radical modernism.[63] The perception of the relationship between artist and society as being inherently problematic thus became firmly established in the early decades of the twentieth century.

Many of the modernist composers of the *fin-de-siècle* decades were suspicious of any wish for wide public acceptance; Jim Samson comments that modernism 'took the form of an inward-looking crisis of expression, alienated from the public, jealous of the integrity of art and protective of its "truthfulness"'.[64] This self-conscious estrangement became manifest in the works of the leading avant-garde composers in Germany and Austria, the prime example being Schoenberg, and, as well as following the aesthetics of the nineteenth century, was a reaction to the cultural circumstances of the time. Reinhold Brinkmann has argued that Schoenberg's atonal music is not only part of a music-historical process, but was the 'reflection of a very specific and problematic historical, social, cultural and psychical situation' of *fin-de-siècle* Vienna. Schoenberg's music is 'at once a subject of this state of mind and its complex symbolic representation'.[65] Many of Schoenberg's Expressionist works, for instance *Erwartung* or *Die glückliche Hand*, feature characters in a traumatic situation, and display a turning-inward that seems to leave little room for consideration of the outside world; Brinkmann notes that *Erwartung* is a *mono*-drama.[66]

According to Brinkmann, Schoenberg's introspection 'could be demonstrated in compositional terms'; he cites Schoenberg's 'antimonumental, antisymphonic poetics of the "critical years" around 1910'. Schoenberg

---

63 Ibid., 68.

64 Samson, 'Music and Society', 43. Samson is here discussing the situation in Vienna specifically, but as German-speaking countries were in many ways unified in cultural terms at this time, his comments can be taken as indicative of the situation throughout Germany and Austria.

65 Brinkmann, 'Schoenberg the Contemporary: A View from Behind', in Juliane Brand and Christopher Hailey (eds), *Constructive Dissonance: Arnold Schoenberg and the Transformations of Twentieth-Century Culture* (Berkeley, Los Angeles and London: University of California Press, 1997), 197.

66 Ibid., 200. Also see Robert W. Witkin, *Adorno on Music* (London and New York: Routledge, 1998), 131. Schoenberg's pupil Berg engaged with the same theme of isolation in his opera *Wozzeck*.

withdrew from large genres and the complicated formal constructions of the Viennese and German tradition, instead writing in 'lyrical genres such as lied and character piece'.[67] Brinkmann calls these works, along with the comparable short pieces by Berg and especially Webern, 'intense moments of inwardness'. Jonathan Dunsby writes on the same theme, commenting of *Pierrot Lunaire* that the *commedia dell'arte* figures were employed by writers of the era because 'their disembodiment, usually as marionettes or puppets; and their lack of rootedness...symbolized the cruel alienation of the times'.[68] Not only Schoenberg's compositions but also his paintings point to his estrangement; Brinkmann says that his series of paintings of eyes are 'pictorial realizations' of the '"cry of despair" of the isolated individual', while his 'Self-Portrait from Behind' similarly stresses the subject's rejection of his surrounding environment, with his back turned to the viewer.[69] Perhaps the quintessential example from Schoenberg's oeuvre of a work dealing with individual isolation is his *Moses und Aron*, although unlike some of his other pieces, this opera deliberately explores the place of such an individual within society through the contrast of the prophet Moses, who is in contact with God yet cannot express his vision, with Aron, who can communicate with the people but distorts the message in doing so.[70]

Schoenberg's belief that isolation was necessary for true art is a theme accentuated in his writings throughout his life, for instance in his well-known comment from 1946 that 'if it is art, it is not for all, and if it is for

---

[67] Brinkmann, 'Schoenberg the Contemporary', 200.

[68] Dunsby, *Schoenberg:* Pierrot Lunaire (Cambridge: Cambridge University Press, 1992), 7.

[69] Brinkmann, 'Schoenberg the Contemporary', 199 and 202. This is even more apparent in an early sketch for the painting which Brinkmann discusses, in which Schoenberg is surrounded by, yet isolated from, a city landscape.

[70] This contrast between individual and society has led some writers, for instance John Bokina and Peter Tregear, to hold that *Moses und Aron* is an artist-opera, despite the fact that Moses is not an artist (Bokina, 'Resignation, Retreat and Impotence: The Aesthetics and Politics of the Modern German Artist-Opera', *Cultural Critique* 9 (Spring 1988), 183 (reprinted in his *Opera and Politics: From Monteverdi to Henze* (New Haven and London: Yale University Press, 1997)); Tregear, *Ernst Krenek and the Politics of Musical Style* (University of Cambridge: Ph.D. dissertation, 1999), 139 and 175).

all, it is not art';[71] it found practical expression in his Society for Private Musical Performances. A similar sentiment was expressed by Schoenberg's contemporary, Busoni, who wrote that 'it is absolutely necessary for one to have the highest ideals to be able to appreciate the highest things. The artist should therefore receive money to be able to avoid popularity, since it is only in relative isolation that he can continue to aim at higher things'.[72] In his revealingly titled essay of 1937, 'How One Becomes Lonely', Schoenberg expresses his belief that his adoption of serialism, which led to increased isolation, was a matter of necessity, compelled, it seems, by higher forces. 'While composing for me had been a pleasure, now it became a duty. I knew I had to fulfil a task; I had to express what was necessary to be expressed and I knew I had the duty of developing my ideas for the sake of progress in music, whether I liked it or not; but I also had to realize that the great majority of the public did not like it'.[73] At the same time, Schoenberg gives indications that he is ambivalent towards his audiences and their reactions to his music. In 'My Public' of 1930, he contends that it is only a 'small but active "expert" minority' which objects to his music during concerts.[74] On the contrary, he says, the public 'as a whole...[is] always rather inclined to enjoy something they have devoted time and money to', and goes on to report the positive reactions he has received towards his music from an army sergeant, a night porter, a taxi driver, a hired man and a lift man.[75]

Schoenberg's pronouncements are typical of a tendency which persisted as the twentieth century progressed, and of which he was one of the earliest representatives. This is the inclination to see art as necessarily separate from society if it is to be 'true', and, concomitantly, the requirement that the artist himself or herself remain apart from the world. Modernist composers followed the implications of the idea of transcendent Art, inherited from the previous century, and in doing so, disregarded the potential, and actual, effects this would have upon their public. 'By rejecting the bourgeois audience that had created the social possibility of nineteenth-century

---

[71] Schoenberg, *Style and Idea*, 124.

[72] Busoni, *Selected Letters*, trans., ed. and intro. Antony Beaumont (New York: Columbia University Press, 1987), 211 (18th August 1915).

[73] Schoenberg, *Style and Idea*, 53.

[74] Ibid., 97.

[75] Ibid., 98.

music, [the radical artist] condemned himself to the role of the uncompre-hended outsider, with only ironic counterfeits, mystic invocations and penitential silences with which to beg his keep from those same consumers of art that he had previously rejected'.[76] One of the principal exponents of this aesthetic doctrine was Adorno, who made the imperative isolation of modern art a cornerstone of his theory. According to Adorno, the crisis of modernity was characterised by the disjunction between the individual and society, with society holding a dominant position over the powerless sub-ject. The measure of the truth-value of an artwork lay in how far it was able to reproduce this disparity within itself.[77] Modern artworks must, therefore, be autonomous from society if they are to be 'true', as only then can they reflect society as it is, and avoid becoming a 'commodity'; autonomy must be achieved through the use of a complex, 'difficult' musical surface.[78] Adorno viewed Schoenberg's music in particular as fulfilling his criteria for 'true' art, even if, simultaneously, he was sceptical about the twelve-tone technique.[79]

The dominance of modernism in histories of twentieth-century music, and concomitantly the perpetuation of an aesthetic which demands the spiritual, and even practical, isolation of the artist, has often disguised the fact that this aesthetic has never been a given, but has been hotly contested, especially in the early years of the twentieth century.[80] While the Schoen-bergian and Adornian army may have won the battle, it was not the only participant. Other composers engaged with the theme of the place of the artist in society during these years and, as we will see, produced widely varying positions. In the years following World War I, we may discern a population of composers which took disparate stances towards the problem of art and society. Broadly speaking, these groups ranged from the most conservative, in both style and outlook, including Pfitzner and Richard Strauss (at least discounting the latter's brief foray into the avant-garde with *Salome* and *Elektra*), through the Second Viennese School, to the

---

[76] Peter Franklin, *The Idea of Music: Schoenberg and Others* (London: Macmillan, 1985), 164.

[77] Witkin, *Adorno on Music*, 4.

[78] Martin Jay, *Adorno* (Cambridge, Mass.: Harvard University Press, 1984), 159. Also Wit-kin, *Adorno on Music*, 11 and 17.

[79] See ibid., 132.

[80] See Franklin, *The Idea of Music*, xiii.

youngest composers, who only became active after the war, such as Hindemith, Weill and Krenek. In their various ways, all of these composers took up distinctive stances towards the question of the artist and society, whether by actively engaging with it, or by trying to ignore it. By turning to three of these composers, Pfitzner, Krenek and Hindemith, we may trace an alternative story to modernism, one which also engages with the era's prevalent concerns with art, the artist, and society. While Pfitzner's opera *Palestrina* was written at a time when many of the effects of industrialisation, and particularly of new technology, were yet to be fully felt, the composer was nevertheless aware of the changing nature of society, as well as being affected by the alterations in the aesthetic landscape brought about by modernism. Pfitzner also experienced the social upheaval of the era of World War I, as I will show in Chapter 2. In contrast, Krenek's *Jonny spielt auf* was written when the embracing of modern life was at its height, while Hindemith's *Mathis der Maler* came during the period of backlash against this phenomenon. The three operas therefore accompany the various aspects of the changing environment for composers in the early decades of the century, and in different ways attempt to renegotiate a position for the artist in the modern world.

Artist-Operas as Self-(re)presentation

The artist-opera is a particularly apposite genre with which to investigate changing ideologies of artistry in the early twentieth century, because of the way in which the composers of such works construct relationships between the fictional individuals in the piece and their society. The fact that a central character of a *Künstleroper*, often the hero, is an artist may seem like an invitation to equate him (or more rarely, her) with the creator of the artwork, and seems to comment on the relationship of the real composer of the work to his own society.[81] An artist-opera could, therefore, be read as 'autobiographical'; however, 'autobiography' implies that the fictional version of the artist somehow traces the facts of his creator's life, and his beliefs, in a quasi-objective manner. In an artist-opera, I will argue, this is

---

[81] I use the male pronoun here as, to the best of my knowledge, no *Künstleropern* have been written by women.

not the case: the composer does not so much reflect his life within such a work as construct it, through the persona of the fictional artist.[82] How far the composer is conscious that his fictional artist may be compared to himself is open to speculation; however, he nevertheless presents a view about art which may be based on his stated aesthetic premises. (In this respect, it is significant that the composers of the three operas studied here wrote their own libretti.)

We may understand the *Künstleroper* in psychoanalytical terms: the central artist-character acts as a projection by the composer and embodies an attempt at self-definition.[83] Stephen Frosh, in his book *Identity Crisis: Modernity, Psychoanalysis and the Self*, theorises the formation of individual identity, saying that the modern state of mind is 'forged in the context of instability', and marked with its own internal instabilities, which the individual must seek to resolve.[84] Frosh draws on the work of Daniel Miller, who describes this process of resolution as 'objectification'. In Miller's theory, 'the full cycle of development...is one in which internal elements are projected outwards in material form, where they appear to sustain a life of their own...but are then reabsorbed to enrich the inner being, increasing its complexity and also making sense of its experience'.[85] To try and understand the world, the subject continually 'externalises' and then sublates, or reabsorbs, creating 'a dynamic of externalising and internalising'. The self 'develops in response to the economic and political contexts that

---

[82] My use of the word 'persona' differs from its use by Edward T. Cone in his *The Composer's Voice* (Berkeley, Los Angeles and London: University of California Press, 1974). For Cone, the persona is something which 'speaks' in the music itself, and which is controlling the course of the music. In contrast, I am not arguing for a persona *within* the music; rather, my usage is to do with the articulation of identity, and in itself need not have anything to do with music.

[83] Such ideas surface occasionally in writing on *Künstleropern*; for instance, Bokina says that Pfitzner 'projects a twentieth-century psychology of resignation, onto the...figure of Palestrina' (*Opera and Politics*, 138), while Peter Franklin, discussing the same opera, comments that it is a 'psychoanalytic "case-study"' ('Palestrina and the Dangerous Futurists', in *The Idea of Music*, 135). Also see Kienzle's *Das Trauma hinter dem Traum* for a psychoanalytical interpretation of Schreker's opera *Der ferne Klang*.

[84] Frosh, *Identity Crisis: Modernity, Psychoanalysis and the Self* (London: Macmillan, 1991), 7.

[85] Ibid., 18.

surround it, through a process of internalising or appropriating the materials of culture and social relations in which the individual is embedded'.[86] Frosh argues that artistic creation can help in the search for self-identity. He says that an inner experience of identity crisis is 'circumvented' through the creation of an external object which 'embodies the inner disturbance and so makes it possible to take up a stance towards it, to have a relationship with it out of which some emotional and perhaps intellectual sense can be made'. He continues that 'something internal and partially unknown is externalised and worked on until it has recognisable shape, then it is taken back inside and appropriated as a representation or embellishment of "identity", a path to the construction of a more integrated and elaborated self'.[87]

The composer of an artist-opera may be interpreted as attempting to create his own internal unity through creating a form of unified autonomous self which is objectified in the fictional artist. He formulates a mirror-image of himself where the fictional character's problems are solved:[88] although the plot of a *Künstleroper* often depicts an artist for whom the relationship with society is problematic, and whose thoughts and actions are therefore disunified, these problems are always resolved in some way. An artist-opera is thus an exploration and a statement of self-identity, directed both internally, to the composer himself, and externally, to the world around him. A further way of viewing the artist-opera is in terms of 'performativity'; this term, which I take from Judith Butler's work, is an apt one to describe how the composer acts out a version of himself on stage, thereby illustrating how he also presents himself in real life. An artist-opera shows us how an artistic identity, like any identity, is not fixed, but performative; that is, instead of having any prior ontological status, identity only comes into existence through being acted out. There is no single fixed being to be expressed; instead, an identity is only constituted from the actions of the

---

[86] Ibid., 17.

[87] Ibid., 191–2.

[88] Mention of a 'mirror-image' in this context may invoke Jacques Lacan's 'mirror-stage' theory. However, in Lacan's theory, the individual is altogether more passive than active – the ego-identity is formed when the individual sees himself or herself in a 'mirror' (real or metaphorical). The composer of a *Künstleroper*, though, is actively creating an alter ego.

subject.[89] Thus, while a composer is always in the process of moulding, or performing, his own identity, in his artist-opera we can see this process being fictionalised – literally performed – on stage. (I will return to this issue in Chapter 5.)

Precursors of the Twentieth-Century Artist-Opera

The theme of art or the artist has always been a common one in opera. The many instances of the Orpheus myth may be mentioned, for example, as well as others: Mozart's *Der Schauspieldirektor* and Salieri's *Prima la musica, poi le parole* in the eighteenth century, or Berlioz's *Benvenuto Cellini* and Wagner's *Tannhäuser* and *Die Meistersinger von Nürnberg* in the nineteenth, amongst others. In the early decades of the twentieth century, though, a surprisingly large number of operas were written which feature a prominent artist character, with nineteen such works by what are now considered major composers being written in the years between 1912 and 1935.[90] The focus of the plots of such operas changed subtly over the centuries: in earlier examples of the genre, the plot of the work may centre on something other than art (such as a love story), or art may be an important aspect but not a specifically problematic one. Operas in this vein continued to be written during the nineteenth and twentieth centuries; for instance, in Strauss's *Intermezzo*, the fact that the principal character is an artist is unimportant to the plot, while in Weill's *Der Protagonist*, the main character's artistry is relevant to the plot, yet this character does not explicitly reflect on his position towards society. During the course of the nineteenth century, however, and into the twentieth, an explicitly problematic relationship between the artist and his art, or his society, began to be thematised. This antagonism between artist and society has often been seen as the defining aspect of the genre.[91]

---

[89] See Judith Butler, *Gender Trouble: Feminism and the Subversion of Identity* (New York and London: Routledge, 1990), 25.

[90] See the Appendix for a list of these works.

[91] See Ulrich Weisstein, 'Die letzte Häutung. Two German *Künstleropern* of the Twentieth Century: Hans Pfitzner's *Palestrina* and Paul Hindemith's *Mathis der Maler*' in Claus Reschke and Howard Pollack (eds), *German Literature and Music: An Aesthetic Fusion, 1890–1989* (Houston German Studies. Munich: Wilhelm Fink Verlag, 1992), 198; Bern-

The explicit thematicisation of the relationship between artist and society within opera, and particularly within German opera, was to some extent influenced by the sister genre of the *Künstlerroman*. The first instances of *Künstlerromane* were written during the era of German literary Romanticism, spanning from the end of the eighteenth century to the early decades of the nineteenth. Numerous examples were written at this time; some of the most well-known include Tieck's *Franz Sternbalds Wanderungen* (1798), Novalis's *Heinrich von Ofterdingen* (1800), E.T.A. Hoffmann's *Lebensansichten des Katers Murr* (1821), and Goethe's *Wilhelm Meister* (1777–1829).[92] According to scholars of German literature, the explosion in the *Künstlerroman* genre at the turn of the nineteenth century was due to the contemporaneous decline of court patronage, which led to a new artistic sensibility and which was itself fictionalised in *Künstlerromane*. Other factors, such as the advent of industrialisation, also played a role.[93] The heroes of these early nineteenth-century novels show their ambivalence to the society around them, be that the world of the nineteenth century itself or an earlier era; such artists are often characterised as outsiders, for instance Hoffmann's Johannes Kreisler or Goethe's Wilhelm Meister.[94] Christina Brantner writes that the problem of 'the isolation of the artist and his search for a justification of an independent existence' remained a theme of the *Künstlerroman* until Thomas Mann's *Doktor Faustus*.[95] Herbert Marcuse

---

hard Kytzler, 'Moses und Mathis, Aaron und Palestrina. Zur Krise des kreativen Künstler [sic] im mythischen Spiegel der Moderne', in Peter Csobádi et al. (eds), *Antike Mythen im Musiktheater des 20. Jahrhunderts: Gesammelte Vorträge des Salzburger Symposions 1989* (Anif/Salzburg: Verlag Ursula Müller-Speiser, 1990), 196 and 204; and Bokina, 'Resignation, Retreat and Impotence', 158.

[92] Other works by Goethe deal with similar themes, for instance the *Künstlerdrama*, *Torquato Tasso* (1789), or the isolated individual (although not explicitly an artist) in *Die Leiden des jungen Werthers* (1774). See Maurice Beebe, *Ivory Towers and Sacred Founts: The Artist as Hero in Fiction from Goethe to Joyce* (New York: New York University Press, 1964) 27 ff.

[93] Sabrina Hausdörfer, *Rebellion im Kunstschein: Die Funktion des fiktiven Künstlers in Roman und Kunsttheorie der deutschen Romantik* (Heidelberg: Carl Winter Universitätsverlag, 1987), 62 ff. Also see Schubert, *Der Künstler als Handwerker*, 214.

[94] Christina Brantner, *Robert Schumann und das Tonkünstler-Bild der Romantiker* (New York: P. Lang, 1991), 43; Hausdörfer, *Rebellion im Kunstschein*, 18.

[95] Brantner, *Robert Schumann*, 40.

suggests that a conflict between artist and society is an inherent requirement of a true *Künstlerroman*: such a work 'strictly speaking, presents the
attempt of the artist to somehow solve the conflict' between himself and the
world.[96]

The *Künstlerromane* of literary Romanticism were central to the formation of the myth of the isolated artist, which first appeared at this time.
Such novels dealt with now-familiar Romantic themes – ideas, for instance,
of genius, or of the necessity for the artist to sacrifice himself to his work –
and set a pattern which would be followed by subsequent generations of
both writers and composers.[97] Sabrina Hausdörfer comments that 'the early
Romantic period is in many ways what the genre of *Künstlerroman* later
constituted, and has remained present in that which is no longer specifically
tied to the genre, but which thematises the problem of creativity and the
relationship of the artist to the world'.[98] The early Romantic writers were
therefore among the first to exhibit a concern with the nature of artistry and
with the position of the artist in modern society, even if the reality of the
writer's own experience may not have matched up to the mythical artistic
ideal of his works.

The idea that an artist's life may be represented in his or her work also
developed within music criticism in the early nineteenth century. The

---

[96] Marcuse, 'Der deutsche Künstlerroman', 16. Also see 332, as well as Beebe, *Ivory Towers and Sacred Founts*, 6; Hausdörfer, *Rebellion im Kunstschein*, 16–17; Schubert, *Der
Künstler als Handwerker*, 25; and Reinhard Seebohm, 'Triumph und Tragik des Künstlertums: die Stellung von Pfitzners "Palestrina" in der Geschichte des deutschen Künstlerdramas', *Pfitzner* 32 (April 1974), 15.

[97] Hausdörfer, *Rebellion im Kunstschein*, 18–19.

[98] Ibid., 24. Other studies of *Künstlerromane* include Helene Goldschmidt, *Das deutsche
Künstlerdrama von Goethe bis R. Wagner* (Weimar: Alexander Duncker Verlag, 1925);
C.D. Malmgren, '"From Work to Text". The Modernist and Postmodernist Künstlerroman', *Novel – A Forum on Fiction* 21/1 (1987), 5–28; and Jörg Theilacker, *Der erzählende Musiker: Untersuchung von Musikererzählungen des 19. Jahrhunderts und ihrer
Bezüge zur Entstehung der deutschen Nationalmusik* (Frankfurt a.M.: Verlag Peter Lang,
1988). Seebohm's essay, 'Triumph und Tragik des Künstlertums' takes Pfitzner's *Palestrina* as a literary rather than as a musical text, and compares it to works by Goethe and
Grillparzer. Literary investigations such as these are of limited usefulness to an examina-
tion of *Künstleropern*, as their writers focus on the intricacies of the written text in a way
which is impossible to apply to music, at least not without some degree of force.

Romantic aesthetic's lauding of the personality of the artist, particularly the genius, and the value placed on self-expression, led to a situation in which the work of art was often seen not only as an emanation from the artist, but also as a representation of an aspect of his or her life or feelings. An early example of such writing is the interpretation by Franz Joseph Fröhlich of Beethoven's music, particularly his Ninth Symphony, as autobiographical, an idea which, according to Robin Wallace, has since become common-place.[99] According to Fröhlich, whose article was published in 1827, the Ninth Symphony's progression from D minor to D major portrays the composer's struggle to come to terms with his deafness, and his eventual joy in succeeding. On a more small-scale level, Fröhlich saw the progression of the music as reflecting varying moods which portray the composer's personality.[100] The primacy of emotional self-expression in the nineteenth century meant both that existing musical works were retrospectively interpreted as autobiographical, as in Fröhlich's view of Beethoven, and that new works were written by Romantic composers in accordance with this aesthetic, an obvious example being Berlioz's *Symphonie Fantastique*. In this way, a context was created in which the reflection of the composer's feelings and experiences within his art was expected.

Out of this context came the most significant German *Künstleropern* of the nineteenth century, Wagner's *Tannhäuser* and *Die Meistersinger von Nürnberg*. The heroes of both operas are typical representations of the Romantic artist, with their desire to express their feelings in song. The relationship between artist and society is also presented in both, but the idea of artistic estrangement is shown only metaphorically, hidden behind an alternative story. In *Tannhäuser*, the hero's conflict between two women, Venus and Elizabeth, is the focus; this could be seen as presenting a struggle between different types of society and the artist's relationship to each, but only on an allegorical level. Tannhäuser's songs are not the source of his problems, but merely an expression of them. In *Die Meistersinger*, Walther is an outsider who wishes to become part of the bourgeois society of Nuremberg. His motivation is his love for Eva; he achieves his

---

[99] Wallace, *Beethoven's Critics: Aesthetic Dilemmas and Resolutions during the Composer's Lifetime* (Cambridge: Cambridge University Press, 1986), 78. Also see Jim Samson, 'The Great Composer', in Samson (ed.), *The Cambridge History of Nineteenth-Century Music*, 271.

[100] Ibid., 83. Also see Dennis, *Beethoven in German Politics*, 64.

aims through art, but art functions only as a means to his end. In *Die Meistersinger*, unlike later *Künstleropern*, the central artist-character and the character who is aware of society are two different people, Walther and Hans Sachs. Walther is the artist, as it is he who sings in the Guild contests; although Sachs does sing (his cobbling song of Act Two), it is Walther who encapsulates the Romantic aesthetic by using art to express his emotions. In contrast, Sachs is more inwardly concerned than Walther with the folly of the world, as shown in his *Wahn* monologue. Whereas later artist-operas frequently bring these two elements into one person to produce the artist who is concerned with the role of his art within society, in *Die Meistersinger* there is a separation between the artist Walther and the more reflective and socially-aware Sachs.[101]

In *Die Meistersinger*, the focus is on the community, rather than on any conflict between the individual and society: several characters form a nexus at the centre of the drama, so that the work is not specifically about either Walther or Sachs. (The title itself shows this, with its use of the plural.)[102] *Die Meistersinger* may be seen as representative of the kind of society Wagner would have liked to exist: art has a central place in the community, and Walther is presented as an inspired and progressive artist (because he does not follow the Meistersingers' rules) who is recognised by the ordinary people. Bernhard Schubert comments that 'the stage action [in *Die*

---

[101] Some writers suggest that Sachs is an artist, for instance, Bernhard Schubert ('Wagners "Sachs" und die Tradition des romantischen Künstlerselbstverständnisses', *Archiv für Musikwissenschaft* 40/3 (1983), 212–53), and Michael Tanner, who states that this is the case because Sachs pulls the strings and brings Walther's talent to fruition (*Wagner* (London: HarperCollins, 1996), 164). However, on the surface level of plot, Sachs's artistry is secondary to Walther's. Schubert also takes Sachs, Walther and Beckmesser as representing different facets of Wagner's own self-understanding as an artist ('Wagners "Sachs"', 213).

[102] Anthony Arblaster, *Viva la Libertà! Politics in Opera* (London and New York: Verso, 1992), 176. Also see Schubert, 'Wagners "Sachs"', 246–7. This emphasis on the plural is in contrast to the focus of the later *Künstleropern* in which the artist is always the main character, a factor also reflected in their titles which frequently refer to a single person. There is an element of conflict within *Die Meistersinger* with the riot in Act Two, but this differs from later *Künstleropern* in that it is a conflict on the explicit, external level, rather than an internal one on the part of the artist or a struggle between artist and society.

Meistersinger] symbolises the Utopia of a cultural unity, which should have become reality with Wagner's activities in Bayreuth'.[103] With its lauding of community, and the integration of the artist Walther into Nuremberg society, *Die Meistersinger* presents a political message about art and artistry which anticipates later *Künstleropern*. A further political dimension is added in Sachs's speech in Act Three, where he proclaims:

> Take care! Evil trickery threatens us: if first German people and state are divided by false foreign majesty, no prince will understand his people any more, and foreign mists with foreign frippery will be planted for us in German land; no-one will know what is German and true if there is no honour for German masters! Therefore I tell you: honour your German masters![104]

This declamation may be read against the nationalism of Wagner's own era, and thereby offers an insight into contemporary political issues.[105] As will be discussed later, the relationship between artist and society within *Künstleropern* may be read in political terms.

Another, less well-known artist-opera, which falls chronologically between *Die Meistersinger* and the operas to be discussed in the chapters below, is even more directly concerned with art and politics: Richard Strauss's *Guntram* (1893). *Guntram* tells the story of a singer who is a member of a religious group, or *Bund*, of singers called the 'Streiter der Liebe' ('Warriors of Love'). At the beginning of the opera, Guntram meets a group of peasants fleeing their homeland, which is nominally ruled by the Herzog but in actuality by his cruel son-in-law Robert; the hero decides to help them. After chancing to meet the Herzog and Robert, he is invited to their castle, where he sings a song to try to enlighten them and to change their attitude towards the ordinary people. Robert attacks him with his sword, but Guntram retaliates and kills him; he is thrown into prison. He there announces to his friend Friedhold, a fellow member of the 'Streiter

---

[103] Schubert, *Der Künstler als Handwerker*, 96.

[104] 'Habt acht! Uns dräuen üble Streich: zerfällt erst deutsches Volk und Reich, in falscher welscher Majestät kein Fürst bald mehr sein Volk versteht, und welschen Dunst mit welschem Tand sie pflanzen uns in deutsches Land; was deutsch und echt, wüßt' keiner mehr, lebt's nicht in deutscher Meister Ehr! D'rum sag ich euch: ehrt eure deutschen Meister!'.

[105] See Schubert, 'Wagners "Sachs"', 249, for discussion of this political dimension.

der Liebe', that he will turn his back on art. Friedhold reminds him of the purpose of the *Bund*, which is to lead people to God through art; Guntram is impressed by his words, but he has broken the rule that the members of the *Bund* remain pure, and refuses to answer to them for his crime. The opera ends with Guntram being released from prison by Freihild, Robert's wife, with whom he has fallen in love; despite her reciprocation of his affection, though, he decides to spend his life in solitude as a penance for his crime.

   Guntram's foregrounding of an explicitly political issue in relation to art and the artist created a new current within the artist-opera genre which was only implicit in the operas of Wagner. Indeed, the opera foregrounds the various uses of art: for Friedhold and his band of religious singers, art is solely for the purpose of turning the listener's thoughts to God.[106] Fried-hold's criticism of Guntram is therefore double-sided: the hero has transgressed the rules of the *Bund* not only through his murder of Robert, but also by using art for political ends, and using it as a weapon. Strauss's opera has never become particularly well-known – it was deemed a failure musically and dramatically after its first performance[107] – and its influence on later composers is therefore difficult to assess. Nevertheless, its concern with the artist's position in society demonstrates how composers of this era were involved in this debate.

The Artist-Opera and Politics

The artist-operas explored in this book all present, and resolve, a conflict between artist and society. In this respect, these works engage with an inherently political problem: the interaction of individuals within society, and the negotiation of various positions between the artist and his environment which invest power and authority in particular individuals or groups. The wishes of such figures as Wagner or Liszt to bring about revolution in order to create a new context for art, or even Schoenberg, in his explicit rejection of mass society, all have an inherently political content; my examinations of *Palestrina, Jonny spielt auf* and *Mathis der Maler* develop this by read-

---

[106] See Friedhold's speech to Guntram in Act 3, Scene 3.
[107] Norman Del Mar, *Richard Strauss. A Critical Commentary on His Life and Works*, Vol.1 (London and Boston: Faber and Faber, 1986), 94 and 118.

ing each work against a specific political context. I will examine the relationship of each opera, and its composer, to ideologies about the political organisation of society current in Germany in the period from World War I to the early Third Reich; these ideologies also found expression within political parties.[108]

In one sense, we may say with some confidence that all art is political, in that it expresses an ideology of some kind. This may be aesthetic, that is, about the nature of art itself, or it may be closer to what we would more readily term 'political', that is, when it is about an aspect of society. Anthony Arblaster, in his book on opera and politics *Viva la Libertà!*, defines the 'political' in two ways. He writes that 'traditionally, politics has been centred on the question of government or rule: what persons or institutions govern and should govern society'. He contrasts this with a wider question, which is 'about power, meaning not only the struggles of individuals to achieve it or hold onto it, but also the distribution of power in society between various groups and individuals, and the relations between the (relatively) powerful and the (relatively) powerless'.[109] These power relationships, which he says may occur 'within families, within groups [and] within institutions', are those more frequently studied in recent musicology, particularly the study of the power relationships between men and women or between races. Examinations of music with specific reference to the more limited area of governments and party politics are rarer, however, and those that do exist often consist largely of empirical documentation of the attitudes of political movements towards music, for instance in the Third Reich or within the socialist and communist workers' music movements. There has to date been comparatively little in-depth consideration of the music which originated within, or which was linked to, such movements.[110]

---

108 While 'Germany' is sometimes used to denote the German-speaking countries, therefore including Austria, my investigation is more precisely focused on Germany itself and its political history in this period. Of the three composers, only Krenek was Austrian, and was living in Kassel, Germany, at the time of the composition and first performances of *Jonny spielt auf*. However, in discussion of the larger cultural context, I will also draw on Austrian sources, as German and Austrian culture were well integrated with each other at this time.

109 Arblaster, *Viva la Libertà!*, 2.

110 Works on the Third Reich include Michael H. Kater, *The Twisted Muse: Musicians and*

Political parties or movements, as defined in Arblaster's first category, necessarily encompass, and focus, the ideologies held by wider groups within society, as described in his second category, for the purposes of ruling a state. The following chapters will compare the philosophies expressed by Pfitzner, Krenek and Hindemith with those espoused by political movements in the period roughly between the First and Second World Wars. The three operas consider not only the nature of art, but also of society, a concern which corresponds with the interests of those involved in politics. Each work manifests a vision of the artist's position in an ideal society, suggesting, in the same manner as a political party, a world for which one should strive.

Their Music in the Third Reich (New York and Oxford: Oxford University Press, 1997); Erik Levi, *Music in the Third Reich* (London: Macmillan, 1994); Michael Meyer, *The Politics of Music in the Third Reich* (New York: Peter Lang, 1991); Potter, *Most German of the Arts*; and Joseph Wulf, *Musik im Dritten Reich: Eine Dokumentation* (Frankfurt a.M.: Ullstein, 1983). On the socialist music movement, see W.L. Guttsmann, *Workers' Culture in Weimar Germany: Between Tradition and Commitment* (New York: Berg, 1990), and Dümling, '"Im Zeichen der Erkenntnis der sozialen Verhältnisse"'. On political questions in opera, see Bokina, *Opera and Politics*, and Jeremy Tambling's *Opera and the Culture of Fascism* (Oxford: Clarendon Press, 1996), which primarily investigates how fascist relationships to conceptions of gender, approached psychoanalytically, may be found in operatic works. Much of his book is therefore less directly about politics than about a particular ideological discourse in opera, concerning gender, which also appeared within a political movement.

2   Pfitzner, *Palestrina*, and the Nonpolitical Composer

Hans Pfitzner wrote his opera *Palestrina* between 1912 and 1915. He had been debating the subject from as long before as 1895, and considered several possible librettists until deciding in 1909 to write his own text. The opera, subtitled 'A Musical Legend', is based on the myth that the Renaissance composer Palestrina 'saved' music from an imminent ban by the Catholic church by writing his *Missa Papae Marcelli*; the beauty of his music convinced the Pope that music was fitting in the praise of God.[1] Pfitzner's opera was first performed in Munich in 1917, and was immediately hailed as a great success for the composer. Many of Pfitzner's contemporaries suggested that the hero of the opera was intended as a representation of Pfitzner himself; Wilhelm Furtwängler, for instance, said to the composer, 'You yourself are Palestrina', while Bruno Walter stated later that Palestrina's personality depicted that of Pfitzner.[2] Thomas Mann, in his book *Betrachtungen eines Unpolitischen* (*Reflections of a Nonpolitical Man*), which was written in the same years that Pfitzner was composing his work and which was published shortly after the première, said that he believed the opera to be 'confessional'. Mann even pointed out the similarities in the physical appearances of Pfitzner and Karl Erb, the singer of Palestrina at the first performance; this fact validated to Mann that the opera was autobiographical.[3] A drawing of Pfitzner by Karl Bauer made a year

---

[1] A description of the origins of this myth may be found in Owen Toller, *Pfitzner's* Palestrina: *The 'Musical Legend' and its Background* (Exeter: Toccata Press, 1997), 218 ff. Also see Gottfried Scholz, 'The Image of Giovanni Pierluigi da Palestrina in Pfitzner's *Palestrina*', *Musical Quarterly* 85/1 (Spring 2001), 78.

[2] Furtwängler and Walter quoted in Johann Peter Vogel, *Hans Pfitzner: Mit Selbstzeugnissen und Bilddokumenten* (Reinbek bei Hamburg: Rowohlt, 1989), 71.

[3] Mann, *Reflections of a Nonpolitical Man*, trans. and intro. Walter D. Morris (New York: Frederick Ungar Publishing, 1983), 302 and 312. Photographs of the two men can be

after the first performance is clearly influenced by the scene in the opera where the mass is dictated to Palestrina by a chorus of angels: Pfitzner is shown in contemplative mood while two angels play the organ and violin above his head (fig.2.1). Pfitzner's portrayal of Palestrina seemed to catch the imagination of his contemporaries, who readily identified the real composer of the work with the fictional composer in the opera.

The fact that Pfitzner could so easily be equated with his main character, both by writers who experienced the first performance and those coming to the opera subsequently, might suggest that this view was corroborated by Pfitzner himself.[4] However, in an essay he wrote some years after the composition of *Palestrina*, Pfitzner hinted that the work was not intended to be autobiographical, saying 'I didn't think in the least at that time about wanting to identify myself with the title hero, although certain features and

---

found in Vogel, *Hans Pfitzner*, 68–9.

[4] More recent musicological discussion of the opera includes Bernhard Adamy, *Hans Pfitzner: Literatur, Philosophie und Zeitgeschehen in seinem Weltbild und Werk* (Tutzing: Hans Schneider, 1980); Tim Ashley, 'In Sympathy with Death', *Opera*, January 1997, 33–9; Paul Attinello, 'Pfitzner, *Palestrina*, Nazis, Conservatives: Longing for Utopia', *Journal of Musicological Research* 15 (1995), 25–53; Bokina, 'Resignation, Retreat and Impotence'; Leon Botstein, 'Pfitzner and Musical Politics', *Musical Quarterly* 85/1 (Spring 2001), 63–75; Reinhard Ermen, *Musik als Einfall: Hans Pfitzners Position im ästhetischen Diskurs nach Wagner* (Aachen: Rimbaud Presse, 1986); Franklin, '*Palestrina* and the Dangerous Futurists'; Donald Henderson, 'Hans Pfitzner's *Palestrina*: A Twentieth-Century Allegory', *Music Review*, 1970, 32–43; M. Owen Lee, 'Pfitzner's *Palestrina*: A Musical Legend', *Opera Quarterly* 4/1 (1986), 54–60; David J. Levin, '"Father Knows Best": Paternity and Mise-en-Scène in Hans Pfitzner's *Palestrina*, *Musical Quarterly* 85/1 (Spring 2001), 168–82; Joseph Müller-Blattau, *Hans Pfitzner: Lebensweg und Schaffensernte* (Frankfurt a.M.: Waldemar Kramer, 1969); Gottfried Scholz, 'The Image of Giovanni Pierluigi da Palestrina'; Michael P. Steinberg, 'Opera and Cultural Analysis: The Case of Hans Pfitzner's *Palestrina*', *Musical Quarterly* 85/1 (Spring 2001), 53–62; Owen Toller, *Pfitzner's* Palestrina; Johann Peter Vogel, *Hans Pfitzner*; Marc A. Weiner, *Undertones of Insurrection: Music, Politics and the Social Sphere in the Modern German Narrative* (Lincoln: University of Nebraska Press, 1993); and John Williamson, *The Music of Hans Pfitzner* (Oxford: Clarendon Press, 1992).

Fig.2.1 Hans Pfitzner, by Karl Bauer: from *Jugend* (1918) (Photo: AKG London)

parallels crept imperceptibly into such a creation'.[5] The suggestion that these parallels crept in 'imperceptibly' seems perhaps *faux naïf*, although profession of such a sentiment is consistent with Pfitzner's maintenance of a degree of mystique around the creative process. I will examine here the extent to which these 'features and parallels' appear in the work, and how far the fictional Palestrina may function as a persona for Pfitzner, a kind of 'wish-fulfilment', through which he seeks to construct both an ideal artist-figure, and an ideal environment for the artist. Pfitzner fought for the preservation of nineteenth-century values regarding art and society in the face of the 'threat' of modernity; thus, Palestrina's relationship to his society can be read against Pfitzner's position towards his own culture. The opera demonstrates the concern about the relationship between artist and environment which preoccupied many at this time, and attempts to uphold a politically and aesthetically conservative discourse.

The Context of *Palestrina*

Political Conservatism c. World War I

Although conservatism was well-established in late nineteenth- and early twentieth-century Germany, its predominance began to be challenged in the years leading up to World War I, and there was a steady growth in support for the SPD (*Sozialdemokratische Partei Deutschlands*, or German Social Democratic Party) which campaigned for greater democracy.[6] (Indeed, the growing threat of the SPD is seen by many historians as one factor, amongst others, which precipitated the German government's decision to go to war in 1914.)[7] Prior to this, the cultural and societal norms of Ger-

---

[5] Pfitzner, 'Palestrina. Ein Vortrag über das Werk und seine Geschichte', in *Reden, Schriften, Briefe*, ed. Walter Abendroth (Berlin: Hermann Luchterhand, 1955), 31.

[6] In the 1912 Reichstag elections, the SPD had seen an increase in their seats from 43 to 110, and with the left-leaning portions of the centre parties (the Centre Party and the Left Liberals) could command a majority coalition. This state of affairs continued throughout the war until the 1918 revolution.

[7] See E.J. Passant, with W.O. Henderson, C.J. Child and D.C. Watt, *A Short History of Germany 1815–1945* (Cambridge: Cambridge University Press, 1962), 132, and Volker R. Berghahn, *Imperial Germany, 1871–1914: Economy, Society, Culture, and Politics*

many, and its structures of power, had been long institutionalised. In the princely states which had existed in Germany before their unification in 1871, a hereditary aristocracy had been the system of governance; after this date, the Prussian monarch was Kaiser of Germany.[8] This dominant governmental system, where there was one absolute and ultimate source of power, was so long established that, for many, it was simply accepted as normal and 'correct'. Alternatives to this state of affairs were not to be considered, and threats to the established regime, such as democracy, were generally dismissed as foolish aberrations. This was despite the nominal existence of an elected Reichstag, or parliament, since 1871; this Reichstag was little more than token representation as it was subsidiary in importance to the Federal Council (*Bundesrat*), and both could be overruled by the Kaiser.[9] While the Reichstag was elected on the basis of universal male suffrage, the Bundesrat (representing the *Länder*) had a different electoral system skewed heavily in favour of the right wing.[10] Because of this situation, the Reichstag was, perhaps, tolerated. Even so, some thought the parliament too 'democratic', and would have preferred a return to absolutism: the German Conservative Party, for instance, thought democracy was a sin against 'Divine Law'.[11]

(Providence and Oxford: Berghahn Books, 1994), 278.

[8] Hans-Ulrich Wehler, *The German Empire 1871–1918*, trans. Kim Traynor (Providence and Oxford: Berg, 1985), 54.

[9] David Blackbourn, *The Fontana History of Germany, 1780–1918: The Long Nineteenth Century* (London: Fontana Press, 1997), 257 and 266; Berghahn, *Imperial Germany*, 190 ff. The Reichstag, which represented the whole of Germany from 1871, was preceded by the 'North-German Confederation', founded in 1867, as well as by other, smaller elected assemblies on city or state level; these could generally be overruled by the appropriate aristocrat, however.

[10] The voting system for the Bundesrat varied between different states: in Prussia, for instance, a vote from a man in the highest tax bracket carried between 16 and 26 times more weight than a man in the lowest tax bracket; 10% of the population fell below the minimum tax threshold and were not allowed to vote. With partialities such as this, it was not surprising that the conservatives generally gained the most seats, so for example, in the 1908 Bundesrat elections, the conservatives won 47.9% of the seats even though only 16.7% of the electorate voted for them. Ibid., 210.

[11] Ibid., 217. Also see William Carr, *A History of Germany 1815–1945* (Second Edition. London: Edward Arnold, 1979), 196 ff.

Prevalent rhetorical discourses gave these power structures validity. The dominant culture deemed that that which was consistent with the prevailing view was 'right' and 'natural', and especially, truly 'German'. Turn-of-the-century nationalist associations, such as the Pan-German League and the 'Reich Association against Social Democracy', for instance, conveyed their arguments in favour of 'Germanness' 'as scientific "insights" gained from Nature and History', rhetoric which convinced many people of their accuracy.[12] The conservative and monarchist political climate had been perpetuated by (and because of) its inscription into the whole social and educational milieu. For example, on the command of Wilhelm II, the school curriculum was drawn up in 1889 in order to 'instil a conservative image of existing conditions in the young', children being educated in traditional and monarchical values.[13] The higher an individual progressed in the educational system, the more conservative the institution became, so that those men with university educations – the ones who would go on to positions of power and influence – were the ones who were most thoroughly indoctrinated with reactionary ideas. Churches similarly propagated conservatism, while two years of national service brought thousands of young men into the reactionary environment of the armed forces.[14] This culture therefore ensured its own perpetuation through its establishment as the principal frame of reference within the whole social structure.[15]

In these circumstances, progressive left-wing parties such as the SPD made no headway into the Reichstag for many years. The SPD favoured democracy because it was an egalitarian system which would enfranchise everyone; such beliefs could be readily aligned by those on the Right with socialism. Democracy threatened centuries of privilege for the upper classes; its egalitarianism may have been only for electoral purposes, but was deemed to set a dangerous precedent. If all citizens were equal in voting rights, where would their demands for equality end? Democracy was therefore to be resisted, as it represented the potential overthrow of the existing social structure.

---

[12] Berghahn, *Imperial Germany*, 228.

[13] Ibid., 90.

[14] Ibid., 93.

[15] Passant, *A Short History of Germany*, 92. Also see Blackbourn, *The Fontana History of Germany*, 424 ff.

While conservatism formed the dominant social context for the years up to World War I, towards the end of the war it began to look increasingly likely that, in addition to losing, Germany would experience a fundamental change in its whole political system, because of the growing power of the SPD. During the war, the politicians of the left had been happy to suspend their principles on political reform for the sake of patriotism; they had joined with the Right in a *Burgfrieden*, a political truce that meant that all sides would work together in their belligerent aims.[16] However, when defeat began to look likely, the Socialists, now increased in number in the Reichstag, became a threat to those on the right.[17] Inspired by the Russian Revolution in 1917, and able to point to the daily hardships which the war had induced, the Left could again assert its demands for a more responsible governmental system. The opposition by the SPD within the Reichstag to the existing status quo was accompanied by unrest amongst ordinary citizens, who became increasingly critical of the perpetuation of a war which they realised they were unlikely to win. Civil discontent, in the form of general strikes, began to take place in several cities from 1917.

Conservative Politics and Art (1): Thomas Mann's Betrachtungen eines Unpolitischen

The growing threat of the left wing and the shifts in the German political landscape gave rise to a flood of invective and apocalyptic predictions by those who were part of the previously unquestioned ruling classes. This threatened class included Pfitzner, whose reaction was exemplified in *Palestrina*, and the writer Thomas Mann, whose book *Betrachtungen eines Unpolitischen* (*Reflections of a Nonpolitical Man*) crystallised the conservatives' objections to the new political currents.[18] Mann readily

---

[16] Carr, *A History of Germany*, 266.

[17] More radical left-wing parties also appeared at this time, such as the *Unabhängige Sozial-Demokratische Partei* (USDP, or Independent Social-Democratic Party), a breakaway group from the SPD, and the Spartacus League, the forerunner of the *Kommunistische Partei Deutschlands* (KPD, or German Communist Party).

[18] The book is a diatribe against Mann's brother, the author Heinrich Mann, with whom Thomas was in conflict at this time. Nevertheless, Mann's opinions have a wider political implication. See Ernst Keller, *Der unpolitische Deutsche: Eine Studie zu den 'Betrachtungen eines Unpolitischen' von Thomas Mann* (Berlin: Francke Verlag, 1965), 5 ff., and

acknowledged his right-wing stance in the book, and it is an effective way of understanding conservative thought of the era, providing an important insight into this political discourse which is highly relevant to Pfitzner's opera.[19] Hugh Ridley says that the book 'provides a good summary of many of the deeply held but largely unconsidered convictions which the German intellectuals of the Second Reich held concerning their political and social function. It is a crucial text for the transfer of pre-1914 attitudes into the Weimar Republic...and for demonstrating the continuity of conservative ideology across the divide of the war'.[20]

To fully understand Mann's political position, we must first understand his use of the word 'politics' in *Betrachtungen eines Unpolitischen*, as it has a very particular meaning. As becomes apparent during the course of the book, 'politics' signifies only those tendencies to which Mann is opposed – broadly speaking, liberal and left-wing ones. Conversely, the beliefs which he espouses are termed 'nonpolitical', as alluded to in his title. The dichotomy between the 'political' and 'nonpolitical' may be seen as implicit in conservative thought of the era more widely, and Mann acts as a focal point for this ideology. His book encapsulates the negative and positive beliefs of conservatism, discernible throughout the cultural and political environment of contemporary Germany, in the neat and explicit dualism of 'political' versus 'nonpolitical'. Mann's employment of this dichotomy is complex, and as a result initially difficult to understand, because he amalgamates two spheres, the political and the aesthetic. The book is a diatribe against the 'politicization of the intellect', not only against politics *per se*, although the two are intimately connected.[21] Mann sets up

---

Erich Heller, *Thomas Mann: The Ironic German* (Cambridge: Cambridge University Press, 1958).

[19] Mann was to change his political position later in his life, abandoning his anti-democratic stance in the 1920s and starting to defend the Weimar Republic (a *volte face* which was later to lead him into difficulties with the Nazis). Part of Mann's important pro-democracy essay dating from the twenties, 'Von deutscher Republik', can be found in Anton Kaes, Martin Jay and Edward Dimendberg (eds), *The Weimar Republic Sourcebook* (Berkeley, Los Angeles and London: University of California Press, 1994), 105–9.

[20] Ridley, 'The Culture of Weimar: Models of Decline', in Michael Laffan (ed.), *The Burden of German History 1919–1945: Essays for the Goethe Institute* (London: Methuen, 1988), 16.

[21] Ibid., 17. The reasons for this come back to Mann's dispute with his brother Heinrich;

two contrasting domains. What is termed the 'political' is concerned with the worldly: society, the state, governmental systems (specifically democracy), as well as 'lower' types of art which Mann terms 'civilisation' and 'literature'. These apparently neutral words are used by him in a derogatory fashion. Against this 'political' realm is contrasted the 'nonpolitical' sphere, which is concerned with matters spiritual and metaphysical, the individual (which he terms the 'personality' and, confusingly, contrasts with the denigrated term 'individual') rather than the social, and with 'culture' and 'art'.[22] Ridley comments that, for Mann, 'the artist is concerned with the timelessly human and with the traditional rather than with the modern or with the ephemeral, time-serving issues of politics'.[23] This 'nonpolitical' sphere also has a 'higher' kind of government, namely monarchy, which is supposedly distanced from the worldly. Dichotomies between what is seen as 'political' and what is 'nonpolitical' are fundamental to Mann's argument; as Hans Eichner says, Mann 'returned time and again to such antitheses as "Kultur" and "Zivilisation", the individual and society, "Dichtung" and "Literatur", the "Obrigkeitsstaat" and democracy, and every time he presented the first of these alternatives as more German and better'.[24] Both the 'political' and 'nonpolitical' realms described by Mann

---

Heinrich advocated that artists should be more explicitly involved with politics, a view which Thomas rejected. The latter's attempt at an 'unpolitical' stance is therefore based in opposition to Heinrich's 'political' point of view. See Hans Eichner, 'Thomas Mann and Politics', in Hans H. Schulte and Gerald Chapple (eds), *Thomas Mann: Ein Kolloquium* (Bonn: Bouvier Verlag Herbert Grundmann, 1978), 11, and Heller, *Thomas Mann*.

[22] Thus Mann is inconsistent in his use of such terms. 'Individual' has a positive connotation when contrasted with 'society', but a negative one when set against 'personality'. He also sometimes uses other terms inconsistently.

[23] Ridley, 'The Culture of Weimar', 17.

[24] Eichner, 'Thomas Mann and Politics', 10–11. According to Stephen Lamb and Anthony Phelan, Mann believed that the terms 'culture' and 'civilisation' had been used imprecisely. As a remedy, Mann explained the meaning of 'culture' in partly militaristic terms, such as 'unity, style, form, self-control, and discipline'. He contrasts this with 'all the French liberal traditions of *Zivilisation*: liberty, equality, and fraternity, all of which he dismisses as the "cosiness of the social contract"' ('Weimar Culture: The Birth of Modernism', in Burns (ed.), *German Cultural Studies*, 54). The contrast of 'culture' with 'civilisation' is a recurrent idea at this time, also to be found in the writings of Houston Stewart Chamberlain and Moeller van den Bruck; see Robin Lenman, John Osborne and Eda Sagarra, 'Imperial Germany: Towards the Commercialization of Culture', in Burns

in fact combine the political (in that they espouse a particular ideology and a system of government) and the aesthetic. However, this fact is disguised somewhat by Mann's persistent use of 'political' to denote only worldly matters, and, comparatively, 'nonpolitical' to denote a metaphysical, higher realm, ostensibly defined by aesthetic, spiritual matters, and supposedly distant from ideology despite its own inherent ideological roots.

Mann admits to his own conservatism while holding that it is nonpolitical; simultaneously, he demonstrates how 'politics' are those beliefs which conflict with conservatism. Mann's objections to the 'political' are strongly grounded in his environment: what he defines as 'political' are those views held by the contemporary socialist and liberal parties, principally the SPD. Mann does not actually name the SPD, nor any other particular group; however, he attacks the notion of 'democracy', and seen against the context of the time, it is clear who his enemies are. 'Politics' and 'democracy' are treated as synonymous, as Mann states unequivocally:

> When, in the following discussions, the identity of the concepts 'politics' and 'democracy' is defended or treated as obvious, it is done with an extraordinarily clearly perceived right. One is not a 'democratic', or, say, a 'conservative' politician. One *is* a politician or one is not. And if one is, then one is democratic. The political-intellectual attitude is the democratic one; belief in politics is belief in democracy.[25]

Mann's dichotomy between the 'political' and the 'nonpolitical' is augmented by that between the 'social' and the 'metaphysical', which operates along the same axis. 'Democracy' is grounded in the 'social', in its concern for the worldly; according to Mann, this concern with practical matters is wrong and misguided. The 'metaphysical' element is more important than the social. He points to the 'irrevocable conflict between individual and society', but says that 'politics', which is 'namely enlightenment, social contract, republic, progress toward the "greatest good for the greatest number"' – that is, the liberal, progressive tendency – cannot resolve this conflict. The only reconciliation possible is on the metaphysical level, 'in the sphere of personality'.[26] It is, he says, 'wrong to confuse the supra-

---

(ed.), *German Cultural Studies*, 20, and Keller, *Der unpolitische Deutsche*, 136.

[25] Mann, *Reflections*, 15–16. Also 190: 'democracy is not only political, *it is politics itself*'.

[26] Ibid., 185.

individual element with the social one, to place it completely in the social sphere: in the process one neglects the metaphysical supraindividual element'.[27] Reconciliation between individual and society is possible 'only on a spiritual path, never on a political one'.[28] Mann sees the 'personality', which has a metaphysical essence, as being of primary importance, and of no concern with the state: 'the state...cannot be the bearer of personal life'.[29]

Mann extends his distinction between the 'social' and the 'metaphysical' to the nation as a whole. 'The nation, too, is not only a social but also a metaphysical being; the bearer of the general (*des Allgemeinen*), of the human quality is not "humanity" as the sum of individuals, but the nation... . Here we have the difference between the mass and the *Volk*, the difference between which is that between individual and personality, civilization and culture, social and metaphysical life. The individualistic mass is democratic, the nation aristocratic'.[30] Because of his contrast of the 'political' or 'social' with the 'nonpolitical' or 'metaphysical', a term such as 'democracy', aligned as it is with 'politics', has a wider meaning for Mann than simply as an electoral system. He understands it as a method of social reform having fundamental ramifications for the structure of the nation (along with its further debasing aesthetic connotations of 'literature' and 'civilisation'). For Mann, democracy means the 'dominance of the people' (*Volksherrschaft*), a phrase which, he says, 'has its terror'.[31] Power would be wielded by the people – who are implicitly the working classes – rather than by those qualified by birth or education. If all of the population were given an equal vote, he believes, then everything would be reduced to the lowest common denominator; the different strata of society would be levelled out into a homogeneous mass. Democracy therefore leads to a social, and socialist, levelling process. In contrast to the homogenising effects of socialism, to be German is to prefer social inequality: 'German-national means "free", inwardly and outwardly, but it does not mean "equal" –

---

[27] Ibid., 179.

[28] Ibid., 185.

[29] Ibid., 188.

[30] Ibid., 179–80. I have made some minor alterations to the translation and added the phrase about the 'mass and *Volk*', which is missing from the English version (*Betrachtungen eines Unpolitischen* (Frankfurt a.M.: S. Fischer Verlag, 1956), 240).

[31] Mann, *Reflections*, 192 and 267. The translation of *Volksherrschaft* in *Reflections* is 'rule of the people', but *Herrschaft* has more of a connotation of power and dominance.

neither inwardly nor outwardly'.[32] In Germany, which Mann calls 'the land of great men', the levelling which comes about through socialism is particularly dangerous. The 'great man' by definition stands above the mass, on a higher plane of achievement, but democracy would level out such disparities between individuals, and the great men to be found in Germany would disappear.[33] Mann thinks that superiority and expert authority are anathema to the democrats, because they want equality: 'democracy...is equality and therefore hatred, ineradicable and jealous republican hatred of every superiority'.[34]

'Democracy' is held by Mann to be 'hostile to Germany'; it is 'in itself something un-German, anti-German'.[35] To the conservative Mann, democracy was a foreign invention, championed by some of the very countries with which Germany was then at war – Britain, France and the USA. Mann inveighs against the idea of Germany as a republic in language associated with the French Revolution, and especially the writings of Rousseau: 'Germany as a *republic*, as a virtue-state with a social contract, a democratic people's government and the "complete absorption of the individual in the totality"; Germany as a *state* and nothing more, and the German human being as a Jacobin and *citoyen vertueux* with the citizen's certificate in his pocket – this would be a fright! And especially: it would no longer be Germany'.[36] The traditional German system of government, monarchy, is held to be the superior one, and the idea of democracy is characterised as 'international' and 'foreign': 'democratic and international are one and the same'.[37] Hatred of democracy is explicitly linked to being truly German, because democracy is threatening to 'real' and 'true' German values, and is 'foreign and poisonous to the German character'. Mann is 'deeply convinced that the German people will never be able to love political

---

[32] Ibid., 201.

[33] Ibid., 265 ff.

[34] Ibid., 219.

[35] Ibid., 16 and 190.

[36] Ibid., 202. Also see Keller, *Der unpolitische Deutsche*, 48. Mann uses 'virtue' throughout the book in a derogatory way.

[37] Mann, *Reflections*, 189. Eichner comments that the Allies also saw themselves fighting 'to keep the world safe for democracy...against the fact and the idea of a monarchy, against the paternalistic state which the Germans...called "Obrigkeitsstaat"' ('Thomas Mann and Politics', 9).

democracy...the much decried "authoritarian state" is and remains the one that is proper and becoming to the German people, and the one they basically want'.[38]

The conservative, 'national' position is held by Mann to be not only 'nonpolitical', but suprapolitical: it is simply 'higher', natural, true and superior. He explains that 'it is not just patriotic prejudice when one imagines and perceives in the strangely organic, unforced and poetic word combination, *deutsches Volk*, something not only national, but also essentially different, better, higher, purer, yes, holier than in the expression, "English people" or "French people"'.[39] Mann's ability to see such nationalism as 'nonpolitical' is symptomatic of the supremacy of such thinking within contemporary German society, in which conservatism was the norm and therefore taken to be 'unpolitical'; only that which challenged the dominant state of affairs was deemed 'political'.

Conservative Politics and Art (2): Pfitzner's Aesthetics

Pfitzner, like Mann, was situated firmly within the dominant conservative context of his time, and made no secret of his political convictions. His polemical writings, as well as his letters and the texts he set to music, betray beliefs close to those expressed by Mann in his *Betrachtungen*, in their opposition to left-wing, progressive political forces and his view of nationalism and conservatism as 'natural' and automatically 'correct'. A central concern for Pfitzner, exemplified in his two important essays 'Futuristengefahr' ('The Dangers of Futurism', 1917) and 'Die neue Ästhetik der musikalischen Impotenz' ('The New Aesthetic of Musical Impotence', 1919), is the fate of true 'German' music in the face of new developments such as atonality and jazz. Pfitzner creates an opposition between what he deems 'good' and 'bad', and, like Mann, explicitly politicises that which he is against. In 'Die neue Ästhetik', he describes 'good' art as 'German and true', 'national and true' and 'magnificent and deep'.[40] He suggests that music itself is above politics, saying at the end of the essay that 'the melody

---

[38] Mann, *Reflections*, 16–17.

[39] Ibid., 208 and 267.

[40] Pfitzner, 'Die neue Ästhetik der musikalischen Impotenz', *Gesammelte Schriften*, Vol.2 (Augsburg: Dr. Benno Filser-Verlag, 1926), 130 and 251.

of a Schubertian linden tree lives longer than the empires of Alexander and Napoleon', and thereby infers that music is 'nonpolitical'.[41]

Pfitzner felt he was at the end of the great German tradition of art music. Like Hans Sachs in *Die Meistersinger*, who expresses the sentiment 'Honour your German masters', the conservative Pfitzner revered his compositional forebears. His 'Masters' included composers such as Wagner, Hoffmann, Beethoven, Schubert, Weber, Marschner, and Schumann, about whom he wrote numerous essays, as well as conducting their works. For Pfitzner, these great composers uncovered 'the deepest mysteries of the national life of the soul (*Seelenleben*), music as soul of the nation'.[42] Pfitzner's commitment to the German musical heritage of which he was a part was frequently expressed by the composer, for instance in a letter he wrote in 1946:

> I...remain true to this land in spite of all; the land of Luther in which the B minor mass and Faust originated, the land that brought forth 'Freischütz' and Eichendorff, the 'Pastoral', and 'Die Meistersinger', the land in which the 'Critique of Reason' and 'The World as Will and Representation' were conceived – *I shall remain true to this land until my last breath.*[43]

In contrast, Pfitzner saw modern art as a manifestation of left-wing, 'un-German' politics; like Mann, he demonised trends to which he was opposed, for instance in 'Die neue Ästhetik' which uses explicitly political and anti-Semitic terms to inveigh against modern music. Here, atonal music is described as 'communist', 'Jewish' and as 'free-and-easy, new, international, socially-constructive power-art' (*frisch-fröhliche, neue, internationale, gesellschaftsbildende Kraftkunst*).[44] Pfitzner says that 'the atonal

---

[41] Ibid., 252.

[42] Ibid., 130 and 233.

[43] Pfitzner, *Reden, Schriften, Briefe*, 325 (5th October 1946), Pfitzner's emphasis. Translation as Jon Newsom, 'Hans Pfitzner, Thomas Mann and "The Magic Mountain"', *Music and Letters* 55/2 (1974), 138.

[44] Pfitzner, 'Die neue Ästhetik', 250–51. Translation partly based on Attinello, 'Pfitzner, *Palestrina*, Nazis, Conservatives', 31. Attinello's translation of 'Kraftkunst' as 'power-art' is literally correct, but Pfitzner's original has a further meaning because of its reference to a phrase used by Paul Bekker, *gesellschaftbildende Kraft*. I will discuss the idea of *gesellschaftbildend* music further in Chapter 3.

chaos, along with the corresponding forms in the other arts, is the artistic parallel of the bolshevism which is threatening the European states'.[45] He continues that 'the fate of our national art, especially music', is under threat from the proponents of atonality: 'internationalism, which is the enemy of the *Volk*...not only wants to break up states, but also poisons the innermost life of the *Volk*, their heart, as it were'.[46] Modern music is led by the 'Jewish-international spirit' (*Geist*), and to the Germans is a 'wholly strange madness of destruction and devastation'.[47] He calls jazz 'American-international vulgarity': it is a 'jazz-foxtrot-flood', which 'kills the soul, and flatters the body, which is why its danger remains unnoticed as it is welcomed in'.[48] In 'Die neue Ästhetik', he complains that modern music is 'impotent' because it is not based on inspiration, and turns its back on the fundamentals of music such as harmony and melody; again, he uses a specifically political comparison: 'One can...abolish aristocracies, kill, banish and exile kings and Kaisers, but one cannot kill or abolish the aristocracy of nature and art'.[49] In 1919, when Pfitzner was writing, these words would have had a particular resonance: the November Revolution of 1918, which led to the founding of the Weimar Republic, saw the abolishment of the German monarchy.

With language such as this, Pfitzner signifies his political views as well as his aesthetic ones. His antipathy towards the political forces which he links with progressive musical styles places him squarely on the conservative wing of contemporary politics.[50] Pfitzner's polemics are not only

---

[45] Pfitzner, 'Die neue Ästhetik', 115. On the rhetoric of musical bolshevism, see John, *Musikbolschewismus*.

[46] Pfitzner, 'Die neue Ästhetik', 109.

[47] Ibid., 230. It is interesting to note that other writers of the time aligned modernism in music with democracy, which was disparaged by them as it was by Mann; for instance, an anonymous author in the *Illustrierte Wiener Extra-Blatt* wrote that Schoenberg produced 'democrat-noises' (*Demokratengeräusche*). Reger and Strauss were elsewhere criticised for being musical 'social democrats' (John, *Musikbolschewismus*, 22).

[48] Pfitzner, 'Die neue Ästhetik', 250 and 115. Also see 119: 'The un-German, in whichever form it appears, as atonality, internationalism, Americanism, German pacifism, assaults our existence and our culture from all sides, and European culture along with it'.

[49] Ibid., 229.

[50] See Ulrich Kurth, '"Ich pfeif' auf Tugend und Moral". Zum Foxtrott in den zwanziger Jahren', in Sabine Schutte (ed.), *Ich will aber gerade vom Leben singen...: Über*

representative of right-wing beliefs of the era, but also indicate the anxiety of this group in the face of threats to society in its existing form. Marc Weiner comments that 'the terror with which Pfitzner perceived [jazz]...underscores its function as a symbol of forces threatening to change an established social order'; his comment also goes for the other changes in musical style at this time.[51] Pfitzner exemplifies a disquiet about changes in society amongst conservatives which would eventually lead to political reaction and Nazism.

In his other important essay, 'Futuristengefahr', a denunciation of Busoni's treatise *Entwurf einer neuen Ästhetik der Tonkunst* (*Sketch of a New Aesthetic of Music*), Pfitzner again shows his participation within pre-existent, traditional musical norms, in his treatment of tonal music as a 'given' and as 'natural'. Here, he takes issue with Busoni's proposal that a change in the materials of music is the best way forward, and proposes his alternative to modernism, namely, a return to established aesthetic 'truths'. As Franklin notes in his essay on this polemic, Pfitzner holds to the belief 'that the *means* of artistic expression develop in accordance with changes in what artists feel that they have to say; with the nature of their "inspiration"'.[52] It is useless to change the material of music in the attempt to create new art, Pfitzner argues, as Busoni suggests; this would be to put the cart before the horse.[53] Pfitzner rubbishes the Futurist's desire for the new and modern and replies that 'systems, rules, forms in music grow from music itself, just as with species of animals and plants in nature; some die out there, many survive. The rule against fifths has its own eternal correctness, as every real musician feels'.[54] He pours scorn on musicians who

---

populäre Musik vom ausgehenden 19. Jahrhundert bis zum Ende der Weimarer Repubik (Reinbek bei Hamburg: Rowohlt, 1987), 375.

[51] Weiner, *Undertones of Insurrection*, 67. For a discussion of contemporary right-wing politics in the *Zeitschrift für Musik*, see Sachs's 'Some Aspects of Musical Politics in pre-Nazi Germany'. Many of the arguments presented by this journal, around the ideas of 'Germanness' versus 'internationalism', 'Bolshevism', 'Americanism' and modernism, are clearly part of the same discourse as that expressed by Pfitzner.

[52] Franklin '*Palestrina* and the Dangerous Futurists', 126. Also on Pfitzner's response to Busoni, see Ermen, *Musik als Einfall*, 87 ff., and Adamy, *Hans Pfitzner*, 90 ff.

[53] Franklin '*Palestrina* and the Dangerous Futurists', 127.

[54] Pfitzner, 'Futuristengefahr', *Gesammelte Schriften*, Vol.1 (Augsburg: Dr. Benno Filser-Verlag, 1926), 194.

look for new techniques; speaking of Busoni – although by implication, all 'Futurist' musicians are included – he says that:

> He sits at the piano. How stubborn of the keyboard that no gentler transition is possible between the B and C. This limitation must go! He hears an orchestra: that is still almost the same clarinet and trumpet and violin that appeared in the orchestra of Beethoven's and Wagner's time. How boring is this limitation! He opens scores: what was the tyrannical and pedantic composer thinking of to expect me to play hundreds of bars in the same tempo? I cannot endure longer than eight bars! It curtails my freedom!...I can well believe...that if one has a bad spiritual and physical disposition, one could find it strange and intolerable that for as long as one lives, each day arrives in the morning and leaves in the evening; that the body always takes up the same space; that one must pay for every minute of one's life with a breath; that one could find it highly tedious to always have the same nose on one's face.[55]

By holding the progressive composer up to ridicule in this manner, Pfitzner indicates that tonal music is the established, 'natural' and 'right' way of composing; one can no more escape it than one can escape breathing. Such a view again situates Pfitzner as a conservative: in the same manner as the traditionalist political view in his Germany, exemplified by Mann and termed 'nonpolitical', tonality was so ingrained that it was accepted as the norm. In contrast to the 'bolshevik' and 'international' modernists, Pfitzner's music is governed by eternal laws, allegedly above the realm of the political.

Conservatism in *Palestrina*

As well as having similar political and aesthetic stances, Pfitzner and Mann were personally acquainted: they knew each other socially (although they were not close friends), and Mann admired *Palestrina* in particular.[56] In his *Betrachtungen*, Mann says that *Palestrina* is 'completely...to the point of this book', saying that he has made the opera 'into my own, my intimate

---

[55] Ibid., 222–3.

[56] Vogel, *Hans Pfitzner*, 84. In 1918, Mann founded a 'Hans-Pfitzner-Society for German Music', which would not only promote Pfitzner, but sought to educate the populace through popularising German music and folk music (Adamy, *Hans Pfitzner*, 231).

possession'.[57] Pfitzner's opera may be read in relation to Mann's *Betracht-ungen* and its dichotomy of the 'political' and the 'nonpolitical'.[58]   Both men used their works to construct a conservative position, aesthetically and politically; Pfitzner creates this dualism in his opera through the presentation of the solitary, 'nonpolitical' environment of the composer Palestrina in Acts One and Three versus the worldly, 'political' Council of Trent. This division was described by Pfitzner in his essay 'Palestrina. Ein Vortrag über das Werk und seine Geschichte'; he said that the opera is 'a kind of triptych in form: a first and third act for the real world of Palestrina, and in the middle, the picture of the hustle and bustle (*bewegtes Treiben*) of the

---

[57] Mann, *Reflections*, 297.

[58] A number of writers on *Palestrina* have made reference to Mann's *Betrachtungen* in their work, but this is usually limited to Mann's comments about *Palestrina*, specifically where he refers to Palestrina's positioning outside the everyday world and the work's backward-looking nature; see, for instance, Ashley, 'In Sympathy with Death', 33; Franklin, '*Palestrina* and the Dangerous Futurists', 119; and Newsom's 'Hans Pfitzner, Thomas Mann and "The Magic Mountain"'. The latter considers Mann's novel in more depth than the *Betrachtungen*. The only studies which do mention Mann's 'political'-'nonpolitical' dualism are those by Botstein, Adamy and Toller. Botstein comments only briefly on Mann's and Pfitzner's views of genius as being opposed to egalitarianism ('Pfitzner and Musical Politics', 69). Adamy devotes little space to the theme, and does not draw out its implications for Pfitzner's wider context; he sees Palestrina's 'nonpolitical' position as an aesthetic rather than as an intrinsically political one. Moreover, he concurs implicitly with Mann's belief that conservatism is 'nonpolitical', saying that Pfitzner's conservatism 'excludes any real political engagement in his life' (*Hans Pfitzner*, 238). Toller fundamentally misinterprets Mann because he overlooks the negative implications which Mann attaches to 'politics' and the concepts he aligns with the 'political'. Perhaps influenced by Mann's later, anti-Nazi stance, Toller states that 'Mann's political inclinations were progressive' and that there is a 'gulf between Pfitzner's and Mann's views of progress'; therefore he says that Mann saw *Palestrina* as reactionary and opposed to his own liberal tendencies (*Pfitzner's* Palestrina, 103–4). A closer reading of the *Betrachtungen* shows that this is inaccurate. Toller likewise writes that Mann takes 'almost any general expression of the situation of humanity to be essentially political', a comment which is also incorrect. Toller himself believes that 'there is no justification for political arguments to influence creative artists in the abstract field of music' (ibid., 104).

outside world, which is always an enemy to the quiet creation of the genius'.[59]

Palestrina's configuration of two distinct worlds demonstrates the essential opposition of artist and society that lies at the heart of the work. The Council, as symbolic of society, is painted in negative terms, and is contrasted with the solitary and contemplative milieu of the composer. Mann, in his commentary on Pfitzner's work in his *Betrachtungen*, explicitly designated the Council 'political', calling the second act of *Palestrina* 'nothing other than a colorful and affectionately studied satire on politics, specifically on its immediately dramatic form, the parliament'.[60] Within the context of his book, the reference to 'politics' is, of course, coloured: it is not a neutral term to describe a governmental system, but is used in a derogatory fashion. If the Council is 'political', with all the negative connotations Mann, and Pfitzner, lent to this term, then in contrast, Palestrina himself may be read as signifying the 'nonpolitical'. Palestrina's abstention from involvement in society is shown to be fundamentally necessary: it is through his preclusion from participation in the outside world that he is able to partake fully of his existence on a higher spiritual plane, in touch with angels and with God. Palestrina is 'nonpolitical' in two ways: firstly, he is literally uninvolved in political matters, and secondly, his contrast to the 'political' realm of the Council positions him as 'nonpolitical' in Mann's sense: conservative and concerned with the individual and the 'metaphysical'.

The Character of Palestrina as 'Nonpolitical'

The representation of Palestrina as 'nonpolitical' works on a subtle level. The primary way in which his character is established is through his separation from the world around him – 'society' in Mann's language – and his placement instead in the realm of the 'metaphysical'. Palestrina is completely divorced from society, as represented by the Council: we never meet him outside the room in Rome where he first appears in Act One, and the Council is geographically distant from him. He exists in a secluded world, either alone or with only a few other characters around him. The

---

[59] Pfitzner, *Reden, Schriften, Briefe*, 27.
[60] Mann, *Reflections*, 301.

composer's largely solitary existence in one room symbolises his separate, 'inner realm' of artistic and spiritual experience; his later imprisonment similarly accentuates his distance from society.[61] Pfitzner's conception of the separation of the artist from the world outside is shown in a quotation from Schopenhauer which he used to preface the score of the opera:

> [The] purely intellectual life of mankind consists in its advancing knowledge through sciences and in the refinement of the arts, both of which slowly continue across the ages and the centuries, and to which the individual generations bear their contribution as they pass by. This intellectual life, like an ethereal adjunct, like a fragrant aroma produced by fermentation, hovers above the bustle of the world, above the real life of the nations, which is guided by the will; and alongside the history of the world there proceeds the history of philosophy, of science and of the arts, guiltless and untainted by blood.[62]

The construction of the character of Palestrina is consistent with Mann's belief in the 'irrevocable conflict between individual and society', and his conviction that this antagonism can only be resolved 'in the sphere of personality'. Palestrina does not display any transparently conservative, antidemocratic or nationalist tendencies of his own (even though Mann stated that he 'tends in attitude toward conservatism');[63] instead, he is constructed as 'nonpolitical' through his separation from the 'political'.

Palestrina's isolation from the world alters in status during the course of the opera. It is problematic to him in Act One; since the death of his wife Lukrezia, when he lost all inclination to compose, he has felt his separation acutely. He enunciates his loneliness most clearly during his long monologue in Act One Scene Four, which follows his refusal to write the test mass and Borromeo's angry departure. Here, Palestrina despairs of his estrangement from the world, and wonders how he could ever have created art. He says 'how strange and unknown are people to each other!', and declares that he is now like someone who watches the rest of the world rushing by like 'strange creatures'.[64] Although he could create when his wife

---

[61] Franklin, '*Palestrina* and the Dangerous Futurists', 133.

[62] No attribution is given for this quote in the score of *Palestrina*, but it is taken from the philosopher's *Parerga and Paralipomena*.

[63] Mann, *Reflections*, 308.

[64] 'Wie fremd und unbekannt sind sich die Menschen!'; 'fremde Larven'.

was with him, he now feels that everything is 'meaningless, completely meaningless', and it is all the same 'whether they [my works] are eaten up quickly by flames or slowly by time'.[65]

As he is at his most despairing, though, Palestrina is visited by 'Nine Dead Masters of Composition', who (unsuccessfully) encourage him to write the mass, and subsequently by a choir of angels, whose song inspires him to compose. Both the Masters and the angels are sent from God, and belong to a higher order of reality than that of the mundane world. It is thus suggested that Palestrina also exists on this level. He is an artist of genius, ordained by God and implicitly 'true' and 'correct'. The Masters tell the composer quite explicitly that he must write the mass because God wishes it: in answer to Palestrina's question 'who commands it?',[66] they answer:

> The old Master of the world, who is without name; who is likewise a servant of the ancient Word on the edge of eternity. He creates his work as you do yours, he forges rings, figures, stones, into the shimmering chain of ages and into the events of the world. ...Be ready to add the structure's final stone... . Then you will shine brightly, you will sound purely, Pierluigi, you will be the last stone on his beautiful chain.[67]

Palestrina only suffers while he 'kicks against necessity', the Masters tell him.[68] He must accept his fate, which is to create great art as God wishes; once he has assented to this, his place as 'the last stone on [God's] chain' is assured. This meeting and Palestrina's experience of angelic intervention seems to lead him to accept that his artistic calling makes it necessary for him to live apart from other mortals: in Act Three, he is content with his lot.

---

[65] 'sinnlos, gänzlich sinnlos'; 'ob die Flamme sie [meine Werke] rasch oder die Zeit sie langsam frißt'.

[66] 'wer befiehlt's?'.

[67] 'Der alte Weltenmeister, der ohne Namen ist, der gleichfalls untertan uraltem Wort am Rand der Ewigkeit. Er schafft sein Werk, wie du das deine, er schmiedet Ringe sich, Figuren, Steine zu der schimmernden Kette der Zeiten der Weltbegebenheiten. ...Den Schlußstein zum Gebäude zu fügen sei bereit... . Dann strahlst du hell, dann klingst du rein, Pierluigi, du, an seiner schönen Ketten der letzten Stein'.

[68] 'löck[t] wider den Stachel'.

The angels' dictation to Palestrina of the substance of his mass illustrates his connection with the divine and his removal from the world. Their music is set apart texturally from the music which led up to it: the previous comparatively 'empty' texture and tonally ambiguous music which follows the meeting with the Masters is replaced by the expansive A-major of the Kyrie, with high sopranos, first one singing solo and later a whole chorus, and a richer orchestral texture. The orchestration of the angels' music draws on traditional signifiers for the angelic or divinely supernatural found in music of the nineteenth century, for instance, in Mahler's Eighth Symphony, Liszt's 'Faust' Symphony, or the end of *Parsifal*. It is distinguished particularly by prominent harp arpeggios and high solo violins, as well as by the lofty vocal lines. The music which the angels sing is based on the *Missa Papae Marcelli* by the real, historical Palestrina, although Pfitzner adapts this music substantially. For example, he suggests the 'angelic' and literally 'higher' nature of the mass by shifting the whole register up from the historical Palestrina's original into a higher tessitura. In Pfitzner's version, the choir of sopranos and altos never descends below middle C, in contrast to the more bass-dominated SATTBB of the original. The angels are also frequently situated above the stave in Pfitzner's reworking, even reaching the stratospheric heights of c''', while Palestrina's original music never goes above g''. Palestrina's inspiration by the angels is depicted through his literal repetition of the angels' motifs. Pfitzner uses the head motives from the Kyrie, Christe and Credo of the real *Missa Papae Marcelli*, but does not use the motives 'straight', staying close to the historical Palestrina's original music. Rather, he adapts them into his own style, embellishing the original through adding extensions and melismas to Palestrina's phrases, as well as adding the lavish orchestral accompaniment, transforming the tempered Renaissance music into an effusive jubilation.[69] (Ex.2.1 shows the melodic correspondences between Palestrina's original and Pfitzner's reworking.) As the scene progresses, Palestrina

---

[69] For the words 'Gloria in excelsis Deo', Pfitzner uses a phrase from the original Credo. A detailed analysis of the affinities between Pfitzner's music and the *Missa Papae Marcelli* can be found in Williamson, *The Music of Hans Pfitzner*, 189 ff.; also see Toller, *Pfitzner's* Palestrina, 163 ff., and Scholz, 'The Image of Giovanni Pierluigi da Palestrina', 79.

a) Palestrina - opening of Kyrie

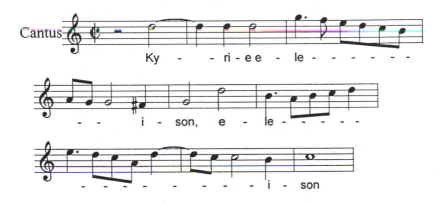

Pfitzner - beginning of Angels' Kyrie (Act 1, fig.161+7)

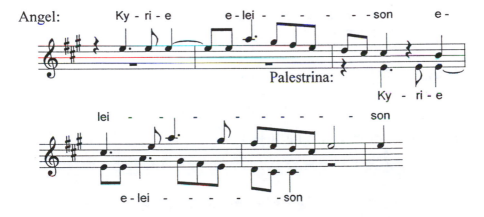

Ex.2.1 Comparison of Palestrina's *Missa Papae Marcelli* and Pfitzner's reworking (Reproduced by kind permission of Schott Musik International)

b) Palestrina - opening of Christe

Pfitzner - Christe (Act 1, fig.164-3)

Ex.2.1 (contd.)

Ex.2.1 (contd.)

sings more of his own music, without copying the angels; this original music is used to express his own sentiments. It may be derived from the angels' music, and may work in conjunction with it, for instance, the passage from fig.164+1 where Palestrina imitates the angels' 'Christe', and then sings his own line in chorus with the angels. This suggests how Palestrina is inspired by the angelic music, but at the same time is able to act independently of it, demonstrating the ability of the genius to be originally creative once inspired.[70]

---

[70] Similar 'angelic' music to that found in this scene is used almost leitmotivically elsewhere in the opera, appearing whenever angels are mentioned, such as in Act One, as Borromeo sings 'Die Engel halten Wacht' ('The angels keep watch'), or when the Cardi-

This dictation scene is of critical importance to the entire opera, and indeed, has often been seen as its dramaturgical climax.[71] The scene is also crucial to understanding Pfitzner's placement of himself within the drama, presenting himself, in an idealised version, as a composer of genius inspired by the angelic host. His use of the historical Palestrina's music is, perhaps, an obvious ploy; if one is writing an opera about a composer who once existed, it might seem only natural to use some of his or her music. In one respect this is certainly the case, and we could leave the matter at that, understanding Pfitzner's use of the *Missa Papae Marcelli* as merely localised historical colour. However, this does not answer the question completely: it is, after all, not absolutely necessary for Pfitzner to use Palestrina's actual music. Moreover, if Pfitzner merely wished for localised colour, then he could have quoted Palestrina's music literally. Instead, though, he tampers with it, thereby inscribing himself into that music. Pfitzner's music becomes a vicarious version of Palestrina's music, because of the ways in which he rewrites Palestrina's original. What is notable about the quotation of the mass is both its alteration by Pfitzner, and its positioning within the opera: it is not included as part of a performance, which would be perhaps the most obvious context for it, but as part of the scene of inspiration, indicating that it has a more strategic dramatic role than a simple quote.[72] As the figure of Palestrina on stage represents the real composer of the *Missa Papae Marcelli*, by merging his music with that of the historical composer, Pfitzner merges himself both with the stage version of Palestrina, and with the actual Palestrina. He becomes conflated with Palestrina, 'taking over', as it were, the shell of his predecessor; it is impossible to say decisively where one composer's music stops and the other one's starts. The amalgamation of Palestrina's music with Pfitzner's means that it is not simply a quote for historical colour; rather, Palestrina's mass becomes possessed by the spirit of Pfitzner, the two personalities sharing the same musical body. In producing this compound, Pfitzner writes himself 'into' the opera; he is not merely outside as a controlling 'presence' but an actor in the drama himself. In so doing, he can construct

---

nal Morone sings in Act Two, 'der hohe Papst er sprach zu uns: "Engel des Friedens seid!"' ('the holy Pope...he told us: "Be angels of peace!"').

[71] See Erman, *Musik als Einfall*, 102.

[72] Weisstein considers the mass itself, rather than Palestrina, to be the focus of the opera, which explains its prominent positioning ('Die letzte Häutung', 208).

an 'alternative' life: the image of Palestrina at the end of the opera, acclaimed by the world but still more inwardly concerned with his art, may be interpreted as a manifestation of the ideal state of affairs to which Pfitzner aspired, where the man of genius is reconciled with a world which understands and accepts him. As Vogel comments, 'Pfitzner had certainly imagined for himself an old age in the style of his *Palestrina*, released in the main from daily duties, generally surrounded by attention and above all, constantly performed on German stages'.[73]

After this scene, we next meet Palestrina in Act Three, where he has become comfortable with his lot. He is still in the same room as in Act One, and remains isolated from the world around him; on the surface, it seems that little has changed. However, his inspiration by the angels and the creativity he experienced has reassured him that his true destiny is to produce art. The composer's continuing separation from the world is emphasised by his behaviour in this act. He assumes the posture of the slightly-distracted Romantic genius, with his thoughts on a higher level: he moves slowly, 'gazes straight ahead', and is 'lost in thought'. The music of the final bars of the piece (from fig.59-2) further articulates Palestrina's continuing isolation.[74] Two musical worlds, signifying the composer and the society outside him, are here vividly juxtaposed; as the composer sits down at his organ in contemplation, 'lost in thoughts of music', cries of 'Long live Palestrina!' ('Evviva Palestrina!') can be heard outside. The musical style associated with Palestrina, comprised of one of the motifs associated with him throughout the work, appears at the beginning and end of the passage, in the orchestra; in between, Palestrina plays the organ on stage using the same style. This material is instrumental, predominantly polyphonic and based around a pitch centre of D. Set against this is the distant music of the people on the street, whose interruptions are in a choral, homophonic texture, with a simple mandoline accompaniment; this music is centred around a C/E dyad. The division of texture, tonal centres and instrumentation between Palestrina and the world outside reinforces the separateness of the two realms, while the final closure, Palestrina's organ

---

[73] Vogel, *Hans Pfitzner*, 106. Vogel calls Palestrina Pfitzner's '*Idealgestalt*' (ibid., 71).

[74] According to Hans Rectanus, in his study of the music of the opera, this passage encapsulates the separation of artist and world expressed in the Schopenhauer citation at the beginning of the score (Rectanus, *Leitmotivik und Form in den musikdramatischen Werken Hans Pfitzners* (Würzburg: Konrad Triltsch Verlag, 1967), 107).

playing a sustained D, indicates whose world is the more important and lasting.

The musical characterisation of Palestrina   The employment of several significant leitmotifs during the opera forms a distinct musical 'world' for Palestrina. For instance, a nexus of five leitmotifs is used to signify his genius.[75] The motif opening the first act Prelude is germinal for other motifs (ex.2.2(a)). Its 'archaic' fifths, which allude to the historical Palestrina's own compositional style, give rise to other related ideas, such as the motif of ex.2.2(b), and a transposed and rhythmically altered version, ex.2.2(c). Another motif used to invoke the composer and his world is found in the Prelude, ex.2.2(d); its harmony and use of suspensions again suggest the musical style of the historical Palestrina.[76] The same passage of the Prelude includes a cadential figure, ex.2.2(e), which assumes its own motivic status during the ensuing music. It is difficult to tie any one of these motifs down precisely to a definite 'meaning', because of their appearance in a variety of contexts.[77] However, all seem to pertain to the creation of art, by either Palestrina or his predecessors, and to Palestrina's place in his compositional lineage. Taken together, this group of motifs may be seen to present a musical picture of Palestrina the genius; they

---

[75] Williamson points out that the term 'motif' is not strictly accurate here, as it implies a fairly short and distinct musical entity (*The Music of Hans Pfitzner*, 174). Within this nexus, however, the motifs are not easily differentiated, as some of them are derived from each other and often appear together in longer musical passages, with one motif leading seamlessly into another. Nevertheless, I shall continue to use 'motif' as a generic term.

[76] Ibid.

[77] Some writers on the opera have sought to categorise these motives: Rectanus calls the motif of ex.2.2(c) the 'creation theme' (*Leitmotivik und Form*, 111); Williamson comments that ex.2.2(a) 'connotes a variety of states and ideas, representing an ideal substance lurking behind them: ecstasy, inspiration, music, and creation' (*The Music of Hans Pfitzner*, 179). Franklin suggests that this motif 'stands both for the ideal and the memory of the "old times" that are symbolized for Palestrina by the noble polyphonic style' ('A Musical Legend', in the programme book for the Royal Opera House production of *Palestrina*, Jan.–Feb. 1997, 15). Williamson designates the motif of ex.2.2(b) the motif of the 'Masters of the Past', and also says that ex.2.2(d) belongs to the Masters, as well as being related to Palestrina (*The Music of Hans Pfitzner*, 183 and 176).

(a) Prologue, b.1

flutes

(b) Act 1, Fig.121+4

D.B.

(c) Act 1, Fig.122+3

viola

(d) Prologue, Fig.B+3

flutes

Ex.2.2 Motives associated with Palestrina (Reprinted by kind permission of Schott Musik International)

(e) Prologue, Fig.E-5

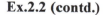

Ex.2.2 (contd.)

establish a separate musical plane for the composer, stylistically distinct
from the music elsewhere in the opera, and constitute a musical
environment in which he lives and with which he interacts. The motifs in
the orchestra circle around Palestrina, his words and his actions, sometimes
accompanying the composer himself, or occasionally occurring with
characters with whom he is associated, such as Borromeo, Ighino or the
Masters, when they talk about his creativity and his heritage.

After their introduction in the Prelude of the first act, these motifs occur
principally in four passages. The first is during Ighino's conversation with

Silla about Palestrina in Act One Scene Two, the second in Borromeo's
scene with the composer in Act One Scene Three, the third during Palestrina's meeting with the Masters, and the last at the end of Act Three. The
music accompanying Ighino's and later Borromeo's speeches creates the
musical environment of the doubting composer, and fixes the association
between his music and the composers of genius of the past. In Ighino's
speech, the motifs of ex.2.2(a) and ex.2.2(e) are used in connection with
Palestrina's former compositional creativity, such as when he says 'he
created work after work his whole life'.[78] Sometimes this functions through
a negative association, such as when Ighino tells how Palestrina can no
longer compose: 'so everything in him became still and empty'.[79] The
music here contradicts Ighino's words, suggesting how Palestrina remains a
genius despite his current lack of inspiration. In Borromeo's speech, associations are made particularly between Palestrina and his predecessors: the
motif of ex.2.2(b) appears as Borromeo tells him how 'the dead Masters lift
their hands [to you]' and at 'if there is no love in your heart for those to
whom you are so indebted'.[80] The music of the opening of the Prelude
(ex.2.2(a)) accompanies Borromeo as he says that Palestrina will create the
mass in order to 'save' music: 'Come, Master! For the sake of your eternal
fame, for the saving of music in Rome'.[81]

Palestrina's place in a line of great composers is accentuated in the
scene of his meeting with the Masters. Here, the significance of the nexus
of genius motifs is underlined through their use by the Masters in association with text which describes Palestrina's talent and his connection to his
predecessors. For instance, the ex.2.2(b) motif is used by the Masters with
the words 'you are familiar to us too'.[82] The same motif is used in the
orchestra when the Masters affirm that they really exist ('Wir sind'),
supporting them and underlining the fact that they are really 'alive' through
the motif's insistence on the presence of creativity. Similarly, the orchestral
voice asserts this presence when Palestrina asks the Masters 'have you not

---

[78] 'Ein Menschenalter schuf und schuf er Werke'.
[79] 'Da ward es still in ihm und leer'.
[80] 'die toten Meister heben ihre Hände'; 'wenn denn in Eurem Herzen keine Liebe für Jene,
denen Ihr soviel verdankt'.
[81] 'Auf, Meister! Euch zum ew'gen Ruhme, zur Rettung der Musik in Rom'.
[82] 'Auch du uns vertraut'.

already died?';[83] the motif of ex.2.2(b) contradicts him, being heard in the orchestra in answer to Palestrina's question. In this scene, the music depicts the dramatic tension between the Masters and Palestrina through the separation of the characters in terms of musical material. Only the Masters use the genius motifs; Palestrina himself uses and is accompanied by different music, signifying his resistance to their endeavours to persuade him to write the mass. However, Palestrina's assimilation into the world of the Masters is demonstrated at the end of Act Three, after his 'conversion' by the angels. In the final scene of the work, as Palestrina sits contemplating at his organ, he offers a supplication to God: 'Now forge me, the last stone on one of your thousand rings, oh God! And I will be content and at peace'.[84] Here the motif of ex.2.2(a) is used, as well as the motif of ex.2.2(b) and its inversion. The motif of ex.2.2(d) forms the music for the final bars, surrounding Palestrina's organ playing and its juxtaposition with the 'Evvivas'. The previously conflicting voices of the Masters scene between the Masters and Palestrina are therefore reconciled, as Palestrina accepts his fate as a composer and genius.

Another important motif in addition to the 'genius' motifs is what we may designate the 'loneliness' leitmotif, first found at fig.113-3 played by a solo viola.[85] The melody is particularly predominant during Palestrina's monologue in Act One Scene Four, following Borromeo's departure. It first appears preceding the phrase 'how strange and unknown are people to each other! The essence of the world is solitude', and later at 'how terrible suddenly to find oneself alone deep in a wood'.[86] (It also recurs in the viola during the final part of the monologue.) In addition, the motif occurs at the beginning of the sixth scene, just before the appearance of the angels, as Palestrina sings 'alone in deepest darkness, I, a poor man full of fear, lift my voice upwards'.[87] The use of the 'loneliness' motif by the solo viola,

---

[83] 'starbt Ihr nicht schon?'.

[84] 'Nun schmiede mich, den letzten Stein an einem deiner tausend Ringe, du Gott! Und ich will guter Dinge und friedvoll sein'.

[85] Toller, *Pfitzner's Palestrina*, 156. Also see Rectanus, *Leitmotivik und Form*, 113 and Williamson, *The Music of Hans Pfitzner*, 182–3.

[86] 'Wie fremd und unbekannt sind sich die Menschen! Das Innerste der Welt ist Einsamkeit'; 'Wie schrecklich, sich plötzlich einsam tief im Wald zu finden'.

[87] 'Allein in dunkler Tiefe voll Angst ich armer Mensch rufe laut nach oben'. The motif is heard again in the last act, when Palestrina remembers his night of creative fervour: 'I

and its relationship to the rest of the orchestra in the passage from fig.113-3 to fig.124+7, may be read as depicting Palestrina himself. The viola becomes a kind of alter ego, an instrumental version of the composer; its relationship to the orchestra signifies the composer's relationship to the world. The viola is almost literally alone in its placement with the other instruments: it appears either completely unaccompanied or with a very sparing accompaniment, and even when it is accompanied, it stands out against the rest of the texture, 'strange and unknown' to the rest of the orchestra. The characterisation of the viola as an alter ego for Palestrina is accentuated by the instrument's use of the same melodic material as Palestrina, particularly the 'loneliness' motif, either simultaneously or in dialogue. When the solo viola returns later in the scene, at fig. 121+2 (after passages which use different musical material), it again shares notes and motifs with the voice. Despite his loneliness at this point of the opera, though, Palestrina learns the necessity of isolation for the great composer through the visitation of the Masters and the angels.

Pfitzner and the concept of genius   Pfitzner's characterisation of Palestrina as a genius illustrates the fictional composer's 'nonpolitical' position, above the activity of the world. According to Pfitzner, the genius must necessarily remain apart from society, on a 'metaphysical' level, in order to be able to create, thus becoming what Mann would term 'nonpolitical'. We may recall here Mann's belief that democracy would flatten out the achievements of 'great men' for the sake of homogeneity: if the 'political' is against the concept of genius, it therefore follows that the genius must be 'nonpolitical'. Just as Mann characterises conservatism as ideology-free and 'natural', and opposes this to the 'political', Palestrina's genius places him not only above society and politics, but as implicitly 'right'. Pfitzner's ideas of genius draw on nineteenth-century aesthetics, and in particular were influenced by Schopenhauer, who stated that the supremely gifted man stands apart from, and above, his fellow mortals. For Schopenhauer, the genius must remain separate from the world in order to create: 'genius lives essentially alone. It is too rare to find its like with ease, and too different from the rest of man to be their companion'.[88] In particular, the genius

---

wrote it [the mass] in one night' ('Ich schrieb sie [die Messe] in einer Nacht').
[88] Schopenhauer, *The World as Will and Idea*, vol.3, trans. R.B. Haldane and J. Kemp

must disassociate himself from politics, and instead should work 'without regard for any reward, approbation or sympathy, and in solitude and with no attention to his own well-being...he is urged to think more of posterity than of the contemporary world by which he would merely be led astray'.[89]

Unlike Palestrina, who does not initially realise his superior talent, Pfitzner appears to have believed in his own genius absolutely. He frequently wrote about the concept of genius in terms which seek to portray a familiarity with the phenomenon that comes from personal experience.[90] Pfitzner believed that genius is essential for true artistic creation, saying that 'the conception of a genius is the alpha and omega of all art'; as he believed his own art to be 'true' art, his own qualities of genius therefore had to be acknowledged.[91] Pfitzner referred to his own superiority, for instance, by calling his works *Meisterwerke*, while in 1933 he said that 'No-one knows how long the "Third Reich" will exist, *but I know that my works will last, according to an eternal law*'.[92] However, he felt that his genius was unrecognised, leaving him on the margins of musical society, a fact which caused him displeasure through much of his life. He expressed his despondency in a letter of 1909:

> Every new work of mine is a failure. ...I have to drag my greatest stage works around to hack-theatres (*Schmieren*) – the economy craves easy fare. ...Hope

---

(Sixth Edition. London: Kegan Paul, Trench, Trübner and Co. Ltd., 1909), 156; also see the section 'On Genius', 138–66, and *Parerga and Paralipomena: Short Philosophical Essays*, Vol.1, trans. E.F.J. Payne (Oxford: Clarendon Press, 1974), 330. For more details on Pfitzner's relationship to Schopenhauer, see Williamson, *The Music of Hans Pfitzner*, 32 ff.; Ermen, *Musik als Einfall*, 52–7; and Adamy, *Hans Pfitzner*, 141–69.

[89] *Parerga and Paralipomena*, Vol.II, 72 and 86. The idea of genius itself has many political implications, not least that the 'great man' can be positioned as a kind of *Übermensch*, or a *Führer*. (See Jochen Schmidt, *Die Geschichte des Genie-Gedankens in der deutschen Literatur, Philosophie und Politik, 1750–1945* (Darmstadt: Wissenschaftliche Buchgesellschaft, 1988) and Adamy, *Hans Pfitzner*, 236.) These have their own particular resonances for the period under question, but Palestrina is quite definitely not constructed as a leader; his opposition to the political prohibits him from taking such a role.

[90] See Pfitzner, 'Über musikalische Inspiration', in *Sämtliche Schriften*, Vol.4, ed. Bernhard Adamy (Tutzing: Hans Schneider, 1987), 300, or *Briefe*, 794 (18th December 1937).

[91] Pfitzner, 'Zur Grundfrage der Operndichtung', *Gesammelte Schriften*, Vol.2, 10.

[92] Pfitzner, *Briefe*, 152 (12th February 1909) and 638 (1st October 1933), Pfitzner's emphasis.

after hope deceives me; but in spite of that, I wring from myself a work like the Quartet, in the most unfavourable circumstances – it meets with incomprehension, and was almost booed off stage in Berlin.[93]

During the Third Reich, he complained that he was 'improperly neglected': 'I should be...the foremost man in the country in artistic matters, i.e. in the highest position', but 'of all the great names in music, I am the only one who has not yet once been given a worthy place'.[94] This lack of recognition helps to explain why he felt moved to idealise an image of himself in a composer who is recognised as the 'saviour of music'.

The idea of inspiration, as presented so centrally in *Palestrina*, is a fundamental part of the concept of the solitary genius, and consistently with his philosophical heritage, Pfitzner held that inspiration 'is the only point of view by which the higher worth of any music can be judged; it is the highest criterion of any music'. One moment of inspiration, he stated, is better than 'a hundred thousand notes of musical work!'.[95] The idea that inspiration merely arrives unsolicited, and that the artist can do nothing to anticipate nor to prevent it, recurs frequently in Pfitzner's writings:

> Just as the essence of art lies in the concept, so the essence of the concept lies in the involuntary (*im Unwillkürlichen*)... . If there were a machine that could exactly indicate the degree of voluntariness or involuntariness, the borders of reflection and inspiration...then the key to all aesthetics would certainly have been found. For, strictly speaking, every argument can only be concerned with that which one cannot decide in practice, [i.e.] what is voluntary or involuntary in artistic creation.[96]

---

[93] Ibid., 151 (12th February 1909).

[94] Ibid., 902 (13th March 1942), 647 (17th January 1934) and 643 (5th December 1933). Also on Pfitzner's belief in his neglect, see Adamy, *Hans Pfitzner*, 52 ff.; on his problematic relationship with the authorities of the Third Reich, see Michael H. Kater, *Composers of the Nazi Era: Eight Portraits* (New York and Oxford: Oxford University Press, 2000), 154 ff.

[95] Pfitzner, 'Über musikalische Inspiration', 300, and Pfitzner quoting Reger, in Adamy, *Hans Pfitzner*, 116. Also on the importance Pfitzner attached to inspiration, see Adamy, *Hans Pfitzner*, 20, and Mosco Carner, 'Pfitzner v. Berg, or Inspiration v. Analysis', *Musical Times* 118 (May 1977), 379–80.

[96] Pfitzner, 'Zur Grundfrage der Operndichtung', 13. Also, 'The work demands to be born,

Consistent with the idea of the involuntary nature of inspiration is the belief that inspiration comes from a higher source, and therefore that the artist has no control over it. The word for inspiration in German, *Einfall*, suggests how something 'falls in' to the artist's mind from outside; logically, the thing which has 'fallen in' must have originated from somewhere 'higher'. The genius, therefore, is implicitly in touch with the divine; inspiration is, according to Pfitzner, 'the breath of God'.[97] The influence of this nine-teenth-century ideology of genius may be traced in Pfitzner's presentation of Palestrina. Palestrina himself realises that his ability to compose is dependent upon higher factors when he is intransigent in the face of Borromeo's requests to write the trial mass. The composer states that the Pope 'can command, but can never command my genius, only me'.[98] The visitation of the angels, who dictate to the composer the music of his mass, is a fairly literal representation of the concept that the genius is in touch with the divine, and illustrates the twentieth-century composer's *Weltan-schauung* concerning his own artistic abilities.

Although the genius's inspiration comes from a higher source, accord-ing to Pfitzner the divine manifests itself through the artist's unconscious; by being aware of his unconscious the artist becomes aware of the divine. Pfitzner said that the unconscious is the 'womb of inspiration', and stated that he was 'convinced that every real creative person, thus every true phi-losopher, composer or poet, sees the unconscious as the real creative force in the artist'.[99] The importance given to the realm of the unconscious may be traced back to the philosophy of Immanuel Kant, who defined the ability to create art whilst in touch with the unconscious as a gift belonging only to the artist of genius; this idea, bolstered by the growing importance of the idea of the irrational, persisted in philosophy and aesthetics throughout the nineteenth century and into the twentieth.[100] In *Palestrina*, the importance of the unconscious for the composer serves to accentuate his separation

---

it doesn't ask after the cost', *Gesammelte Schriften*, Vol.3, 345, quoted in Adamy, *Hans Pfitzner*, 32.

[97] Pfitzner, 'Über musikalische Inspiration', 284.

[98] 'kann befehlen, doch niemals meinem Genius – nur mir'.

[99] Ibid., 282 and 284. Also see Adamy, *Hans Pfitzner*, 121. The interesting use of gendered terminology here, as in Pfitzner's concern with musical 'impotence' in 'Die neue Ästhetik', is discussed further by Eckhard John, *Musikbolschewismus*, 71 ff.

[100] Schmidt, *Die Geschichte des Genie-Gedankens*, 364.

from the world outside. Paradoxically, Palestrina does write the mass which the world, as represented in the Council, wants from him, but he does not do this with conscious intention, as the manner of his inspiration makes clear: he writes in the ecstasy of inspiration, as a 'vessel' of God, and then forgets having done so. The outcome, where the Pope is convinced not to ban music in church, is almost by accident as far as Palestrina is concerned. Palestrina's separation from the world remains intact because he has not *consciously* tried to serve society with his art. The premise that consciousness is inimical to artistic creation is articulated in the Masters scene, where the contrast of the conscious and the unconscious is expressed through the ideas of light versus dark. Palestrina says that 'the light of consciousness, which glares fatally, which rises to disturb us like the bold day, is enemy to sweet dreams, to artistic creation'.[101]

The importance of the unconscious is constructed further in Palestrina's 'loneliness' monologue at the beginning of the Masters scene. Here, the motif of ex.2.2(b), one of the 'genius' motifs, appears in canon in the double basses, with six imitative entries during the last part of the monologue (from fig.121-1), the polyphony forming an obvious allusion to the historical Palestrina's own compositional style. Palestrina says here that everything is 'meaningless, completely meaningless',[102] but the double bass accompaniment flatly contradicts this. Pfitzner plays on the idea of Palestrina's unconscious, constructing a conceit around the fact that, despite his protestations and despair, Palestrina *is* a composer of genius. The passage of polyphony is barely audible, either as polyphony or as the genius motif. Within the context of the whole passage, one hears the low rumble of the double basses, but because of the extremely low register, it is difficult to distinguish the individual entries. Nor are the last two entries, in bass clarinet and cellos, any easier to hear, as by this time the texture is filled out with woodwind and more strings. The allusion to the 'unconscious' here is therefore twofold: the low register at the start of the passage almost literally suggests the 'depths' of the unconscious, while the fact that the quotation is barely audible, perhaps even completely inaudible as a

---

101 'des Bewußtseins Licht, das tödlich grelle, das störend aufsteigt wie der freche Tag, ist feind dem süßen Traumgewirk, dem Künsteschaffen'. The language here is reminiscent of the light-dark dichotomy of *Tristan*, indicating the importance of Wagner for Pfitzner.

102 'sinnlos, gänzlich sinnlos'.

distinctive motif, suggests that it can be heard by the listener only on a subconscious level, rather than recognised as an obvious leitmotif.[103]

A further facet of the concept of artistic isolation, the association of the genius with immortality, is demonstrated in Pfitzner's aesthetics. The composer stated that 'the greatest achievements of the genius...defy temporality (*Zeitlichkeit*)', and 'ability, talent, genius is eternal, out of time, inexplicable'.[104] Because he believed himself to be a genius, it follows that Pfitzner would think himself immortal thanks to his works, as his comment '*I know that my works will last, according to an eternal law*' makes clear.[105] Again, this aesthetic is expressed in his opera. Although Palestrina's visitors are called the 'Nine Dead Masters of Composition', this title is, perhaps, something of a misnomer: they may be dead, but because of their works, they are also living. When Palestrina asks them to tell him, a 'poor soul, caught by mortality', whether these apparent ghosts 'really exist', they answer in the affirmative.[106] The Masters' invitation to Palestrina to join their circle demonstrates that he will become immortal like them. In Act Three, when Palestrina has completed his mass, Ighino comments on the composer's now assured immortality: 'You're now the most famous of all, in distant times they will still speak your name. And not only speak your name, but sing your works!'.[107] Composers of genius are different from ordinary mortals because they rise above the usual constraints of death; this confirms the separation of the man of genius from the world around him.

---

[103] Technically, there is a difference between the subconscious and the unconscious, the former being accessible to the conscious mind under certain conditions, the latter not accessible at all. However, the appeal to the listener's subconscious with this device can nevertheless be seen as representative of the unconscious.

[104] Pfitzner, 'Eindrücke und Bilder meines Lebens', *Sämtliche Schriften*, 646; 'Über musikalische Inspiration', 300.

[105] Pfitzner, *Briefe*, 638. For a discussion of immortality from a more philosophical angle, see Pfitzner's 'Über die persönliche Fortdauer nach dem Tode', *Reden, Schriften, Briefe*, 59–66.

[106] 'arme[r] Geist, in Sterblichkeit befangen'; 'wirklich [sind]'.

[107] 'Du bist jetzt der Berühmteste von allen, in fernsten Zeiten wird man dich noch nennen. Und nicht nur nennen, deine Werke singen!'.

The Council of Trent as 'Political'

While Palestrina represents the 'nonpolitical' in Mann's dualism, the Council of Trent, according to the writer, is a satire on the 'political'. The Council is set in opposition to Palestrina through contrasts of music, geography, and through the *dramatis personae*. The disorder of the Council is constructed in various ways as a representation of the 'hustle and bustle of the outside world', as Pfitzner terms it in his 'triptych' description. For instance, the conflicts between the different factions of the Council, from the opening bars of the act, depict its primarily argumentative nature. The divisions follow national lines: Spanish, Italian and French. Derogatory references to nationalities are rife, for instance, Severolus's 'the Spaniards! Always a hindrance and a thorn', Madruscht's complaint when he sees 'yet another Italian', or Budoja's 'we're blessed with French itches and Spanish scabs'.[108] At the beginning of the act, the conflicts between groups are expressed through free-flowing insults, but these are contained at this stage within groups of fellow-countrymen. As the Council meeting proceeds, the antagonism becomes increasingly vehement, as an argument breaks out about the order in which the items on the agenda should be discussed. As this quarrel escalates, the earlier insults against nations are made explicit: Count Luna of Spain comes into open conflict with the French Cardinal of Lorraine, who questions the way the Count has 'irregularly' been given a chair. The Spanish provoke the Italians and the French, with Luna saying that 'if Spain wants it, then the world wants it' and then crying that he will invite the Protestants to the debate.[109] At these remarks, chaos breaks out, and the meeting is adjourned, the various Council members still arguing as they leave. After they have dispersed, the conflict augments yet further, as the servants of the Council members break out into open riot. The servants '[act] out on their own level the drama Their Eminences have staged for us on theirs'.[110]

The quarrels within the Council come about because of the disputed power relationships between the various participants. The political relations of the different nations – particularly the relationship between Spain and

---

[108] 'die Spanischen! Stets Hindernis und Dorn'; 'ein Italiener mehr!'; 'wir [sind] gesegnet... mit französischer Krätze und dem spanischen Grind'.

[109] 'wenn Spanien es will, so will's die Welt'.

[110] Lee, 'Pfitzner's *Palestrina*', 57.

the Holy Roman Empire – are in flux, and as a result, arguments are based on these national questions. The Council members themselves display no small degree of hunger for power; as John Bokina states, 'Pfitzner lampoons the world of politics... . This is not a world of spirituality, justice, or reconciliation. Rather, politics is associated with self-interest, pomp, and deceit; not far in the background lurk force and violence'.[111] Within this context of power-playing and ill-temper, the rare references to God seem ironic. The speech by the Cardinal Legate Morone, for instance, which contains the most extended exposition of the Council's purpose, is juxtaposed with some rather pompous self-praise, despite his call for 'humility':

> We beg the Holy Ghost, who leads councils and also guides today's meeting, to descend to us and prepare a good conclusion for our work. The holy Pope, whose servants we legates are, he told us: 'be angels of peace!'. Carrying these words in my heart, I pray to God that the work of peace may succeed with you... . Reverend fathers! Beloved brothers! With all humility, which graces Christians, think today on this: We are the flower of all humanity. We are called to build the tower for its salvation that will defy all eras. Although we are truly small before God, yet we are great in the eyes of all people.[112]

As the reverse side to their wishes for power, many of the churchmen are portrayed as shallow and obsessed with trivia, focusing on minor details rather than on important issues in an effort to exert their authority. Instances of this concern with trivia are shown by Bishop Budoja, who worries about whether his expenses will be paid, and by the lack of agreement between Council members regarding the order of the agenda.

The portrayal of the Council's 'hustle and bustle' is further achieved simply through the large number of people who appear in the second act. This stands in direct contrast to the more sparsely populated environment

---

[111] Bokina, *Opera and Politics*, 136. Also see Henderson, 'Hans Pfitzner's *Palestrina*', 36.

[112] 'Den heilgen Geist, der die Konzilien leitet, der auch die heutige Versammlung lenkt, wir bitten ihn, daß er auf uns sich senkt und unserm Werk ein gutes End' bereitet. Deß' Diener die Legaten sind, der hohe Papst, er sprach zu uns: "Engel des Friedens seid!" Dies Wort im Herzen tragend, bitt' ich Gott, daß mir das Friedenswerk bei Euch gelinge... Ehrwürd'ge Väter! Liebe Brüder! Bei aller Demut, die den Christen ziert, seid heute eingedenk: Wir sind die Blüte alles Menschentums. Wir sind berufen, ihm zum Heile den Turm zu baun, der allen Zeiten trotzt. Wir, vor dem Herrn zwar klein, doch vor den Menschen aller Völker groß'.

of Palestrina in Acts One and Three. The Council of Trent is a chaotic hubbub, with a panoply of different characters coming and going, all in clerical garb, and many with the same voice type. Out of twelve solo characters in the act, Morone, Luna and Borromeo are all baritones, Madruscht, Brus and Lorraine are basses, Severolus and Avosmediano are bass-baritones. The potential difficulty of distinguishing between characters is exacerbated by the rapid pace of events in the act, particularly in the first section before the Council meeting officially starts. This section is a rush of activity, with one churchman arriving shortly after another, and sometimes barely being introduced before his successor appears.

The quarrelsome nature of the Council is portrayed musically in the Prelude to the act, of which Mann commented in *Betrachtungen eines Unpolitischen* that it is 'perhaps the most splendid musical piece of the evening, [and] has a completely stirring effect: this crashing, storming, falling, breath-taking agitation...tragically illustrates Palestrina's statement about the "movement that life constantly whips us into"'.[113] The music suggests the Council's chaotic and argumentative nature through the unstable and agitated nature of the components of its musical texture. Rather than starting on the tonic chord, E^b, the Prelude begins with four bars of cadential-type music, beginning on a diminished chord and an upbeat.[114] It then moves to the first inversion of the tonic chord before Pfitzner asserts some measure of stability with a conventional perfect cadence onto the tonic in the fourth bar. The unsteadiness of the opening harmonic progression is strengthened through the continuing obscuration of the tonal movement: although the overall key of the passage is E^b, this is concealed in the bars between the cadence in the fourth bar (fig.1-7) and that at fig.2-3. In many passages of the Prelude, particularly near the beginning, it is difficult to ascertain a particular tonal centre at all, and while there are some more stable harmonic progressions later, the larger-scale harmonic movement is not clearly established until some way into the Prelude. The effect created by this obscuration of tonal centre is supplemented by the chromatic, moto perpetuo melody of the horns, bassoons and lower strings, which refuses to

---

[113] Mann, *Reflections*, 301.
[114] Toller points out that E^b is the key at the furthest possible point from the A of the angels in Act One (*Pfitzner's* Palestrina, 119).

settle even at the cadence. Compared with the archaisms of Palestrina, such writing seems singularly 'modern'.

Much of the first half of the Prelude is based on the moto perpetuo quavers, which form the principal melodic material or act as an accompaniment to other melodies. This material is constructed around a number of motivic cells, many of which are predominantly chromatic or made up of a combination of semitones and whole tones. Their pitch structure does little to establish a definite tonal centre and thus reinforces the music's unsettled nature. (Ex.2.3 shows the formation of these cells at the opening of the Prelude.) The repetition and lack of any particular melodic development may be further read as representative of the inherent nature of the Council: like the arguments in the Council chamber, the musical argument here goes round in circles and does not progress. At fig.1-3, the feeling of instability is augmented by the trumpet melody (if it may be called such). This begins on the dominant, B^b, but then alternates between that note and its semitonal neighbour, A, forming a tritone with the tonic. The trumpet then gradually descends to the tonic through an unconventional route, although the bulk of the descent does not take place until the last moment (see ex.2.3). The trumpet melody's unsettled nature is added to by the continuing moto perpetuo chromatic bass quavers underneath.

The instability of the music is heightened through its rhythmic construction, particularly the way in which the quaver cells are grouped. The grouping often appears to lie across the strong beats of the bar, as can be seen in ex.2.3: at the beginning of the extract, the first quaver of each group tends to be not on the first or third beat of the bar, but on the second or fourth. Later groups fall into odd numbers, such as the suggestion of a Bartókian 2+3+3 rhythm at fig.1-3 to 1-2. The melodies of the first section of the Prelude function similarly: for instance, the violin melody of fig.2+4, itself derived from the motivic cells of previously, which does not conform to an expected beat but evades any regular metre by slurring over barlines and grouping quavers irregularly. The trumpet melody similarly plays consistently off the beat.

The Council not only represents the 'political' in a literal sense, as a political forum, but has the further quality of representing the 'political' in Mann's sense: it attempts to be democratic, as it is intended that the issues at hand are discussed and a consensus reached. Admittedly, elements of the Council seem on the surface to contradict the presentation of democracy.

Ex.2.3 Prologue, Act 2 (Reprinted by kind permission of Schott Musik International)

Ex.2.3 (contd.)

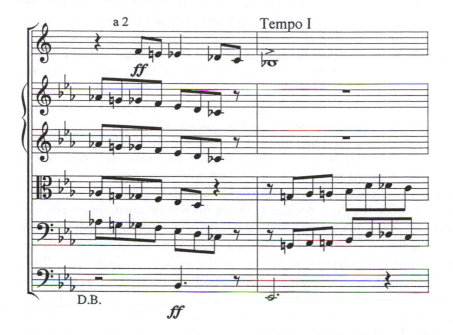

Ex.2.3 (contd.)

Some of the Council members are given more importance than others, for instance, exercising different degrees of privilege (Count Luna is given a throne, for example). This semi-democratic nature of the Council is shown as ridiculous; as Franklin says, the Council is portrayed as a 'garish and often comic pantomime of democracy'.[115] Nevertheless, the Council can be seen as *representative* of a democracy, and of 'politics' in Mann's sense. As well as being concerned with the 'political', the Council is also international, with members coming from a mixture of countries, while the lack of differentiation between these characters forms a palpable representation of the supposed homogeneity which follows when democracy is implemented. The Council functions as a double satire: firstly, Pfitzner's

---

[115] Franklin, 'A Musical Legend', 17. Also see '*Palestrina* and the Dangerous Futurists', 123.

presentation attacks the idea of democracy itself. Secondly, at the time when the opera was written, such democracy did not exist in Germany, and so, as in Mann's *Betrachtungen*, this kind of government is aligned with the 'foreign', the satire being directed at those countries with democratic governments. This 'foreignness' is supplemented by the Council's physical separation from the world of Palestrina.

Pfitzner's attack on the 'foreign' and 'un-German' finds a further outlet in his depiction of characters of various nationalities; the majority of the Council members, with their bad behaviour and petty squabbles, are Italian, Spanish and French. In contrast, there are few Germans, and those that do appear are depicted rather differently. The most important German character in terms of the plot is the Emperor Ferdinand. It is through Ferdinand's persuasion that the Pope decides to waive his ban on music in church until a trial mass has been composed; the 'saving' of music is at least partly thanks to him. The Emperor is thus presented as a man on the side of culture against the potential barbarities of the Italians, a thoroughly fitting position, perhaps, for a German. Significantly, Ferdinand never appears in person, but is only talked about: like Palestrina, the German Emperor is separate from the world of 'politics'. German clerics (with one exception) are also absent from the Council meeting, as Novagerio tells Borromeo: 'the Germans...have stayed away from the synod'.[116] The Council does take place on nominally German soil, in 'uncomfortable, German Trent';[117] although in present-day Italy, at that time Trent would have been under the rule of Ferdinand as part of the Holy Roman Empire (in German, the 'Altes Deutsches Reich'). This explains the presence of German servants at the end of the act, whose designation as German might otherwise be puzzling; rather than having travelled with their masters, they are the habitual inhabitants of the city. Significantly, the Germans play a smaller part in the brawl than the Italians and Spaniards, and utter few insults in comparison. The fact that the Germans are mostly absent from the Council indicates their 'nonpolitical' nature, and demonstrates Pfitzner's belief, like Mann's, that Germans have no place in 'political' democratic assemblies.

Trent's geographical location as part of Germany explains the presence of the only German cleric we meet in the Council, Madruscht, the Prince-

---

[116] 'die Deutschen...[sind] von der Synode fortgeblieben'.
[117] 'Trident, der deutschen, unbequemen'.

Bishop of Trent. His presentation is more ambivalent than Ferdinand's. The stage directions present him as 'a strong man who, despite his clerical clothes, gives the impression more of being a military man or a nobleman', these latter two occupations perhaps being suitably Germanic for Pfitzner. The way Madruscht behaves, though, is ambiguous; depending on one's point of view, it could be taken as either positive or negative. He is opposed to the way in which Council business is rushed through, and stands some-what aloof from those clerics who try to curry favour with him (for in-stance, in his conversation with Novagerio at Madruscht's first entrance). This stance could be interpreted as positive, even an attempt at remaining 'nonpolitical'. More problematically, at the end of the act it is Madruscht who orders that the rioting servants should be shot. This order may seem obdurate to us, but within the militaristic society of Pfitzner's time may have seemed reasonable, or even advisable. The German cleric's presenta-tion is therefore equivocal at best; he does not unambiguously stand out as an exemplar of nobility and magnanimity, and nor does he especially invite our sympathy.[118]

One problematic case in this portrayal of nationalities is the figure of Palestrina himself, an Italian, a fact which prompts the question of why the Germanophile Pfitzner chose this nationality for the hero. A simple answer may be found in the fact that Palestrina is located apart from the world: his separation from society makes him suprapolitical, and his own nationality is therefore irrelevant. An investigation of the status of the Renaissance composer within late nineteenth- and early twentieth-century German musicology is also revealing: just as Shakespeare was claimed by the Ger-man Romantics as being more 'German' than English, at the turn of the twentieth century Palestrina, too, was viewed as being part of the German race. This view is demonstrated in the works of several writers on the com-poser from the early years of the twentieth century: Otto Ursprung, for in-stance, argued for the influence of north-European music on Palestrina, saying that he 'stood incredibly close' to German musical culture; the same view was expressed by Houston Stewart Chamberlain.[119] Ludwig Woltmann

---

[118] Peter Franklin observes that Madruscht represents 'what in the nationalistic Pfitzner was dangerously in accord with that element in his society that would shortly replace demo-cratic inoperancy with Fascist intolerance' (ibid., 132).

[119] Ursprung, *Palestrina und Deutschland,* in Karl Weinmann (ed.), *Festschrift Peter Wagner zum 60. Geburtstag* (Leipzig: Breitkopf und Härtel, 1926), 192; Chamberlain,

held that the motivating force behind the Italian Renaissance was the migration to Italy of the *Germanen*, the ancient Germanic race. Palestrina, he continued, was undoubtedly of 'mixed race', the north-European and the Mediterranean.[120] Furthermore, these same musicologists stress that Palestrina is supranational: Ursprung wrote that 'the art of Palestrina stands over time and over space' (*überzeitlich und überweltlich*), while another scholar, Phillipp Spitta, maintained that Palestrina belonged not to a nation but to the whole world, just like Homer and Shakespeare.[121]

The appearance of one Council member, Abdisu, the Patriarch of Assyria, highlights the real nature of the meeting by acting as a foil to the other, self-important, members. Unlike the other delegates, Abdisu is not concerned with consolidating his own power, but is the one man who seems truly in touch with God, wishing to serve him and the Pope, and to help to bring about decisions that will be in the best interests of the Church. As he first enters the Council, he sings with a sentiment which is more pious and religious than anything expressed by other Council members:

> From afar I have travelled, through misery and pain, yet my feet have carried me here gladly. That I should experience the day of the Lord, and that my old eyes should still see this work: the rebirth of all Christianity – my heart rejoices and is pleased. And now I'd gladly take leave of this beautiful world.[122]

Abdisu cuts a slightly ridiculous figure: he is old, partly senile, and spends most of the meeting asleep. Nevertheless, his peacefulness and quietness,

---

The Foundations of the Nineteenth Century, trans. John Lees (London, 1912), quoted in Ruth A. Solie, 'Beethoven as Secular Humanist: Ideology and the Ninth Symphony in Nineteenth-Century Criticism', in Eugene Narmour and Ruth A. Solie (eds), *Explorations in Music, the Arts and Ideas* (New York: Pendragon Press, 1988), 12. I am indebted to James Garrett for pointing me to this information.

[120] Woltmann, *Die Germanen und die Renaissance in Italien* (Leipzig: Thüringische Verlagsanstalt, 1905), 3–4 and 130. Also see David B. Dennis, *Beethoven in German Politics*, 54.

[121] Ursprung, *Palestrina und Deutschland*, 192; Philipp Spitta, 'Palestrina im sechzehnten und neunzehnten Jahrhundert', *Deutsche Rundschau* 79 (1894), 94–5.

[122] 'Von weither wandert' ich, durch Mühsal und Beschwerde, doch meine Füße trugen froh mich her. Daß ich den Tag des Herrn erleben darf, daß meine alten Augen dieses Werk noch schau'n: die Neugeburt der ganzen Christenheit – dess' freuet sich und jubiliert mein Herz. Und gerne scheid' ich nun von dieser schönen Erde'.

although taken to extremes, form a strong contrast to the raucous argument of the rest of the Council.

Abdisu is 'otherworldly' in a double sense: he has his mind more on matters spiritual than mundane, and is literally from another 'world', the distant and strange land of Assyria. His portrayal as distanced from the society around him, and in touch with the divine, is comparable to the character of Palestrina. The Patriarch only sings twice, first when he enters the Council's hall, and later, in a moment of comedy, when he stands to comment on the discussion about Palestrina (although the discussion has already moved on) and gets the composer's name wrong. The fact that the only time Abdisu speaks during the meeting, he talks about Palestrina rather than any other Council business hints at an affinity between the two men. Furthermore, like the composer, Abdisu is accompanied by a parallel, distinct, musical world, which suggests a connection with Palestrina by virtue of its 'otherness' and through similarities of orchestration and melody. Its peculiar harmonies and instrumentation form a small section of musical exoticism distinguished from the music around it. Abdisu's song divides into an ABA' form: the A sections are the more harmonically peculiar, with a minimum of functional harmony, and instead a shifting between adjacent chords. The occurrence of false relations and alternations between major and minor versions of a chord contribute to the lack of conventional functionality in the harmony. Melodically, the sliding upwardly-resolving suspensions in the clarinet, later taken over by the violin, add to the strange effect. (Ex.2.4 shows the first A section of the song with its distinctive harmonies and melody.) The second, B, section (fig.102+5 to fig.103+4) is unequivocally in C major for much of its duration, apart from a two-bar interlude (fig.103-3 and -2), but becomes more ambiguous at the end of the section. The B section's C major passages are those which are most directly concerned with text about God: 'That I should experience the day of the Lord...the rebirth of all Christianity'.[123] These situate Abdisu as otherworldly in a spiritual sense, just as the A sections' exoticism places him as geographically separate.

The instrumentation of Abdisu's song parallels the orchestration of the angels' scene in Act One. For instance, there is prominent use of the 'angelic' harp, and the high solo violin, accompanied in this instance by the

---

[123] 'Daß ich den Tag des Herrn erleben darf... . Die Neugeburt der ganzen Christenheit'.

Ex.2.4 Abdisu's song (Act 2, Fig.102-4) (Reprinted by kind permission of Schott Musik International)

doch mei-ne Fü-ssen tru-gen   froh   mich her.

C# maj   +7   C maj

Ex.2.4 (contd.)

piccolo. The instrumental range is also particularly high at first, with a pre-ponderance of instruments playing above middle C, and only the occasional punctuating bass note, suggesting, as is the case with Palestrina's angelic dictation, the 'higher' standing of Abdisu spiritually. The B passage, which is distinct melodically from the A sections, introduces melismatic writing, while the intervals between notes are expanded from intervals of a major third or smaller in the A sections (with only one exception, at 'gerne'), to more frequent fourths and fifths in the B section. Both these rising fourths and fifths and the melismas may be compared to the music of the angels' Kyrie in Act One, as shown in ex.2.5. In the same way that Palestrina's music sets the composer apart from society, Abdisu's music situates him as distinct from the rest of the Council; the two characters are both separated from the everyday world through their closeness to the divine.

The representation of new music in Palestrina   A further aesthetic preoccu-pation of Pfitzner is demonstrated in Act Two, namely his opposition to modern music which, as we have seen, he demonised as being 'political' in contrast to 'true', 'nonpolitical' German art. The Prelude at the beginning of Act Two, discussed above, points to the twentieth-century composer's

(a) Abdisu (Act 2, Fig.102+4)

(b) Abdisu (Act 2, Fig.103-1)

Ex.2.5 Comparison of Abdisu's and Angels' lines (Reprinted by kind permission of Schott Musik International)

(c) Angels (Act 1, Fig.161+6)

Ex.2.5 (contd.)

opposition to new music. As Franklin points out, the Prelude is the 'most advanced and "modern" music in the opera'; he describes it as a 'Shostakovich-like fracas'.[124] The Prelude may be read as Pfitzner's portrayal of 'modernist' music. Although its music, taken out of context, may not strike us as particularly unusual for its time, its avoidance of a stable tonality and its rhythmic instability have definite 'modern' implications when viewed against the archaic evocation of Palestrina's music in Acts One and Three. (It also contrasts with the generic, late-Romantic, style of the opera as a

---

[124] Franklin '*Palestrina* and the Dangerous Futurists', 132.

whole.) Through such devices, the Prelude portrays the 'modern' in music, but more broadly, it aligns the Council with the progressive and new-fangled. When this 'modernity' is interpreted in political terms, it signifies parliamentary democracy; like 'democracy' or 'socialism', modern music challenged an established cultural norm. Thus, the music of the Prelude, like the Council as a whole, acts as a representation of all those factors to which Pfitzner, like other conservatives, was opposed.

The conflict between old and new styles of music is further shown in *Palestrina* in Pfitzner's portrayal of Silla, Palestrina's pupil. As well as the danger of a ban by the church, Palestrina's music is threatened by the new music of the Florentine Camerata, represented through Silla, who yearns to join them. The Renaissance composer says that the threat to his music comes from 'dilettantes in Florence' who 'have devised artificial theories for themselves from heathen, ancient writings'.[125] We hear an example of this 'modern' music with a song in the 'new style' by Silla, which is supposed to be a humorous invocation of 'bad' music, like Beckmesser's song in *Die Meistersinger*. It is full of such things as consecutive fifths and octaves, odd seventh chords, and strange voice leading. Paul Attinello comments that it is 'amusingly incompetent: the awkwardness of "Da-a-a-me," the weight of the inappropriate melismas, and the tendency of the harmony to backtrack against its own functional processes are enjoyably ridiculous'.[126] The style of the song forms a direct contrast to Palestrina's own music later in the act, with the new monophony of the 'modernists' being juxtaposed with the traditional polyphonic style of Palestrina. (It is also set against the musical style of the opera as a whole.) Silla's 'modern' music represents that with which the fictional Palestrina is in conflict, and acts as a metaphor for the music Pfitzner himself opposed. Mann himself, in his *Betrachtungen*, calls Silla 'political', and sees his enthusiasm for the new musical style of the Florentine Camerata as being aligned with 'democracy'. He scorns Silla's wish for liberation from Palestrina's school, saying that such a wish for liberation, expressed in 'insidious verses', is

---

[125] 'Dilettanten in Florenz'; 'aus heidnischen, antiken Schriften [haben] sich Theorien künstlich ausgedacht'.

[126] Attinello, 'Pfitzner, *Palestrina*, Nazis, Conservatives', 35.

'individualistic emancipation in idealistic connection with the endless progress of the human race, that is politics, *that is democracy*'.[127]

The opera demonstrates in no uncertain terms Pfitzner's suspicion of
new music and his belief in himself as being, like Palestrina, the 'saviour of
music', fighting a battle in order to rescue true German music from the
clutches of atonality. The overall tenor of Pfitzner's opera, though, is
pessimistic: while one of Pfitzner's principal arguments against the 'Futurists' is their wish to break away from the pre-existent tradition of music, he
himself believes he is at the end of a tradition. As he asks in 'Futuristengefahr', 'What if our last century or century and a half represented the
flowering of Western music, the climax, the real golden age, which will
never return and which is now passing into decline, into a state of deca-
dence, as after the age of Greek tragedy? My own feelings incline... to this
view'.[128] Nevertheless, according to Pfitzner, the 'truths' of this tradition
should still be upheld. Pfitzner's sense of his position at the end of the tradition of German music is demonstrated by the comparison he made between his opera and *Die Meistersinger*, which Mann reports in the course
of his remarks on *Palestrina* in his *Betrachtungen*:

> we compared Ighino with David, Palestrina with Stolzing and Sachs, the mass
> with the prize song... . Pfitzner said: 'The difference is expressed most clearly
> in the concluding scenic pictures. At the end of the Meistersinger there is a
> stage full of light, rejoicing of the people, engagement, brilliance and glory; in
> my work there is, to be sure, Palestrina, who is also celebrated, but in the half-
> darkness of his room under the picture of the deceased one, dreaming at his
> organ. The Meistersinger is the apotheosis of the new, a praise of the future and
> of life; in Palestrina everything tends toward the past, it is dominated by *sym-
> pathy with death*'.[129]

---

[127] Mann, *Reflections*, 305. Mann's emphasis.

[128] Pfitzner, 'Futuristengefahr', 221. Translation taken from Franklin, '*Palestrina* and the
Dangerous Futurists', 128. Franklin suggests that Pfitzner also expresses some degree of
hope, with his comment at the end of his essay that 'all around there stretch beautiful
green pastures'; this suggests the ability of artists to continue creating great work, if
only they hearken to their deepest inspiration and do not pursue the wild-goose chase of
sterile technical innovation ('Futuristengefahr', 223, and Franklin, '*Palestrina* and the
Dangerous Futurists', 130).

[129] Mann, *Reflections*, 311. Mann's emphasis. Mann had used the phrase 'sympathy with

This culminatory feeling pervades the whole of *Palestrina*; Mann describes the opera as 'the grave[-]song [*Grabgesang*] of romantic opera'.[130] The fictional composer's place within a teleology of music, and specifically as the culmination of that progression, is asserted by the Masters' reference to Palestrina completing their 'noble circle'; Palestrina is 'the last stone on [God's] beautiful chain'.[131]

The character of Palestrina may be read as a psychological reconciliation, a kind of wish-fulfilment; it is a means whereby Pfitzner could play out his preferred conclusions and attempt to come to terms with his conflict with threatening aspects of the modern world, as well as with what he saw as the lack of recognition of him as a composer. With its invocation of genius, inspiration, immortality, heritage, and notions of tonality and musical convention, Pfitzner's self-construction through the persona of Palestrina creates an ideal of the artist which establishes him as distinct from society, and which may therefore be read, in Mann's terms, as 'nonpolitical'. His picture of the isolated composer works to assert a musical, and social, order, in which the privileged place of the genius is assured, in the face of the threat from the progressive atonal composers he criticised in his writings. The conclusion of *Palestrina* represents the triumph of art over politics, and by extension, the triumph Pfitzner wished for of conservatism over liberalism, socialism and democracy. In this respect, the opera encapsulates Pfitzner's own political position, and the hopes of conservatives for the future of the German nation, namely, that it would remain precisely as it was.

---

death' himself in one of his short stories, the predecessor to *Der Zauberberg*.

[130] Ibid., 313.

[131] 'an seiner schönen Ketten der letzte Stein'. Also see Franklin, 'A Musical Legend', 12, and '*Palestrina* and the Dangerous Futurists', 120, 123 and 130–31.

3   Krenek spielt auf: *Jonny*, Jazz and the Modern Composer

Ernst Krenek's *Jonny spielt auf*, written in 1926, brought the composer almost instant renown. It transcended the bounds of the usual operatic repertoire to achieve wide popular appeal: there were forty-five stagings in German-speaking countries in the 1927-8 season alone, with later productions reaching across the rest of Europe and to New York.[1] It also achieved the most unusual feat, for an opera, of becoming something of a cultural phenomenon: not only were sheet music and recordings of numbers from the opera sold in huge numbers, but there was even a brand of cigarettes produced called 'Jonny'.[2] Unusually for an artist-opera, *Jonny spielt auf* contains not just one artist, but three: the title character Jonny, a jazz musician, Max, a composer in the classical tradition, and Daniello, a violinist; this fact is indicative of the way the opera reflects varying personae of its composer. Of the three characters, Daniello is the most minor; he appears less often and only functions as a prop to the main plot. He is also a performing musician, rather than a creative one as Jonny and Max are. From a structural point of view, Jonny is clearly the main character of the opera: the climax at the end of Act One and the dénouement in the final scene are based on the events surrounding Jonny. However, despite the opera's title, it may be argued that the principal character is Max. It is certainly he who occupies the central position if we regard the work in terms of a *Künstleroper*: as is typical for the hero of such a work, Max feels distant

---

[1] Eva Diettrich, 'Auf den Spuren zu Jonnys Erfolg', in Otto Kolleritsch (ed.), *Ernst Krenek* (Vienna: Universal Edition, 1982), 119; Wolfgang Rogge, *Ernst Kreneks Opern: Spiegel der zwanziger Jahre* (Wolfenbüttel and Zürich: Möseler Verlag, 1970), 63–4.

[2] Hailey, *Franz Schreker*, 242. Krenek himself seemed to have been well aware of the 'marketability' of his work: see Grosch, *Die Musik der neuen Sachlichkeit*, 111–12.

from society and lacks inspiration. Jonny acts as a representative of, and a metaphor for, the society with which Max is in conflict.

It is not only the multiple artist-characters which make *Jonny spielt auf* unusual. The work is set in a time contemporaneous with its composition, rather than in a historical past, something found in only a few other *Künstleropern* of this period.[3] The up-to-date setting, and the way in which a persona for the composer of the work is situated within a contemporary environment, necessarily creates a degree of engagement with society, rather than the distance which results when a historical past is invoked. Partly because of its setting, *Jonny spielt auf* is frequently cited as the quintessence of *Zeitoper* (that is, an opera set in the modern world of the 1920s) and has been since its first performance. According to Susan C. Cook, in her overview of contemporary definitions of the term, a *Zeitoper* was 'an attempt to mirror or depict the age, to infuse opera with the tempo of modern culture, and to bring to the fore aspects of everyday life, all of which came about through the conscious effort of composers to find inspiration from the time in order to create a new relationship with their audience'.[4] A *Zeitoper*'s emphasis on contemporaneity means that its participation in cultural trends may be read with reference to the interaction of these movements with political ones, and the deliberate situation of the *Zeitoper* within contemporary life in itself offers a statement on society.[5] Existing

---

[3] The only other *Künstleropern* unambiguously set in a contemporary era are Schreker's *Christophorus* and Strauss's *Intermezzo*, as well as, possibly, Schreker's *Der ferne Klang*.

[4] Cook, *Opera for a New Republic*, 4.

[5] In their review of Weimar culture, the writers Jost Hermand and Frank Trommler criticise *Zeitopern*, saying that most are banal and shallow; they comment that they were 'rarely really [socially] committed' and that the genre 'merely wanted to reflect back its time, instead of holding a critical mirror up in front of it' (Hermand and Trommler, *Die Kultur der Weimarer Republik*, 317). Similarly, Diettrich holds of *Jonny spielt auf* that it 'contains no socio-critical tendencies of any kind' ('Auf den Spuren zu Jonnys Erfolg', 120). In Hermand and Trommler's estimation, only the works of Kurt Weill are valuable, because of their more explicit social criticism. However, the *Zeitoper* is not only a 'mirror' of the twenties (as the title of Rogge's book also terms it), but, necessarily, a comment upon it; rather than merely reflecting society, as Hermand and Trommler accuse it of doing, the *Zeitoper*'s depiction of society cannot fail to have an ideological content. After all, what a composer chooses to reflect, along with the way in which he or she reflects it, is necessarily the presentation of a particular ideological viewpoint. Also on *Zeitoper*, see

writing on *Jonny spielt auf* rarely discusses the political implications of its use of popular music, though, nor the ideological currents of which the opera was a part.[6] I will explore both of these subjects in this chapter, and will discuss how the opera's connection to the world in which it was written was part of the on-going debate at that time about art's place in modern society.

The Context of *Jonny spielt auf*: Politics and Culture in the Weimar Republic

The unrest on the political landscape around the time of World War I, which had led to the reactionary outbursts by figures such as Mann and Pfitzner, escalated at the end of the war. The Allies would not agree to an armistice unless Germany became a democratic state, a proposal resisted by the Kaiser, Wilhelm II, and his government. As a compromise, the government instead implemented a parliamentary monarchy in October 1918, which partly fulfilled armistice demands, although the Kaiser was still in place. However, in tandem with the Allies' stipulations, discontent amongst the populace spread, spurred on by the war's hardships and defeat, so that, as William Carr puts it, 'by the end of October a revolutionary situation existed in Germany'.[7] More and more voices within Germany began to call for the Kaiser's abdication, while President Wilson's insistence on his removal helped to maintain the pressure from outside by making it plain that

---

Grosch, *Die Musik der Neuen Sachlichkeit*, 101 ff. and 115, and Amidon, *'Nirgends brennen wir genauer'*.

6 This literature includes Diettrich, 'Auf den Spuren zu Jonnys Erfolg'; Rogge, *Ernst Kreneks Opern*; Tregear, *Ernst Krenek*; and Susan C. Cook's *Opera for a New Republic*. There is also a significant amount of work on Krenek which focuses primarily on his later, serial music and which all but ignores the existence of *Jonny* altogether; for instance, Lothar Knessl's *Ernst Krenek* (Vienna: Lafite, 1967); Walter Gieseler's '"Was an der Zeit ist". Versuch einer Annäherung an Kreneks Musikdenken' (*Musica* 34/2 (1980), 127–31); Claudia Maurer Zenck's *Ernst Krenek: Ein Komponist im Exil* (Vienna: Lafite, 1980); the collection of essays edited by Klaus Metzger and Rainer Riehn, *Ernst Krenek* (Musik-Konzepte 39/40, Munich: edition text + kritik, 1984); and George Perle's essay 'Standortbestimmung' (*Österreichische Musikzeitschrift* 48/3–4 (1993), 152–60).

7 Carr, *A History of Germany*, 247–8.

the emperor was an obstacle to peace. On the 29th October, a group of German sailors in Kiel, infuriated by the continuing war situation, mutinied and precipitated civil unrest which spread across the country.[8] The SPD, who were by now a significant force within the Reichstag, dealt with the growing crisis by withdrawing their support from the government on the 8th November, after their demands for the Kaiser's abdication, and for the Socialists to be given greater representation in the cabinet, were not met. Tapping into the mood of the country at large, they, along with other left-wing political groups, called for a general strike, which began on the 9th November. Faced with this pressure from both home and abroad, the Kaiser was forced to abdicate. On hearing the news of the abdication, the SPD was quick to pronounce a republic, with the minister Phillipp Scheidemann making the announcement to the crowds from a Berlin balcony; the SPD leader Ebert became Chancellor on the same day.[9] An interim government was formed from the SPD and the Independent Socialists before the first general election of the Weimar Republic was held on the 19th January 1919. The Socialists did not achieve the overall majority for which they had hoped, winning 37.9% of the vote; nevertheless, they were still the largest party, and formed a coalition with the Centre Party and German Democratic Party.[10]

Although there was not an outright victory for the Socialists in this election, the new constitution of the Weimar Republic, which was drawn up shortly afterwards, enshrined significant changes in social outlook. It provided universal suffrage for all above the age of twenty, equality before the law, the right to assembly, freedom of thought, and the right to form political parties and independent trade unions.[11] State censorship was abolished, while men and women, at least in theory, were to be treated equally and had the same civil rights.[12] The desire for greater equality is indicative of a shift that can be identified in the Weimar Republic away from the old conservatism of the pre-war years. The constitution was a child of the liberal and socialist thinkers of the era rather than of

---

[8] Ibid., 249 ff., and Peukert, *The Weimar Republic*, 21 ff.

[9] Carr, *A History of Germany*, 252.

[10] Ibid., 266, and Peukert, *The Weimar Republic*, 33.

[11] Lamb and Phelan, 'Weimar Culture', 57.

[12] See extracts from the Constitution in Kaes et al. (eds), *The Weimar Republic Sourcebook*, 46–51.

conservatives of the ilk of Mann or Pfitzner, who would never have countenanced such progressive measures. It was 'intended to produce a society based on tolerance, mutual respect, openness, and democracy, where the social, political, and economic conditions that had given rise to the carnage of the First World War would be banished once and for all'.[13] The constitution also ensured the provision of free primary and secondary education for all on the basis of 'ability and inclination, not the social and economic status or religion of the parents', and was intended to promote 'the spirit of German nationhood *and* international reconciliation'.[14]

These changes in the political landscape were accompanied by economic phenomena, to some extent linked to each other. Elections were influenced, as always, by the economic events of the Weimar Republic, with the more extreme parties gaining ground in times of hardship and the more liberal and centre parties in periods of prosperity. The fifteen years of the Republic began with a period of economic crisis, when the poor state of the German economy, badly damaged by the war, was exacerbated by the conditions imposed upon Germany by the Allies in the Versailles peace settlement. Germany was forced to pay millions of marks' worth of reparations, in sums that the country was unable to afford.[15] In the immediate aftermath of the war, and into the early years of the 1920s, the economy was extremely weak, reaching a crisis point in 1923-4, when hyperinflation made the currency all but worthless and left many people in penury. However, in November 1924, a 'new' currency, the Rentenmark, was introduced, and the economy began to stabilise. The period of increased economic stability and prosperity, from the introduction of the Rentenmark until the Wall Street Crash in 1929, has come to be known as the 'Golden Twenties', years taken as synonymous with the idea of the decadent Weimar Republic. As Cook says, 'the stable years of 1924 to 1929 brought with them a general feeling of prosperity, a renewed hope for the future of the Republic, [and] optimism about modern life'.[16]

---

[13] Lamb and Phelan, 'Weimar Culture', 57.

[14] Ibid., 59.

[15] For further details of the economic situation, see Peukert, *The Weimar Republic*, 107 ff. and *passim*.

[16] Cook, *Opera for a New Republic*, 5–6.

Americanism and Politics

One consequence of the economic situation in the twenties was what has been seen as one of the most important cultural movements of the mid-twenties, 'Americanism'. The blockades against Germany, which had been in place since the war, were ended, and this, along with the stabilisation of the mark, meant that there was an influx of American goods into the country. American could be noticed, and it could begin to have an influence on ordinary life in a way that was not possible when the weakness of the German economy discouraged foreign investment. 'Americanism' is used to describe the craze for all things perceived as 'American', and supposedly 'modern', which took place at this time, such as skyscrapers, city life, industrialisation, sport, film and jazz. The historian Detlev Peukert observes that '"Americanism" became a catchword for untrammelled modernity'.[17] America was seen as the epitome of the modern, and synonymous with progress and freedom. It gained an aura of the land of unlimited opportunity, thanks to its economic and financial strength, its lead in mass production and consumption, and its supposed efficiency and innovation.[18] All of these things formed an ideal to which many aspired. America's perceived prosperity contrasted with the poverty and economic instability which Germany had recently suffered, and its supposed *joie-de-vivre* offered a way of recovering from the misery of the war and post-war years. According to Hermand and Trommler, the largely negative attitudes towards the US after Germany's defeat in World War I were turned around, so that by the mid-1920s, 'the USA became...the decisive ideal of the Weimar Coalition as regards the boosting and stabilisation of economic activity'. Economically, the USA was seen as 'a land of pragmatism, of the worship of the factual (*Tatsachenkult*), of objective labour relations, that is, as a soberly planned, thoroughly rationalised society based on industry and performance, whose standard of living was considered superior by all other countries in the world'.[19] At the same time, paradoxically, it was also the land of freedom, liveliness, and a lack of inhibitions, where anything was permitted and anything possible.

---

[17] Peukert, *The Weimar Republic*, 178.

[18] Ibid., 179. On nineteenth-century European conceptions of America, see Tregear, *Ernst Krenek*, 56–7.

[19] Hermand and Trommler, *Die Kultur der Weimarer Republik*, 49–50.

America was particularly important politically: its perceived regard for democracy and equality was that now espoused in the young Weimar constitution, and many thought America to be some kind of 'classless' society that was far removed from the stratified Germany of the Wilhelmine years. According to the Americanism myth, the USA appeared to have transcended class divisions: 'everyone already owned the same houses, the same cars, had the same individual mobility, the same freedom...[and] the same chances in society'.[20] Such egalitarianism was appealing to many of a progressive and left-wing persuasion; according to Hermand and Trommler, newspapers, magazines and books from the mid-twenties depicted the US as 'better, more developed, more modern', where 'a socialisation of technology and with it a democratisation of society had already been achieved'. Julius Hirsch's book, *Das amerikanische Wirtschaftswunder* (*The American Economic Miracle*) of 1926, was typical, presenting the US as a place 'where a true social democracy, under the slogan "Prosperity for All", had been created'.[21] All of the artefacts associated with America therefore became caught up in the representation of this democratic ideal.

This image of America, on a par with many of the aspirations of the more progressive sections of Weimar society, is by modern standards positioned in the centre of the political spectrum. However, to understand the impact of such ideas in 1920s Germany, we must remember that, in comparison to the state of political affairs which had been in place before World War I, the espousal of democracy in the country was a significant step towards the left. Seen against the background of the prevalent conservative climate discussed in the previous chapter, the Weimar Republic was a radical move, and Americanism embodied its values and ideals. Democracy challenged the existing status quo, and was therefore perceived by conservatives as threatening and to be resisted.

Of course, Americanism was not constructed on a view of the real America, but on a myth. Americanism was essentially idealism: it perceived only positive attributes about the country and overlooked the negative ones, therefore basing its idea of the country more on fantasy than on

---

[20] Ibid., 50. Also see Cook, *Opera for a New Republic*, 4, and Grosch, *Die Musik der Neuen Sachlichkeit*, 152.

[21] Hermand and Trommler, *Die Kultur der Weimarer Republik*, 55–6.

fact. Some contemporary critics were aware of this disparity between the real America and the country lauded by Americanism: the writer Rudolf Kayser asked 'Are these phenomena [of Americanism] not much more than the external and revealed symptoms of a more secret, spiritual, soulful essence? Is Americanism not a new orientation to being, grown out of and formed in our European destiny?... . In fact, Americanism is a new European method. The extent to which this method was itself influenced by America seems to me quite unimportant'.[22] Americanism may be read as an attempt at redefinition at a time when the idea of German identity current before 1914 found itself challenged by the large changes in society which Germany experienced following the defeat of World War I. While the conservatives saw this as a threat, and attempted to reclaim the old image, the idea of what it meant to be German could also be reinterpreted. By fabricating an image of 'America' which could be copied at will, an identity of a 'New German' could be constructed, a person whose views were more progressive, liberal and up-to-date than the attitudes which characterised the older, pre-War generation. Aspects of modernity which such Germans wanted for themselves were projected onto the idea of America, and then reassimilated. The construction of an image of America was, therefore, German society's attempt to carve out a niche for itself in the modern world, and to find a collective identity. Peukert writes that 'the public debate about "America" was really a debate about German society itself and the challenge that modernity posed to it. What was at issue was the value to be placed on a "rationalized" form of life emptied of all the ballast of tradition'.[23] The more or less wholly affirmative image of America within the discourse of 'Americanism' constructed a model of a better society, a kind of Utopia, through which the citizens of Weimar Germany attempted to assimilate into their own culture the ideals of a more democratic and more modern nation.

---

[22] 'Amerikanismus', *Vössische Zeitung* no.458 (27th September 1925) in Kaes et al. (eds), *The Weimar Republic Sourcebook*, 395. Also see Grosch, *Die Musik der Neuen Sachlichkeit*, 150–51, and Jack Sullivan, *New World Symphonies: How American Culture Changed European Music* (New Haven: Yale University Press, 1999), xii and xvii.

[23] Peukert, *The Weimar Republic*, 178.

Americanism, Mass Culture and Jazz

As it appeared within Americanism, American culture had an implicit political meaning within the context of 1920s Germany. It was characterised by the phenomenon of mass culture, which by definition is destined for the majority of the population and opposed to the culture of a privileged elite. Mass culture went hand in hand with people's increasing leisure time and greater prosperity in the years after 1924; according to Peukert, the Weimar Republic established a 'framework of leisure' for wage-earners through its introduction of the forty-hour week and the first negotiated agreements covering holidays. Consequently, by the end of the twenties, people from all over the social scale were able to share the same cultural and leisure-time activities.[24] Peukert comments that mass consumption and the new 'culture of leisure' led to 'a certain amount of cultural assimilation', in which, by the end of the decade, people of all social classes listened to the same songs and radio programmes.[25] According to many writers, the influence of mass culture was interpreted by some at the time as pointing to democratisation; the new culture was believed to be egalitarian because it reached all sections of society. The champions of this culture saw that new media such as radio, film, and recording were more readily obtainable by the masses, and through these means, 'they wanted to finally bring art, which formerly had been only at the disposal of the upper ten thousand, into the sphere of the general public, and change it into a democratic art in the widest sense of the word'.[26] In 1930, Albert Einstein lauded radio as heralding true democracy because of its ability to disseminate ideas and art to a wide public.[27] The fact that German radio was owned and run by the government further characterised it as belonging to the whole population, rather than to a monied elite.

The enthusiasm for what was seen as American meant that the supposedly quintessentially American music, jazz, also became highly popular. Jazz and America became synonymous with one another: the music became

---

[24] Ibid., 175–6.

[25] Ibid., 176. Also see Grosch, *Die Musik der Neuen Sachlichkeit*, 4–5.

[26] Hermand and Trommler, *Die Kultur der Weimarer Republik*, 70.

[27] Einstein in E. Kurt Fische (ed.), *Dokumente zur Geschichte des deutschen Rundfunks und Fernsehens* (Göttingen: Musterschmidt, 1957). Quoted in Hailey, 'Rethinking Sound', 14.

emblematic of the country, and vice versa. Albrecht Dümling writes that American popular music in Europe was 'a symbol for America's prosperous advances and expanding capitalism, [a] symbol for the "land of unlimited opportunities"'.[28] He observes that the positive characteristics with which Europeans associated the US, such as 'vitality, freshness, naturalness, liveliness, [and] pleasure-seeking', were also seen as attributes of jazz, and vice versa.[29] In the editorial to a 1925 issue of the journal *Anbruch* dedicated entirely to jazz, Paul Stefan expanded on these positive qualities:

> For us, jazz means: a rebellion of the people's dulled instincts against a music without rhythm. A reflection of the times: chaos, machines, noise, the highest peak of intensity. The triumph of irony, of frivolity, the wrath of those who want to preserve good times. The overcoming of Biedermeier hypocrisy...thus freedom from 'comfortableness'. Richness, happiness, the idea of a lighter music.[30]

For composers, such popular music not only formed a way out of the perceived impasse of atonality, but also bridged the problematic gap between composer and audience.[31] The gap between artist and audience could be

---

[28] Dümling, 'Symbol des Fortschritts, der Dekadenz und der Unterdrückung. Zum Bedeutungswandel des Jazz in den zwanziger Jahren', in Dietrich Stern (ed.), *Angewandte Musik 20er Jahre: Exemplarische Versuche gesellschaftsbezogener musikalischer Arbeit für Theater, Film, Radio, Massenveranstaltung* (Berlin: Argument-Verlag, 1977), 83. Also for discussion of Americanism and jazz in Weimar Germany, see Cook, *Opera for a New Republic*, 42 ff.; Hermand and Trommler, *Die Kultur der Weimarer Republik*, 313 ff.; Bernd Hoffmann, 'Alptraum der Freiheit oder: Die Zeitfrage "Jazz"', in Helmut Rösing (ed.), *'Es liegt in der Luft was Idiotisches...': Populäre Musik zur Zeit der Weimarer Republik* (Baden-Baden: Coda, 1995), 69–81; Michael H. Kater, 'The Jazz Experience in Weimar Germany', *German History* 6 (1988), 145–58; Horst H. Lange, *Jazz in Deutschland: Die deutsche Jazz-Chronik 1900–1960* (Berlin: Colloquium Verlag, 1966); Fred Ritzel, '"Hätte der Kaiser Jazz getanzt...". US-Tanzmusik in Deutschland vor und nach dem Ersten Weltkrieg', in Schutte (ed.), *Ich will aber gerade vom Leben singen*, 265–93; and J. Bradford Robinson, 'Jazz Reception in Weimar Germany', in Gilliam (ed.), *Music and Performance during the Weimar Republic*, 107–34.

[29] Dümling, 'Symbol des Fortschritts', 84.

[30] *Anbruch*, April 1925. Quoted in ibid.

[31] This point is only tangentially acknowledged by writers such as Cook and Rogge. Also

diminished by embracing the new popular culture, and assimilating 'high' and 'low' art; if composers used popular music in their work, then they would instantly communicate with a vast number of people, of all social classes, who would welcome them as speaking 'their' language. Previously, different types of popular music had been limited by class; thus the middle class, who could afford to go to dance halls and hear dance bands, had heard a different kind of music from the working class, who did not have access to such music.[32] Jazz, however, transcended such divides; it became 'a fashion which embraced all classes and levels of society', and a way of 'breaking down the boundaries between "higher" and "lower" art, between art music and entertainment music'.[33]

It is important to note here, however, that what was known in the Weimar Republic as 'jazz' was not the improvised jazz performed in the USA by such musicians as Armstrong and Ellington (which was not widely known in Germany until many years later), but popular dance-band music. The reason for the misnomer is explained by a common misconception at the time. A number of dance bands, originating both from Europe and from the USA, appeared in Germany in these years which called themselves 'jazz bands', although they in fact played American dance music; therefore the public came to assume that what they played was jazz.[34] The music which was designated as 'jazz' at this time is discussed by Robinson; he says that 'jazz to Weimar Germany was an all-embracing cultural label attached to any music from the American side of the Atlantic, or indeed to anything new and exciting'.[35] This widespread misconception of 'jazz' meant that *Jonny spielt auf* could gain its credentials as a 'jazz-opera' despite the fact that it does not contain what is now understood as jazz, but is based on dance music.[36]

---

on this issue, see Grosch, *Die Musik der Neuen Sachlichkeit*, 7–8 and 12.

[32] Ritzel, '"Hätte der Kaiser Jazz getanzt..."', 287–8.

[33] Dümling, 'Symbol des Fortschritts', 84 and 95.

[34] Lange, *Jazz in Deutschland*, 13; Cook, *Opera for a New Republic*, 61.

[35] Robinson, 'Jazz Reception in Weimar Germany', 113.

[36] Krenek saw the famous 'Chocolate Kiddies' review, with music performed by Sam Wooding's orchestra, in early 1926, as well as the Paul Whiteman orchestra at about the same time. He had also heard recordings of Gershwin, Berlin and Youmans (John L. Stewart, *Ernst Krenek: The Man and His Music* (Berkeley, Los Angeles and Oxford: University of California Press, 1991), 31, 81 and 85; Krenek, *Im Atem der Zeit: Erinner-*

The misnomer of dance-band music as 'jazz' helped to perpetuate, and was itself perpetuated by, the myth of America. It indicates the constructed nature of the American image and the way in which it was based upon convenient factors which helped to create the desired ideal. Indeed, the American critic of the New York première of *Jonny spielt auf* in 1929, Herbert Peyser, wrote dismissively that 'the supposedly American features...are about as American as a *Konditorei* on the *Kurfürstendamm*'.[37] The popular music which was known as 'jazz' served the purposes of the myth, as it sounded fresh, lively and sufficiently different from the pre-existing European music to be useful in establishing a new cultural identity in contrast to the old.

Just as democracy was threatening to the existing order, artistic innovations such as jazz challenged established norms, and therefore met with resistance. As Weiner puts it, jazz functioned as 'an acoustical sign of national, social, racial, and sexual difference', opposed to the inherited German culture. It acted as an 'icon of non-German forces', and became an 'acoustical screen for the projection of fears and/or hopes regarding rapid and violent political and social change'.[38] The antipathy towards jazz operated on a number of interrelating levels: musically, it was against the grain of 'real' music; ideologically, it was seen to embody sexual licentiousness and was associated with a supposedly 'inferior' race, 'negroes', who had been identified as such by biological 'science' across Europe since the previous century. The occupation of parts of western Germany after the war by black French Senegalese soldiers exacerbated the hatred felt by conservative Germans.[39] 'American jazz became the acoustical sign of the transplanted black, and thus could refer both to America as the foreign and victorious New World divorced from European traditions, and at the same time to Africa as the purportedly uncivilized Dark Continent from which the feared black was seen to challenge Europe's racial and national hegemony'.[40] Conveniently, jazz could also be perceived as a product of

---

ungen an die Moderne, trans. Friedrich Saathen and Sabine Schutte (Hamburg: Hoffmann und Campe Verlag, 1998), 587).

[37] 'Jonny over there', *Modern Music* 6 (Jan.–Feb., 1929), 32–4. Quoted in Robinson, 'Jazz Reception in Weimar Germany', 109.

[38] Weiner, *Undertones of Insurrection*, 121.

[39] Kater, 'The Jazz Experience in Weimar Germany', 155.

[40] Weiner, *Undertones of Insurrection*, 123. The fact that Jonny is a black American is not

another race regarded with suspicion, the Jews, as the American art composer Henry Cowell pointed out.

> The foundations of jazz are the syncopation and rhythmic accents of the Negroes; their modernisation and contemporary form is the work of Jews, mostly New York Tin Pan Alley Jews. Jazz is negro music, seen through the eyes of these Jews.[41]

The supposed Jewish dominance of trade meant that Jews were also identified as marketing and supplying the 'inferior' jazz music.[42] Thus two racially 'inferior' groups could be demonised in the same music, and held up as challenging the existing status quo.

Opposition to jazz came from the political right, and the educated middle and upper classes, groups that were by and large the same people, as Michael Kater discusses. Such people were 'fiercely loyal to the monarchy...after the shameful armistice of November 1918, they were chiefly inspired by xenophobia and racial bigotry, freqeuntly mixed in with conservative religion'.[43] According to Kater, their attacks on jazz were frequent and widespread. He explains how 'spokemen of distinguished university fraternities' attacked jazz as the 'outgrowth of Americanism, even Bolshevism, and as diametrically opposed to military discipline'.[44] As we have seen in the previous chapter, Pfitzner was at the forefront of the attack on jazz. Writing in 1926 (shortly before the first performances of *Jonny spielt auf*), he declared that the 'soulless' American 'jazz-foxtrot-

---

significant for the present reading, however; on this topic, see Tregear, *Ernst Krenek*, 74.

[41] Cowell, 'Bericht aus Amerika', in *Melos*, 1930, 363 ff. Quoted in Dümling, 'Symbol des Fortschritts', 84.

[42] Kater, 'The Jazz Experience in Weimar Germany', 154.

[43] Ibid., 153. An interesting divergence can be seen between the attitudes of traditional conservatives and the radical right-wing to 1920s popular culture. Most conservatives viewed the new cultural innovations with suspicion, seeing them as symbolising a left-wing and pro-democratic ideology; the National Socialists' official line on jazz was identical. However, many individual National Socialists (often from a younger generation than the conservatives) secretly enjoyed jazz music; see Michael H. Kater, *Different Drummers: Jazz in the Culture of Nazi Germany* (New York and Oxford: Oxford University Press, 1992).

[44] Kater, 'The Jazz Experience in Weimar Germany', 154. Also see John, *Musikbolschewismus*, 284 ff.

culture' had triumphed over European civilisation.[45] Pfitzner saw the move from 'real' German music to 'degenerate' jazz as an indication of the diseased state of the nation, of which democracy was another symptom.[46] He equated jazz not only with Americanism and democracy but with everything else seen as politically suspicious: bolshevism, internationalism, Judaism, and pacifism. Pfitzner's belief indicates how Americanism came to be associated with other left-wing tendencies in the conservative mind.[47] Many conservative musicians echoed Pfitzner's attacks; for example, Georg Göhler, a critic and composer, voiced his antipathy to 'trash' in the *Zeitschrift für Musik*, in terms showing that he too associated it with those who had allegedly perpetrated the revolution:

> The purchasers of trash are to be found in those circles which have come up in the world through the revolution... . If we go even deeper...we find that typically, the tarts and gigolos (*Lebeweiber und -männer*) who go mad about jazz and foxtrots are also enthusiastic admirers of 'Salome' and 'Mona Lisa' and that the intoxication with pleasure of these revolutionary Germans is very closely connected with the moral inferiority of the fashionable works in our opera houses and theatres![48]

The antipathy towards jazz expressed in such comments demonstrates the threat under which the conservatives felt themselves. Jazz, as a symbol for America, encapsulated not only a change in artistic direction, but a far-reaching political ideology. The strength of the attachs upon it demonstrates jazz's potency at this time as a signifier for the liberal Weimar Republic's ideals.

---

[45] Pfitzner, 'Die neue Ästhetik', 115–16.

[46] Ibid., 230 and 244. He also refers to 'the international loss of soul, the pseudo- or a-national Americanism' (ibid., 113); this is an interesting phrase, indicating that Pfitzner sees Americanism not as American *per se* but as a-national.

[47] Eckhard John notes that for some, jazz was linked with both communism and (American) democracy because of the way in which all of the band's players were of equal importance, and had no single leader (*Musikbolschewismus*, 290–91). On how any progressive artist movement was labelled by conservatives at this time as 'left-wing', see ibid., 50 ff.

[48] 'Das "Versagen des Musikverlags" und das "Anwachsen der Schundmusik"', *Zeitschrift für Musik* 9 (1921), 226. Quoted in Ritzel, '"Hätte der Kaiser Jazz getanzt..."', 289–90. *Mona Lisa* (1915) is an opera by Max von Schillings.

Krenek and the Meaning of Popular Music

Krenek's engagement with the discourse of Americanism in *Jonny spielt auf* is obvious: Jonny is a black American jazz musician who triumphs over the 'old world'. The opera interrogates the role of popular music in modern society, and raises questions about the social and artistic ramifications of populism. The contemporary debate about the nature of art in modern life became central to Krenek's thinking in the mid-1920s, when he began to talk about the necessity for the gap between composer and audience to be closed. Modern music must pay attention to its audience, he says, because the idea 'that an artist creates because he must, and therefore doesn't have to concern himself with whether he'll find an ear that wants to listen to him, is so stupid and feeble, that it's hardly worth repeating it. Certainly he creates that which he must, but it will only be living if he feels himself grounded in his home soil'.[49] He said he had begun 'to understand that a living relationship between art and the public was not only possible, but also...desirable, in contrast to an autocratic, abstract radicalism, which refused this relationship from the start'.[50]

Krenek believed that a simplification of musical language was the key to a closer relationship between artist and public; music must be 'kept as simple as possible if it is to be effective', he wrote in his 1925 essay, 'Music of Today'. The artist will 'have to rediscover perceptually and re-shape the universal means of musical expression to one which all are capable of understanding'; this could be achieved, he implies, by the use of dance music: 'it doesn't do us any good...to close our eyes to a phenomenon of the times'.[51] Two years later, he stated that 'the widest possible comprehensibility of the musical substance' is possible if the composer attempts to 'reach out for the "popular nature" (*Volkstümlichkeit*) of the time'; this 'popular nature' in the modern age lies in popular music.[52] In the essay '"Materialbestimmtheit" der Oper', he elaborates on this point, writing that contemporary dance forms 'open an unusually large range of

---

[49] Krenek, 'Jonny spielt auf' (1927–8), in *Im Zweifelsfalle: Aufsätze zur Musik* (Vienna: Europa, 1984), 18.

[50] Krenek, 'Ernst Krenek über sich und sein Werk', *Blätter der Staatsoper und der Städtische Oper* 8/4 (Oktober 1927), 3.

[51] Krenek, 'Music of Today', in Cook, *Opera for a New Republic*, 201–2 and 199.

[52] Krenek, 'Jonny spielt auf', 26. Also see Grosch, *Die Musik der Neuen Sachlichkeit*, 17.

suggestions of a purely musical nature to the musician. Now and then, we hear a rhythmic and harmonic diversity and complexity in the pieces of American bands which thoroughly equals, in purely material terms, the sound structures (*Klanggebilden*) won from the disintegration of the heritage of Romantic harmony. ...[American dance music] is grown in the soil of a living *Gebrauchsmusik*, and despite its apparent complexity is still understood and consumed'.[53] In these years of the mid-1920s, Krenek frequently points out the necessity for music to be grounded in contemporary life because only this, he says, can make an art which is capable of transcending its time. Mozart wrote music based on contemporary dances which 'still lives today, although no-one dances gavottes and minuets any more'.[54] This music 'is living beyond its time because it was created from its time'. Jazz, therefore, is 'immensely useful' and 'topical' to the 'needs of modern people'.[55]

The Influence of Paul Bekker

Krenek's call for the bridging of the composer-audience gap is expressed not only in aesthetic terms but also in political ones; indeed, his political and aesthetic views in the years around *Jonny spielt auf* coalesce. Not only does he argue the case for composers to be closer to their audience, but by doing so, he suggests, they will achieve a political aim. Important in this respect is the essay '"Materialbestimmtheit" der Oper', written in the year in which *Jonny* was premiered. Here, Krenek says that the use of modern dance-music by art composers is not just a ploy for popularity; rather, it is employed because it has *gesellschaftbildende Macht*, 'socially constructive'

---

[53] Krenek, '"Materialbestimmtheit" der Oper' (1927), in *Zur Sprache gebracht: Essays über Musik* (Munich: Albert Langen / Georg Müller, 1958), 27.

[54] Krenek, 'Jonny spielt auf', 29.

[55] Ibid., 30. Also see his comments in later essays; for instance, in 'Zur heutigen Situation der "Neuen" Musik' (1931), he says that the introduction of elements of jazz into art music was 'one of the last attempts...to produce a satisfying relationship between art and its audience' (*Im Zweifelsfalle*, 244). He also wrote that the use of jazz elements, by himself and other composers, was 'prompted by the...desire to establish music as a vehicle of widely intelligible communication' ('A Composer's Influences', *Perspectives of New Music* 3/1 (Fall–Winter 1964), 38). Also see Grosch, *Die Musik der Neuen Sachlichkeit*, 108.

or 'socially forming power'.[56] Krenek's expression *gesellschaftbildende Macht* is one which had previously been used in a number of writings by the critic Paul Bekker. Krenek was Bekker's general assistant at the Kassel State Opera from 1925, where Bekker was *Intendant*, and the two men had known each other for several years beforehand.[57] Krenek certainly knew Bekker's writings before he took the Kassel job, and was highly influenced by them; according to Cook, Bekker was his 'mentor'.[58] Stewart says that in 1923, Krenek had referred to Bekker in a letter, citing the critic's ideas on the 'social role that music had once had' and wondering 'how music would be able to return, as he put it, "to life"'.[59]

The philosophy which Bekker developed to explain the place of music within society was advanced, and controversial, for the time. Cook explains that Bekker 'asserted that a new society...required correspondingly new forms of artistic expression which would be "the truly productive, direct incarnation of the new state."'[60] In *Das deutsche Musikleben*, of 1916, he 'expressed his belief in the engendering power of the musical community', while in his *Kritische Zeitbilder* he claimed that art should not belong to the elite, but should 'reflect all of society'.[61] Bekker's concept of *gesellschaft-*

---

[56] '"Materialbestimmtheit" der Oper', 27.

[57] Stewart, *Ernst Krenek*, 60.

[58] Cook, *Opera for a New Republic*, 14. Also on Krenek's opinion of Bekker, see Krenek, *Im Atem der Zeit*, 379 ff. and 612–13.

[59] Stewart, *Ernst Krenek*, 60. Despite being one of the few writers to mention the connection between the two men, Stewart does not mention Bekker's idea of *gesellschaftbildende Macht* in music specifically, nor Krenek's adoption of it, although he does refer to the same issues in passing. His discussion of Krenek's writings from this period focuses on aesthetic issues, particularly the composer's thoughts on opera as drama, rather than on the broader sociological issues which were also apparent at this time and were strongly influenced by Bekker (ibid., 63).

[60] Cook, *Opera for a New Republic*, 11–12, quoting Bekker, *Kritische Zeitbilder* (Berlin: Schuster and Loeffler, 1921), 217.

[61] Cook, *Opera for a New Republic*, 11; Bekker, *Das deutsche Musikleben* (Berlin: Schuster and Loeffler, 1919); *Kritische Zeitbilder*. Also see Franklin, 'Audiences, Critics and the Depurification of Music: Reflections on a 1920s Controversy', *Journal of the Royal Musical Association* 114 (1989). For a detailed discussion and philosophical critique of Bekker's aesthetic ideas, which goes into areas beyond the scope of the present chapter, see Giselher Schubert, 'Aspekte der Bekkerschen Musiksoziologie', *International Review of Music Aesthetics and Sociology* 1/2 (1970), 179–86.

bildende Macht is neatly expressed in his 1918 book, *Die Sinfonie von Beethoven bis Mahler*, in which he says that the 'need to speak to a *mass public*' is the reason why composers write symphonies.[62] He argues that the performance of a symphony of genius does not merely present a clever collection of themes and melodies, but creates a communal feeling in the audience, an 'experience of community', a *Gemeinschaftserlebnis* or *Volksversammlung*.[63] 'The criterion of the greatest symphonic art...is the specific character and the extent of the power with which this work of art is able to form communities of feeling (*Gefühlsgemeinschaften*), thus its ability...to create a single, definite, individualised being out of the chaotic mass of the public...Thus I call this ability *to create communities* (*gesellschaft-bildende Fähigkeit*) the highest quality of the symphonic work of art'.[64] The idea that music can 'create communities', especially in the context of the 1920s, may be seen as a left-wing position, with its concern for the mass public's relationship to music over the individual's. According to Bekker's model, music rises above the concerns of the individual to create a communal structure in which, it seems, all listeners are equal. In addition, Bekker's belief that an innovating composer is one who 'adopts a critical position towards his society' is indicative of a progressive attitude which, in contrast to conservatism, wishes to move away from the status quo.[65] In *Die Sinfonie von Beethoven bis Mahler*, this hint becomes explicit in Bekker's discussion of Beethoven. In his symphonies, Bekker argues, Beethoven 'created the artistic symbol of a new, ideal consciousness of community (*Gemeinschaftsbewußtsein*)'; the audience for whom he was writing, and who he helped to create, was 'a continuation of the mighty democratic movement, which led from the French Revolution to the German wars for independence'.[66] Bekker's explicit evocation of the 'mighty democratic movement' here points to the ideological implications of his

---

[62] Bekker, *Die Sinfonie von Beethoven bis Mahler* (Berlin: Schuster and Loeffler, 1918), 12.

[63] Ibid., 14 and 16.

[64] Ibid., 17. Bekker's emphasis. Translation based partly on that in Weiner, *Undertones of Insurrection*, 53. Bekker uses *gemeinschaftbildend* and *gesellschaftbildend* interchangeably, and does not appear to differentiate between the two, although the latter appears more frequently.

[65] Franklin, 'Audiences, Critics', 83.

[66] Bekker, *Die Sinfonie von Beethoven bis Mahler*, 22 and 16.

own argument; his emphasis is on community and collective experience, and by his own admission this is democratic, not elitist.

Bekker's ideas came under attack from conservative musical circles, and particularly from Pfitzner in his 'Die neue Ästhetik der musikalischen Impotenz'. Pfitzner objected to the idea that music could be *gesellschaft-bildend*, as, in his view, 'if nothing more depends on the music itself, but only on the "poetic idea", the "program", the power to "form communities", then it is easy to compose'. One does not need any musical talent to write such music, he believes; Bekker's aesthetic therefore 'must delight all musical quacks and dolts; they are protected by it, it justifies them'.[67] According to Pfitzner, Bekker's view that the power to form communities is 'the highest criterion' of a symphonic work of art means that the value of the work comes from something outside the work itself; in his estimation, this could result in the objectionable situation in which the musical material itself could be banal and unoriginal, but where the work may still be valued as *gesellschaftbildend*.[68] One of Pfitzner's quarrels with Bekker is because of what Pfitzner takes to be the latter's censure of Beethoven in *Die Sinfonie von Beethoven bis Mahler*, in Pfitzner's opinion the most 'German' of musicians.[69] Bekker's criticism of the 'pantheon of German music' leads to a diatribe from Pfitzner which is explicitly political: 'In the shame and outrage of the revolution, we experience with sorrow that German works, German people, have let themselves be led by Russian-Jewish criminals and have shown an enthusiasm which they begrudged their German heroes and benefactors. In art, we experience that a German man from the people, of such a sharp understanding and deep knowledge as Herr Bekker...leads the international-Jewish movement in art'.[70] Pfitzner's invective against the

---

[67] Pfitzner, 'Die neue Ästhetik', 155. Translation as Weiner, *Undertones of Insurrection*, 54. Also for discussion of Pfitzner's opinion of Bekker, see Carner, 'Pfitzner v. Berg', 379; Adamy, *Hans Pfitzner*, 102 ff.; and Ermen, *Musik als Einfall*, 129 ff. On how Pfitzner's views of Bekker were shared by other commentators, see John, *Musikbolschewismus*, 63.

[68] Pfitzner, 'Die neue Ästhetik', 241.

[69] Ibid., 243. How far Bekker's comments on Beethoven are in fact a real criticism is debatable; he suggests that Beethoven's themes are not necessarily particularly original. Also see Botstein, 'Pfitzner and Musical Politics', 67.

[70] Pfitzner, 'Die Neue Ästhetik', 244.

'new, international, *gesellschaftsbildende Kraftkunst*' is therefore explicitly aimed at Bekker and his aesthetic concepts.[71]

The altercation between Bekker and Pfitzner, while ostensibly about music, couched two opposed political positions in aesthetic terms.[72] Bekker's belief in music which can appeal to all indicates a conception of an ideal society radically different to Pfitzner's, in which music remains the privilege of the elite. For Pfitzner, music of genius cannot be *gesellschaft-bildend*, only transcendent of the concerns of the world, whereas Bekker argued that the work of art is of genius if it can be easily comprehended and community-forming. The two men are radically different both aesthetically and politically, and characterise the political divide of the Weimar Republic as well as the contemporary debate about music: one is in favour of modernism and democracy, the other fiercely traditional in both music and politics. (It is interesting to note that Bekker appeared in a 1935 National Socialist list of 'Music Bolshevists', the linking of the critic with far-left politics, in the eyes of the right wing, thus being made explicit.)[73] The contrast between Pfitzner and Bekker is summed up at the end of *Die Sinfonie von Beethoven bis Mahler*, where Bekker contrasts the backward-looking art of Pfitzner with what he believes is the forward-looking one of Mahler. 'With [Mahler] the chapter of the Romantic symphony closes; it does not close, as with Pfitzner's Palestrina, in sombre flight from the world, out of grief for one's own fate, but it closes while letting one's own fate be forgotten...with the announcement of the message of all-encompassing love. Therefore it does not belong to the *past* from which we turn away, but to it belongs the *future* towards which we strive'.[74]

Bekker's concept of *gesellschaftbildende Macht* influenced many young composers of the time, and the influence of his philosophy on Krenek is clear; the composer said in later years that at this time 'music, according to my new philosophy, had to fit the well-defined demands of the community

---

71 Ibid., 251. Attinello's translation of the last word of this phrase as 'power-art', while literally correct, therefore misses out on the allusion of Pfitzner's original ('Pfitzner, *Palestrina*, Nazis, Conservatives', 31). Pfitzner includes an 's' in this term (*gesellschafts-bildende*) which Bekker omits (*gesellschaftbildende*).

72 See Weiner, *Undertones of Insurrection*, 53.

73 See John, *Musikbolschewismus*, 360.

74 Bekker, *Die Sinfonie von Beethoven bis Mahler*, 60–61.

for which it was written; it had to be useful, entertaining, practical'.[75]
Krenek saw contemporary popular music as being the means through which
communities could be formed, as is shown in his essay '"Materialbestimmtheit" der Oper', where he says that a composer will be led to use
contemporary forms of dance if he feels the necessity for his music to be
relevant: 'No-one will deny their *gesellschaftbildende Macht*, which we
experience everyday. It touches us through its deeply exciting, irresistible,
purely animal effectiveness on our nerves'.[76]

Artists and Society in *Jonny spielt auf*

Krenek's ideas about the importance of *gesellschaftbildende Macht* in
music, and the implications this has for the relationship of art, artist and
audience, is portrayed through his central opposition in *Jonny spielt auf* of
the characters of Jonny and Max. The two musicians can be compared on a
number of levels: Jonny, for instance, is comfortable interacting with the
world around him, while Max is shown in isolation, often on top of a
mountain. The two have wholly separate plots: Max's is inward-looking
and reflective, concerning his problems with his art and his relationship to
the wider society; Jonny's, in contrast, revolving around the theft of Daniello's violin, is action-driven and dramatically exciting. Instead of agonis-
ing about his life, Jonny lurches from one situation to the next, steering
events rather than removing himself from them. Max's fate only becomes
similarly exciting at the end of the opera, as he rushes to catch the train to
America. Jonny works in close interaction with other characters, while Max

---

[75] Krenek, 'Self-Analysis', *New Mexico Quarterly* 23 (1953), 14. As well as Krenek, Kurt
Weill uses the same terminology in his writings, and his use of popular music may be
seen as an attempt to develop Bekker's aesthetic. See Christopher Hailey, 'Creating a
Public, Addressing a Market: Kurt Weill and Universal Edition', in Kim H. Kowalke
(ed.), *A New Orpheus: Essays on Kurt Weill* (New Haven and London: Yale University
Press, 1986), 27; Kim H. Kowalke's editorial note to Weill's 'Shifts in Musical Composition' ('Verschiebungen in der musikalischen Produktion'), in the former's *Kurt Weill in
Europe* (Ann Arbor: UMI Research Press, 1979), 480; Weill's essays 'Verschiebungen in
der musikalischen Produktion' (ibid.), 'Gesellschaftsbildende Oper' (ibid., 489) and
'Tanzmusik' (ibid., 473); and Amidon, *'Nirgends brennen wir genauer'*, 177 and 187–8.
[76] Krenek, '"Materialbestimmtheit" der Oper', 27.

has little to do with most of them; because Jonny sets chains of events in motion rather than merely reacting to outside circumstances, the other characters circulate around him. This interaction parallels his relationship to art: for Jonny, music is expendable, more current and not treated as an autonomous art-object, as it is by Max. Jonny might be seen as a more superficial character than Max because of the way he reacts more quickly to life; he has none of the heart-searching monologues which Max has but is more happy-go-lucky. Nevertheless, it is Jonny who triumphs, with no sense of irony.[77] Max's soul-searching may be 'deeper', but it sets him apart from the ordinary people around him, because no-one can understand him. Jonny's down-to-earth quality, and his closeness to the other characters, illustrates his participation within all of society, rather than his retreat from it, and this contributes to his music being *gesellschaftbildend*.

The nationalities of the two composers – Jonny is American, Max an unspecified middle-European – are of primary importance to the moral of the story, and the conclusion of the opera focuses this moral in no uncertain terms. After believing the violin to be lost to him, Jonny finally succeeds in obtaining it after Daniello, its owner, falls to his death beneath a train. Jonny is shown triumphant, playing the violin on top of a turning globe. Daniello's violin symbolises the old order, and its eventually successful theft by Jonny indicates the triumph of the New World; the classical violin is stolen by a jazz musician, and pressed into the service of a new style of music. Jonny expresses this idea earlier in the opera, in the song which he sings as he retrieves the violin from its hiding place in Anita's house: 'all that is good in the world belongs to me. The old world created it, but doesn't know what to do with it any more'.[78] The chorus voices this sentiment again at the conclusion of the opera:

> Time is up for the old ways, the new time is at hand. Don't miss your connection, the journey is beginning into the unknown land of freedom. ...The glitter-

---

[77] I therefore disagree with Rogge's statement that Jonny's triumph is ironic (*Ernst Kreneks Opern*, 66).

[78] 'mir gehört alles, was gut ist in der Welt. Die alte Welt hat es erzeugt, sie weiß damit nichts mehr zu tun'.

ing new world comes across the sea and inherits old Europe through the dance![79]

Jonny's engagement with the wider world, and Max's separation from it, is central to the opera's message; the ways in which the two musicians are located within their environments, and their different artistic sensibilities, can be easily compared. Max's isolation is established at the beginning of the opera, where he is shown as wholly set apart from the world around him, on top of a mountain glacier; he is thereafter consistently shown in isolated locations, either on the glacier or in his home. Max feels he has no place in the world, saying he 'cannot live in these towns any more'; in contrast to his estrangement from city life, on the glacier he is 'at home'.[80] The mountain acts as a metaphor for Max himself: it is set apart from, or above, the world around it.[81] He is full of praise for the mountain which lures him away from his work and his fellow men: 'You beautiful mountain! You attract me, you drive me to go away from home, away from work! You send your glacier out to me, great and magnificent, white and sparkling in the midday light'.[82] The idea of Max's isolation is shown again in Scene 7, as the despairing composer prepares to throw himself from the mountain, which then speaks to him: rather than having conversations with real people, the detached Max talks with mountains. Krenek said that Max was modelled on the type of artist 'who doesn't concern himself with whether he will find an ear that wants to listen to him... . What we see is his isolation, his remoteness from life, and his anxious contrast to the basic attitude of the world around him'.[83]

---

[79] 'Die Stunde schlägt der alten Zeit, die neue Zeit bricht jetzt an. Versäumt den Anschluß nicht, die Überfahrt beginnt ins unbekannte Land der Freiheit. ...Es kommt die neue Welt übers Meer gefahren mit Glanz und erbt das alte Europa durch den Tanz!'.

[80] 'kann in diesen Städten nicht mehr leben'; 'zu Haus'. Anita calls Max a 'Gletschermensch' (a 'person of the glacier') in Scene 2.

[81] The glacier leitmotif is also employed as a metaphor for the isolation of the composer. On the appearances of the glacier motif, and its meaning within the work, see Rogge, *Ernst Kreneks Opern*, 57–8.

[82] 'Du schöner Berg! Der mich anzieht, der mich antreibt, zu gehen, fort aus der Heimat, fort von der Arbeit! Deinen Gletscher sendest du mir entgegen, groß und herrlich, weiß und strahlend im Mittagslicht'.

[83] Krenek, 'Jonny spielt auf', 18–19.

Max seems to parody the stereotypical Romantic artist figure, out-of-date and slightly ridiculous. He is situated as such a figure through the rhetoric he characteristically employs. For instance, in Scene 5, as he awaits Anita's return from Paris, his language is overstated in typical nineteenth-century fashion:

> Oh heart, my heart, do not yet thunder so furiously, you must let me still keep some reason. Blood, oh my blood, do not roar so loudly, let me still breathe!... Oh joy, do not kill me yet, not so early, let me still live, let me experience this moment! Oh heart, my heart, do not beat so furiously, you, my heart, have patience![84]

Other factors indicate his status as a Romantic artist, such as his intense relationship with art. He treats his works as his 'children', as he states to Anita in Scene 2 when she is about to leave to sing in his opera: 'How I am jealous of my own child! To serve it, you leave me alone! My own work robs me of you! ...I suffer because of you, yet still you go away'.[85] The work of art is treated in a way typical of nineteenth-century aesthetics: it is given a special status as autonomous, having an existence independent of the composer who created it.

The portrayal of Max as a lonely, Romantic artist figure is, however, complicated by another possible reading of his character. In this interpretation, Max is a modernist composer, as is argued by Cook in *Opera for a New Republic*. She points out how Max clearly parodies specific composers; for example, in the very first line of the opera he exclaims 'Du schöner Berg!' ('You beautiful mountain!'). This allusion to perhaps the most modernist of Krenek's contemporaries is repeated elsewhere in the opera. The first line of the song which Max has composed, 'Als ich damals am Strand des Meeres stand', for instance, refers to Schoenberg's 1909 song, 'Am Strand'.[86] According to Cook, the text of 'Als ich damals' not only

---

[84] 'O Herz, mein Herz, brause noch nicht so wild, noch mußt du mich bei klarem Verstand lassen. Blut, o mein Blut, tose nicht so laut, laß mich noch atmen!. ...O Freude, töte mich noch nicht, nicht zu früh, laß mich noch leben, laß mich noch diesen Augenblick erleben! O Herz, mein Herz, schlage nicht so wild, du mein Herz, gedulde dich noch!'.

[85] 'Was bin ich auf mein eigenes Kind eifersüchtig! Ihm zu dienen, läßt du mich allein! Mein eigenes Werk raubt dich mir!. ...Ich leide so um dich, und doch fährst du weg'.

[86] Cook states that Krenek referred to Scene 4 (*recte* Scene 5), as 'Max in Erwartung', al-

'characterizes Max's personality as an individual uncomfortable with reality', but also 'parodies expressionist texts with their other-worldly senti-ments'.[87] The allusions to modernist composers continue, such as through the image of the mountain as satirically representing the solitary intellec-tual. Webern had a great interest in mountains, and, Cook comments, is described in the Moldenhauers' biography as needing to seek the 'rarified air of the heights'.[88] Cook argues that these allusions to the composers of the Second Viennese School situate Max as a modernist composer stylisti-cally; she says that the instance we hear of Max's own music, 'Als ich damals', 'parodies chromatic, atonal writing'.[89] Cook's view would seem to challenge the portrayal of Max as a Romantic composer. However, this apparent contradiction is resolvable because of the important distinction between aesthetics and musical style. As Franklin points out in his article 'Audiences, Critics and the Depurification of Music: Reflections on a 1920s Controversy', aesthetic 'idealism' was common to both stylistically traditionalist composers such as Pfitzner, and modernist ones like Schoen-berg or Berg. Franklin comments that Berg's 1920 attack on Pfitzner's 'Die neue Ästhetik', entitled 'Die musikalische Impotenz Hans Pfitzners neuer Ästhetik', takes issue only with Pfitzner's allegedly faulty analysis, and that Pfitzner's 'idealism', his belief in music as transcendent, is not dissimilar to

---

though this is not in the score, and she gives no reference (*Opera for a New Republic*, 85). Max does say in Scene 6 that in his dream at the end of that night, 'alles war voll Erwartungen' ('all was full of expectation'), but this is the only use of this word in this section of the opera.

[87] Ibid., 101.

[88] H. and R. Moldenhauer, *Anton von Webern* (New York: Alfred A. Knopf, 1979), 158, quoted in ibid., 85. Also see the references to Webern's relationship to mountains in Kathryn Bailey (ed.), *Webern Studies* (Cambridge: Cambridge University Press, 1996), 18, 62 and 277. The mountain image is particularly apposite for the time in which the opera was written, when mountaineering was popular amongst intellectuals: mountain peaks were understood as symbolising the superiority of the educated elite over more ordinary people. Siegfried Kracauer writes that in the early years of the century, intell-ectuals and students climbed mountains 'full of Promethean promptings...and with infi-nite pride [would] look down on what they called "valley-pigs" – those plebeian crowds who never made an effort to elevate themselves to lofty heights'. Siegfried Kracauer, *From Caligari to Hitler: A Psychological History of the German Film* (Princeton: Prince-ton University Press, 1947), 111.

[89] Cook, *Opera for a New Republic*, 101.

Berg's own philosophy.[90] The aesthetics of the Second Viennese School in particular 'tended no less than Pfitzner's towards the supreme validation of a cherished artistic style or goal as being bound up with Nature'.[91] David Neumeyer similarly writes that 'modernism, paraded about as truly revolutionary doctrine, was fundamentally an extreme extension of postures of the nineteenth-century romantics'.[92] If we understand modernist aesthetics as being an extension of Romanticism, rather than a departure from it, as I have discussed in Chapter 1, then Pfitzner and Schoenberg were closer in aesthetic outlook than their musical styles would suggest. Max can therefore hint in both directions, functioning as a Romantic and as a modernist artist, and is thus particularly pertinent for the context in which Krenek was working.

The configuration of Max as conventionally Romantic is further shown through the source of his artistic inspiration. Initially, he is inspired by nature, and this partakes of a familiar nineteenth-century topos of artistic provenance. He goes to the glacier in order to escape the world, believing that there he will derive strength and inspiration: he says in Scene 6 that the mountain is his source of stability, while in Scene 7, he declares that the mountain 'always sent me comfort and strength...[and] fortified my youth'.[93] His conversation with the glacier in Scene 7 is the ultimate communion with the natural world: Max is not merely close to nature, but in tune with it to such an extent that he can communicate with it on a semantic level. A second common idea for the origination of inspiration may also be found, namely the construction of women as muses to the male creative artist. The muse idea is found in Romanticism in two related manifestations, both of which are present in *Jonny spielt auf*. The muse may be wholly fictional, with the source of inspiration personified in a female figure; in *Jonny*, the glacier is personified in this way, speaking to Max with a female voice. Alternatively, a real woman within the artist's life may assume the status of a muse; the role which would otherwise be given to the fictional muse is projected onto the actual woman in the artist's life. Anita begins to assume the role of a muse for Max as they become more involved

---

[90] Franklin, 'Audiences, Critics', 81 and 85.

[91] Ibid., 86.

[92] *The Music of Paul Hindemith* (New Haven and London: Yale University Press, 1986), 8.

[93] 'mir immer Trost und Kraft gesandt...[und] meine Jugend stärkte'.

with each other. Although it is not made explicit in the text that Anita provides the inspiration for Max's music, it is found implicitly during the scenes between them. Firstly, Max has written an opera for her, part of which we hear them rehearse in Scene 2; secondly, in Scene 5, Max awaits Anita's return, and as he is counting the minutes by, he sits down at the piano to try to work. However, he fails because he is lacking in inspiration, showing how he cannot compose without her; all we hear instead is an echo of 'Als ich damals', the song he has written for her.[94] In contrast to Anita's role for Max as a muse, Jonny has a blasé attitude towards women which is the opposite of Max's idealisation of Anita. Instead of exalting one particular woman, Jonny indicates his ability to move through a variety of them: 'When I change hotels, there are new girls, but the whole thing is just another season'.[95] As Rogge comments, music and women are both an expression of Jonny's vitality: 'music becomes for him an object of his passion, in the same way as women'.[96] This also exemplifies his different sensibility towards art: for Jonny, women and music are both something temporary and expendable, for Max they are both something almost sacred, to be idealised.

The different positions of Max and Jonny are further shown through their own compositions. Max's situation as a composer isolated from society is illustrated through the only composition of his which we hear, the

---

[94] The overall effect of both manifestations of the Romantic muse idea is the same: in both cases the woman, whether real or fictional, is imbued with qualities in the mind of the artist which in reality she does not possess. A number of actual nineteenth-century composers may be seen to have endowed muse-like qualities on real women: Christina Brantner has argued that Clara Schumann functioned in this role for her husband Robert (*Robert Schumann und das Tonkünstler-Bild der Romantiker*). We may also cite Berlioz's infatuation with Harriet Smithson.

[95] 'Wechselt das Hotel, gibt es neue Mädchen, und das Ganze war wieder eine Saison'. Also see Scene 4, where the Hotel Director says to Jonny, 'Do you want even more women?' ('Wollen Sie noch mehr Weiber?'). The relationship between Yvonne and Jonny is less 'serious' than that between Max and Anita; indeed, they split up from each other in the first scene they appear in. Although Yvonne continues to be present, Jonny does not pay her very much attention, and the reason why he suddenly chooses to carry out her request to rescue Max from the police is unclear.

[96] Rogge, *Ernst Kreneks Opern*, 59.

aria 'Als ich damals am Strand des Meeres stand'. The text of the song alludes to his position apart from the world:

> As I stood once on the seashore, homesickness sought a home in me. I sought my home in the land of dreams, so that my grief would be eased. But my dreams gave me no happiness, the sorrow remained the same in sleep. Oh pain which has mortally wounded me! Flow down, oh tears.[97]

While we are told nothing of the character of the song, it may be read as a persona for Max. Max's separation from reality is suggested by the 'land of dreams' he seeks out in the song, in his case this being the world of solitude and the mountains. An indication that the character speaking in the song is identifiable with Max appears later, in Scene 5; Max says to the absent Anita, 'Als du damals am Rand des Gletschers zu mir tratest' ('When you came to me then at the edge of the glacier'), and is accompanied by the melody which appeared in the original version of the song. 'Als ich damals' is constructed as 'Art' by being disconnected from the 'reality' of the rest of the opera. In terms of plot, the song is mostly irrelevant to the dramatic action of the opera, and does not move it forward in any way. It is also presented as geographically separate, being performed in one room and 'heard' only by the performers themselves; the opera's audience is privileged to eavesdrop on their performance. Finally, the song is temporally distinct, bringing the action to a standstill while it is being performed; for Anita and Max, it is a way to pass the time before Anita must leave. The definite and obvious break which separates 'Als ich damals' from the non-diegetic music on either side of it accentuates the contrast between 'art' and 'reality'. The song has the purpose within the opera of portraying Max's musical style and personality, but the way in which it is distinct temporally, geographically, and in terms of plot helps to underline the composer's distance from the 'normal' music around it, and therefore from the world outside.

Jonny, in contrast, is seen making music far more often than Max. While Max only writes and performs one piece of music and then ceases

---

[97] 'Als ich damals am Strand des Meeres stand, suchte das Heimweh mir heim. Ich suchte mein Heim in der Träume Land, daß das Weh mich ließe. Doch ward meiner Träume ich nicht froh, das Leid blieb das Gleiche im Schlaf. O Schmerz, der mich tödlich traf! Drum, o Träne, fließe'.

composing, Jonny plays in no fewer than six different pieces. Three of these are played by Jonny offstage in conjunction with his band ('Shimmy', 'Tango' and 'Jazz'), and one is sung by him onstage, accompanied by his band offstage ('Blues' ('Leb' wohl, mein Schatz')). The other two ('Auf wiedersehen' and 'Jetzt ist die Geige mein') are sung by Jonny alone on-stage. It is never explicitly stated whether these pieces are actually composed by Jonny or just played by him, but they are clearly associated with him; when we read them as being written by him, they demonstrate his compositional fluency, in contrast to Max's sterility. It is also made clear that Jonny is a versatile all-round musician, when he sings 'When I play the violin, strum the banjo, blow the saxophone and trombone...'[98] Jonny's music is clearly tonal, and often has prominent blues thirds and rhythmic syncopation, in a style borrowed from contemporary dance music. (Ex.3.1 shows some typical examples of this style.) In contrast to Max's isolation, Jonny's 'accessible' popular music exhibits the way in which he is inte-grated with the society in which he lives. The preference for Jonny's music amongst the other characters is suggested throughout the opera, and some-times becomes particularly obvious, for instance at the end of Scene 7, when the jazz musician's music is directly contrasted with Max's. Here, Anita's voice is broadcast on the radio, singing 'Als ich damals', to which the reaction of the listeners on stage is: 'Listen to that voice! It sounds so divine! It's a pity she likes singing modern music so much. And yet, when she sings it, one could almost believe it to be music'.[99] When the radio is re-tuned to Jonny's band, there are exclamations of 'thank the Lord!',[100] before everyone starts dancing happily. Thus Jonny's music actively cre-ates a community: it is *gesellschaftbildend*. The contrast in the public's re-actions to the two types of music vividly illustrates the problem, according to Krenek, of the art composer in the modern world; the difference between the negative picture of Max as an out-of-touch aesthete and Jonny's vibrancy could hardly be more explicit. To paraphrase Pfitzner, the old aesthetic is shown to be musically impotent.

---

[98] 'Wenn ich hier die Geige spiele, Banjo zupfe, Saxophon, Posaune blase...'

[99] 'Hören Sie die Stimme an! Sie klingt so göttlich schön! Schade, daß sie so gern moderne Musik singt! Und doch, wie sie's singt, meint man fast, es wäre Musik'.

[100] 'Gott sei Dank!'.

a) Shimmy (I/583)

Ex.3.1 Examples of Jonny's music (© 1927, by Universal Edition A.G., Vienna / UE 8624)

b) Blues (I/959)

Ex.3.1 (contd.)

Perhaps the most significant aspect of Jonny's music, and where it contrasts most strongly with Max, is its status within the opera as a whole. Jonny's music, signifying the 'new world', takes up a large section of the music of the entire work, especially when compared to Max's, showing the integration of his style of music with the world of the opera. Both Max's and Jonny's music appear diegetically; Jonny's music is either sung by him on stage or played by the offstage band. Significantly, though, Jonny's diegetic music reappears within a non-diegetic context, sung by other characters or by Jonny himself. (A summary of the instances of diegetic music, as well as where it recurs non-diegetically, is given in Table 3.1.) The way in which Max's music remains wholly diegetic, while Jonny's music is taken up by all of the characters and incorporated into the musical language of the whole, illustrates the relative positions of the two artists towards society. The music of Jonny's band is unashamedly 'popular'; it is so much a part of everyday life for the characters in the opera that, in contrast to the full stop of 'Als ich damals', this music is employed by the characters on stage in a non-diegetic way, demonstrating its *gesellschaftbildende Macht*. The 'Blues' song, 'Leb' wohl mein Schatz', first played by Jonny's band, is particularly significant in this respect, being taken up by the characters on numerous occasions as part of the plot. The 'negro-spiritual' first sung by Jonny with the words 'Jetzt ist die Geige mein' has a similarly important role.[101] Jonny's style becomes, in part, the musical language of the opera *per se*, and assimilated with the everyday world, illustrating the position of Jonny's music as a part of society rather than distinct from it. This *gesellschaftbildende* power of Jonny's music not only acts fictionally within the realms of the opera itself, but also, it could be argued, in the 'real' world outside the opera: because of its popular character, Jonny's music is stylistically posited to be the music of the everyday world outside the opera house. The employment of stylistically 'popular' music not only suggests the assimilation of Jonny and his music into the society of the opera, but also serves symbolically to bridge the gap between the fantasy world on stage and the reality which the audience ordinarily inhabits, helping to 'normalise' the operatic characters which use this music, and bringing them

---

[101] We hear it first pertaining to the plot before we hear it as an instrumental number, but it nevertheless functions in the same way.

Table 3.1: *Jonny spielt auf* – diagetic and non-diegetic music

Bar	Title/Words	Performers	Status	Location
I/363	'Als ich damals'	Anita & Max	diegetic	onstage
I/585	Shimmy	Jonny's band	diegetic	offstage
I/941	Blues ('Leb' wohl')	Jonny's band [+ Jonny & Yvonne]	diegetic [+ non-diegetic]	offstage [on-stage]ᵃ
I/1138	Tango	Jonny's band	diegetic	offstage
I/1289 & I/1740	*Niggerlied*	*Jonny*	*diegetic*	*onstage*ᵇ
I/1762	[Blues]	[Soloists' ensemble]	[non-diegetic]	[onstage]
II/884	*Neger-Spirituel*	*Jonny*	*diegetic*	*onstage*
II/1335	'Als ich damals'	Anita	diegetic	offstage
II/1411	Jazz	Jonny's band	diegetic	offstage
II/1523	Neger-Spirituel	Jonny's band	diegetic	offstage
II/2183	['DIE STÜNDE SCHLÄGT' = MUSIC OF BLUES]	[CHORUS]	[NON-DIEGETIC]	[ONSTAGE]ᶜ
II/2323	['ES KOMMT DIE NEUE WELT' = MUSIC OF NEGER-SPIRITUEL]	[CHORUS AND SOLOISTS]	[NON-DIEGETIC]	[ONSTAGE]

ᵃ *Square brackets indicate sections which are non-diegetic but which employ music which functions diegetically simultaneously, or elsewhere.*

ᵇ *Italics indicate music which is functioning diegetically, but which nevertheless uses words pertaining directly to the plot.*

ᶜ *Capitals indicate that music heard previously is re-heard with different words.*

into line with the audience's everyday experience.[102] This occurs to a much greater degree than would be the case if the opera were written in a conventionally 'classical' style, in which the music has a limited existence outside the confines of its own performance in the opera house. This is especially true for the time of *Jonny spielt auf*'s composition, when the newest art music was usually little heard by the general public. *Jonny spielt auf* is not simply 'art music', but partakes in a different musical discourse distinct from the usual realm for opera, because of its frequent use of a popular style. This popular music is stylistically identical with that found in the wider cultural environment of the opera, and would later become literally identical when the popular numbers of *Jonny spielt auf* became hits in their own right.

Max's Transformation

While the opera clearly portrays an underlying conflict between Max and Jonny, Krenek resolves this tension during the course of the work. In the early scenes of the opera, Max finds his position outside society unproblematic, but as the plot progresses, a gradual heightening of tension between Max and the world outside him comes about, through the agency of Anita, a singer, with whom Max falls in love in the first scene. Anita mediates between the two environments represented by the two musicians. She is herself a singer, an artist, and therefore has one foot in Max's artistic world; however, as a performer and in communication with audiences, she also belongs to society. When Max falls in love with her, this society begins to exert a pull on him, and simultaneously, he loses his ability to compose (as is shown in the scene, already discussed, when he cannot work while waiting for Anita to return). Consistently with her mediating role, Anita first appears in Max's mountain environment, climbing the glacier herself where she meets the composer. Yet she is also to be found in

---

[102] A split similar to that between the diegetic and non-diegetic music is that between on-stage and off-stage music: much of Jonny's music is performed by the off-stage band, indicating a literal mediation between the fantasy world of the opera and the world outside which parallels that of musical style. Max's music, 'Als ich damals', is originally heard in an on-stage setting, but also partly shifts when it is heard on the radio in Scene 7, indicating the composer's gradual transformation. This issue is considered to some extent by Grosch (*Die Musik der Neuen Sachlichkeit*, 158–9).

Jonny's world, in the hotel where the jazz musician first appears in Scene 3, and in the railway station. While Max stays mostly in one place, their home, Anita moves between there and her singing engagements. Anita's function as an intermediary is shown by her resistance to the role into which Max tries to cast her. She refuses Max's attempts to place her on a pedestal, and becomes exasperated with the way he pours out his Romantic longing for her. Anita tells him that he must reconcile himself to modern life and that the strength he thought he had on the mountain was only an illusion:

> Life, which you cannot understand, is movement, and therein lies happiness. To be yourself in the midst of life, that is everything. To be yourself at every moment, to live it to the full at every moment, and to live each moment as though it were the only one, nothing before nor after, and yet not lose yourself.[103]

The musical language of 'Als ich damals' (which Anita performs, further showing her position as an intermediary) demonstrates the tension which comes to exist between Max and society. The song sets up a separate musical world for Max, in the same manner that Palestrina is characterised by particular leitmotifs. The music of *Jonny spielt auf* divides into sharply differentiated styles: Max's post-Romantic style is contrasted both with a similar but more atonal style which forms the bulk of the non-diegetic music, and with the strongly tonal and rhythmic music influenced by contemporary popular music, associated with Jonny and the everyday world to which he belongs. Max's song, 'Als ich damals', while it possesses little strong harmonic direction, and often no clearly established tonal centre, nevertheless still refers to a number of tonal centres: it opens with an implication of C, which is also referred to in b.381-5, and definitely closes in C at the end. The song also cadences unambiguously on F in b.380 and moves from a cadence on F to C in b.412-6, while also hinting at A in b.394-5. The harmonic style of the song combines conventionally tonal chords, extended chords with the addition of sevenths and added sixths, and some dissonant chords which cannot be explained with reference to conventional

---

[103] 'Das Leben, das du nicht verstehst, es ist Bewegung, and darin ist es Glück. Darin du selbst sein, das ist alles. In jedem Augenblick du selbst sein, in jedem Augenblick es ganz sein, und jeden Augenblick leben, als ob kein andrer käme, weder vorher noch nachher, und sich doch nicht verlieren'.

tonality. Many of these seemingly dissonant chords, though, can be explained in terms of suspensions and anticipations. The non-harmonic notes of the voice part may often be explained in terms of passing and auxiliary notes, although there are also passages in which the voice part does not fit with the harmony implied in the piano, such as in b.391-2, and particularly b.400-3.[104] (Ex.3.2, the beginning of the song, illustrates its musical style.) The opera's association of tonality with everyday society means that the tonal moments within 'Als ich damals' do not remain semiotically neutral; tonality is used in the opera as a marker to the world associated with Jonny, and its employment by Max shows his pull towards that society. The tension in 'Als ich damals' between tonality and atonality can be interpreted as denoting Max's position on the edge of society, neither able to be assimilated into it nor able altogether to escape it.

After meeting Anita, Max becomes aware of his isolation, and uneasy with it; the glacier's previous role as a means of escape from the trials of society is no longer effective for him. In Scene 7, on the glacier, Max is now afraid of the mountains, and shows how Anita has made him aware of his seclusion by using words which allude to her: 'I am afraid. Were those not her words?'.[105] This growing unease is fundamental to the reappraisal he makes of his place in society. Max states to the absent Anita in Scene 5 that when he met her, his ice began to melt: 'When you came to me then at the edge of the glacier, you melted away the ice of my soul. Now I live and suffer. My life is completely in your hands'.[106] He is forced to question his previous existence, which completely ignored a world outside art, and consequently he undergoes a fundamental reorientation of his way of life.

---

[104] Overall, the music of 'Als ich damals' is reminiscent of the style of, for instance, early Berg. Joseph Henry Auner also makes this point, suggesting its similarity to Berg's *Four Songs*, op.2, and Schoenberg's Second Quartet ('"Soulless Machines" and Steppenwolves: Renegotiating Masculinity in Krenek's *Jonny spielt auf*', in Mary Ann Smart (ed.), *Siren Songs: Representations of Gender and Sexuality in Opera* (Princeton: Princeton University Press, 2000), 228). Grosch's arguement that the song alludes to French Baroque opera, however, seems bizarre (*Die Musik der Neuen Sachlichkeit*, 118).

[105] 'Ich habe Angst. Waren das nicht ihre Worte?'.

[106] 'Als du damals am Rand des Gletschers zu mir tratest, schmolzest du hin das Eis meiner Seele. Jetzt leb ich und leide. Mein Leben ist ganz in deiner Hand'.

Ex.3.2 Opening of 'Als ich damals am Strand des Meeres stand'
(© 1927, by Universal Edition A.G., Vienna / UE 8624)

Max's longing to be assimilated into society is suggested by the persona of 'Als ich damals', who is 'homesick'. Scene 7 further depicts Max's problematic position towards society and comments on the sterility, or even death, of the composer who is distanced from the world, through the image of the glacier. This representation is achieved in two ways, through the text and the music. The textual element is constructed in opposition to the opening scene of the opera; here, when Anita said that she was afraid on the glacier because it suggested to her 'unending death',[107] Max had contradicted her: 'but it is alive! ...What life is in its austerity... . To me, it is a symbol of tranquil life'.[108] However, in his moment of crisis in Scene 7, his opinion has changed: not only is he afraid, he now says that 'loneliness forms a vault over me like a death knell. Death itself comes to me'.[109] Max is also constructed as distanced from society and compositionally sterile through musical means. The aridity of Max's musical world is built from a texture which is characterised by comparative emptiness, with slow-moving harmonic progressions and tempi. His isolation is strikingly indicated during the most immobile passage of the scene, beginning in b.1284. Here, Max is at his most wretched. The Glacier has refused to help him, and has ordered him back to life, saying 'you are human. You must live, you must suffer!'.[110] The music becomes less and less active until it seems it will stop altogether. Max's lines reflect his despair; they are progressively contracted, so that the wide-ranging melodic lines which he sang previously, encompassing an octave or more within one phrase (see b.1226, for instance, as well as other scenes), are reduced to chromatic phrases within the C-G fifth in the section from b.1284. Max's voice eventually divests itself of melody altogether, until he repeats a monotone in speech rhythm, to the words 'loneliness forms a vault over me like a death knell'. This suggests Max's depressed state of mind, his compositional emptiness and his distance from society. The accompaniment to Max's singing is even more notable. For about fifty bars (almost two minutes' worth of music), it is made up principally of a sustained harmonium open fifth on C and G, a

---

107 'unendlicher Tod'.

108 'Er lebt doch!. ...In seiner Starrheit welches Leben!. ...Er ist mir Symbol...des gefaßten Lebens'.

109 'die Einsamkeit wölbt sich wie eine Totenglocke über mich. Der große Tod kommt zu mir'.

110 'du [bist] ein Mensch. Du mußt leben, du mußt leiden!'.

sustained low C in the double basses, and the Glacier-Voice repeating its leitmotif, eighteen times in all (b.1284-334). In addition, there is a repeated G in the violins, and from b.1299, a slowly descending scale from C to C in the basses, the downward movement of which can be seen as a conventional semiotic marker for Max's dejection. The orchestral voice depicts here the death-knell-like vault to which Max's words refer: the high harmonium notes with the low bass ones form a 'frame' into which Max's lines fit, which may suggest a vault-like space, while the open fifth's ringing in the harmonium approximates a bell.[111] As this musical vault encloses Max, the contracted nature of his lines give the impression that he is no longer able to break out, either spiritually or musically – he is compositionally and emotionally bereft, as expressed in his monotone. Although he may have gained strength and inspiration from the glacier in the past, the reverse is true by this scene.

Max solves his problematic seclusion by deciding to leave the rarefied world of art for integration with society. Although Jonny and Max never meet, apart from briefly in Scene 7, and their worlds are kept musically distinct, there is an important shift in the music accompanying Max during the course of the work. The change takes place after Max's decision to go with Anita to America (although it is anticipated before then); Anita's character as an intermediary between the two types of world is again apparent at the point of Max's change of heart. It is she who, after having made Max aware of his isolation, brings him into the world of Jonny, through one crucial moment in Scene 7. Here, Max's conversation with the glacier has ended in failure, the glacier telling him that he 'must return to life!'.[112] As he remains alone and pitying his fate, he hears Anita's voice singing 'Als ich damals', which is being carried from the loudspeaker on the hotel terrace at the foot of the mountain. Hearing this song has a profound effect on Max; it makes him decide not to kill himself, but to 'return to life' as the mountain commanded and go back to the world. Anita's voice on the radio effects Max's transition away from the realm of solitude and towards his assimilation into the modern world of Jonny. Max starts singing music

---

[111] In the score, Krenek specifies that the harmonium should be supplemented whenever possible by a glass harmonica, and this adds to the bell-like effect. (The Decca recording of *Jonny* includes the glass harmonica (*Entartete Musik* series, Decca 436 631–2).)

[112] 'Du mußt zurück ins Leben!'.

comprised of 'Als ich damals' in places, suggesting how he is beginning to regain his compositional ability. In contrast to the comparative lack of music which accompanied his most despairing moments, the music hints here that he can now compose again, even if this is only indicated so far by the music he has already written. Max descends from the mountain with renewed optimism, and sets out for the station where Anita is to catch the train which will take her to America.

The catalyst for Max's conversion is when he hears Anita singing 'Als ich damals', but an inconsistency is created by his hearing this song. Max is moved to return to life by hearing his own music, and does not hear what replaces the song on the radio: jazz music, played by Jonny. As Max is returning to life and to society at large, we might expect him to hear instead the music which represents it, rather than what he has written himself. However, the composer's decision on the glacier is only the first of two important moments. After his descent from the mountain, and his subsequent arrest for the supposed theft of Daniello's violin, Max begins to return to his old ways, becoming his old-fashioned and dejected self when he is driven away by the police and a disguised Jonny in Scene 10. Max sings 'now everything is over, the game is at an end. Life has triumphed over me'.[113] However, a second moment of conversion comes during this scene which more decisively throws him back towards Anita; it is accompanied by a corresponding, and significant, re-evaluation of the musical language. While in Scene 7, Max left the mountain before hearing the jazz on the radio, in this scene, his final decision is illustrated precisely through the use of popular music. At the beginning of his monologue in Scene 10, when he is still downcast, his music comprises tonally undirected chromatic lines in the woodwind and in his own part, with an accompaniment of ambiguous string chords. However, the music becomes more and more tonal as the monologue progresses, with a snatch of tonality in b.2115-7, and anchoring pedal-notes from b.2118. At the very point where Max realises his previous mistakes, and makes his decision that the time has come for him to take control of his life, the atonal style becomes infiltrated with allusions to Jonny's style of music for a few bars. First, in the horns (b.2128-9), comes a phrase taken from Jonny's 'Shimmy', followed by a phrase in trumpet and trombone which has not previously been heard, but which clearly

---

[113] 'Jetzt ist alles aus, zu Ende ist nun das Spiel. Das Leben hat gesiegt über mich'.

alludes to the popular style, with its syncopation and percussion accompaniment (b.2130-1). Finally, the violins play part of the 'Leb' wohl' Blues (b.2132-3) (see ex.3.3).[114] Immediately after this music, Max declares 'Now the moment has come!',[115] and orders the driver back to the station. The anomaly set up in Scene 7, when Max did not hear the jazz music on the radio, is thus resolved; his conversion to society is now illustrated through the music which represents it.

This is not the only instance where the music signifies Max's change of direction; his decision to embrace the modern world entails a broader change in some of the musical material accompanying him. Before his revelation on the mountain, we see intimations in Max's accompaniment of the style of Jonny's music. For instance, a descent of a perfect fourth is employed with a dissonant harmonisation to refer to Max, such as in Scene 4, where Anita tells Daniello about her connection with the composer (b.I/1442).[116] (This is related through inversion to the glacier leitmotif). The same descending perfect fourth is found at the opening of the 'Blues', 'Leb' wohl, mein Schatz' (see ex.3.1). Other sections of 'Leb' wohl' are used by Max, such as the cadence at the end of the first phrase, and the cadence in the final few bars of the song, both with the characteristic feature of a 'blue' minor third. The appearances of this cadence in Max's music are all related, through the accompanying text, to the role Anita plays in converting Max. The first instance appears at the end of their first duet in Scene 1 (b.I/202 ff), providing a hint of the future direction their relationship will take, while the next appears in Max's monologue in Scene 5, at the significant words, 'when you came to me then on the edge of the glacier, you melted away the ice of my soul' (II/327 ff).[117] (These correspondences are shown in ex.3.4.)

---

[114] It also hints at the music of the final chorus at the cadence of b.2132 (at 'unbekannte Land der Freiheit').

[115] 'Jetzt ist der Moment gekommen!'.

[116] The same chords are also used in connection with Daniello. Because Daniello is a performer rather than a creative artist, he has a tendency to use music associated with other people. Grosch takes the view that the principal dualism in the opera is in fact between Jonny and Daniello, not Jonny and Max (*Die Musik der Neuen Sachlichkeit*, 158).

[117] 'Als du damals am Rand des Gletschers zu mir tratest, schmolzest du hin das Eis meiner Seele'.

II/2128-2133

Ex.3.3 Act 2, b.2127-32 – Max's realisation (© 1927, by Universal Edition A.G., Vienna / UE 8624)

vln I/II

wwind.

snare drum

bsn. / horn

bass drum

Ex.3.3 (contd.)

These hints in the musical accompaniment flower in the music after Max's conversion, with what was previously only an implication becoming more explicit. In the eight scenes in which Max appears, references to Jonny's style of music are few in those preceding Scene 7. However, these references increase noticeably in the Glacier Scene; while the scene is still predominantly without jazz elements, and remains more atonal than tonal, there are nevertheless significantly more allusions to the popular style than have been found before. The Glacier-Voice's first statement, 'who calls?',[118] is a re-harmonised form of the descending fourth motif of the beginning of 'Leb' wohl'. The Glacier Scene also uses a number of other elements from 'Leb' wohl', sometimes the blues third cadence, and some-times melodic lines from the song (see ex.3.5). After Scene 7, appearances of the blues third in Max's music recur in Scene 9, and are again connected to Anita, as he sings firstly 'I must see her again! Will my heart bear it?' (II/1731 ff.) and 'where, where are you, beloved?' (II/1795 ff.);[119] this is followed shortly after by the 'Leb' wohl' cadence in the orchestra (II/1809).

---

[118] 'Wer ruft?'.

[119] 'Ich soll sie wiedersehen! Wird's mein Herz ertragen?'; 'Wo, wo bist du, Geliebte?'.

**Ex.3.4 Allusions to Jonny's style in Max's music, scenes 1 and 5 (©
1927, by Universal Edition A.G., Vienna / UE 8624)**

Ex.3.5 Allusions to Jonny's style in Max's music, scene 7 (© 1927, by Universal Edition A.G., Vienna / UE 8624)

Ex.3.5 (contd.)

The final appearance of the blues third in this context comes as Anita is waiting for Max, 'why doesn't he come?' (II/1854);[120] this section forms the basis for the music later in the scene (see ex.3.6).

While these examples are all instances of Jonny's music being used in scenes about Max, at other points Max's own music is transformed into the style of Jonny's. For instance, the glacier leitmotif associated with Max is 'jazzed-up' in the interlude between Scenes 1 and 2, its rhythms changed so that they become more syncopated, and the melody merged into the cadence of the 'Leb' wohl' Blues at the end. In this way, the orchestral voice anticipates the association of Jonny's music and the glacier which is spelt out in Scene 7, and hints at the transformation that Max will undergo. What these changes in musical style signify is not difficult to guess: the employment of elements of Jonny's music to accompany Max suggests how the classical composer becomes converted to the ways of the modern world. Jonny's music begins to encroach upon Max's world, and the distance between the two diminishes. At the end of the opera, Max is fully assimilated into the soloists' chorus, singing music based on 'Leb' wohl' and 'Jetzt ist die Geige mein', which demonstrates how he has now become integrated with modern society.

---

120 'Warum kommt er nicht?'.

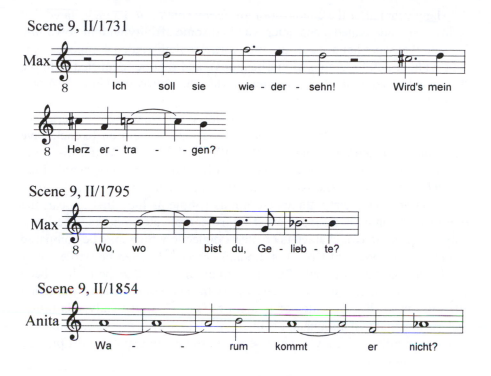

Scene 9, II/1731

Scene 9, II/1795

Scene 9, II/1854

Ex.3.6 Allusions to Jonny's style in Max's music after scene 7 (© 1927, by Universal Edition A.G., Vienna / UE 8624)

Krenek and *Jonny spielt auf*

The creation of two distinctive societies in *Jonny spielt auf* operates, in a parallel fashion to *Palestrina*, by allegorising the preferred position for the artist in modern society, and more broadly, constructs a Utopian vision of what society should be. In diametric contrast to Pfitzner's opera, though, *Jonny* holds up an image of a progressive modern society with which the artist should be engaged, through the use of *gesellschaftbildend* popular music. The opera captured the forward-looking, democratic ideals of the Weimar Republic, while it simultaneously partook of, and perpetuated, the contemporary myth of Americanism.

Many years after the composition of *Jonny spielt auf*, Krenek stated that in Max, he had created a character who had some affinity with his own life. He said that what happens to 'the introvert, problem-ridden composer' was 'not without autobiographical implications', and that he identified with the 'repressed inhabitant of the glacier world, the introverted middle-European'.[121] 'Personal experiences were worked in [to the opera] to some extent', he wrote, although he does not enlarge on what these experiences were.[122] Not surprisingly, given such admissions, writers on Krenek have also pointed to the autobiographical qualities of Max.[123] While his statements would perhaps seem to leave us with a fairly straightforward situation when it comes to assessing the opera's representation of Krenek's own views on art and society, things are not as simple as they first appear; the presence of Jonny as a second artist figure complicates matters. The interplay between the two characters creates a dialectic which may be compared to the circumstances of Krenek's life and career.[124] When he wrote *Jonny spielt auf*, Krenek was only 26. His career up until that point had been successful amongst art-music circles, with his compositions attracting attention from the advocates of modern music.[125] Stylistically, his music had been atonal and dissonant; his opera of 1923, *Orpheus und Eurydike*, is a good example of this style. The opera is based on an expressionist play by

---

[121] Krenek, *Horizons Circled: Reflections on My Music* (Berkeley, Los Angeles and London: University of California Press, 1974), 38. He says the same thing in 'Self-Analysis', 16.

[122] Krenek, 'Jonny erinnert sich', *Österreichische Musikzeitschrift* 4/5 (1980), 187.

[123] Cook, *Opera for a New Republic*, 84; Grosch, *Die Musik der Neuen Sachlichkeit*, 113; Rogge, 'Oper als Quadratur des Kreises: zum Opernschaffen Ernst Kreneks', *Österreichische Musikzeitschrift* 34 (September 1980)', 454, and *Ernst Kreneks Opern*, 54; Stewart, *Ernst Krenek*, 82.

[124] Matters are complicated further by Krenek's own changing opinion towards his work in the years after its composition; in fact, in the years of the mid-1920s, just after the opera was finished, the composer was more negative towards Max (for instance, in the essay 'Jonny spielt auf' (1928), he says that Max's character is based on 'sterile and dead' art-composers who reject their audiences; he also refers to such composers' 'arrogance', 'vanity', 'cowardice' and 'weakness' ('Jonny spielt auf', 18–19 and 21)). He also did not make any claims for Max being autobiographical at this time – this interpretation only came later.

[125] Unfortunately, there is to date no discussion of these early works; the existing writing on Krenek does not examine them in any detail.

Oskar Kokoschka, and its surreality of plot verges on the incomprehensible. Its music is similarly expressionist – Rogge says that it is characterised by 'dissonances which increase without concession'.[126] Krenek later said that he wrote atonal music early in his career because he wanted to be radical, but 'from a technical viewpoint I was dissatisfied with the disorder and lack of organisation which seemed to reign [in atonal music]'.[127]

The seeming change of direction towards the popular which *Jonny* represented (although it later proved not to be) was anticipated in some of the works preceding it, which were also influenced by popular music, albeit to a lesser extent. The influence of the popular may be seen in Krenek's *Tanzstudie* (1922), which contains a 'Foxtrott' movement, and in the last movement, also a 'Foxtrott', of op.13a, *Eine kleine Suite von Stücken über denselbigen Choral verschiedenen Charakters* (1922). Cook says of this op.13a movement that its 'oom-pah oom-pah bass line and dotted, swingable melody shows Krenek's sure understanding of the dance's character, which he combined with his dissonant harmonic idiom'.[128] The opera *Der Sprung über den Schatten* (1923) (which precedes the dissonant *Orpheus*) contains sections influenced by contemporary popular music, although elsewhere it maintains a predominantly dissonant style. One chorus, 'Im freien Land Amerika', is designated a 'Foxtrot', and uses syncopated rhythms and popular-style melodies, with gestures towards blue thirds; other sections use tango rhythms and syncopated melodic lines.[129] *Der*

---

[126] Rogge, *Ernst Kreneks Opern*, 35. Krenek said in his programme notes to the first performance that 'an attempt is made to unite an entire scene from time to time by simple, easily recognizable harmonic, melodic, rhythmic, and coloristic elements' (quoted in Stewart, *Ernst Krenek*, 78).

[127] Krenek, *Music Here and Now*, trans. Barthold Fles (New York: Russell and Russell, 1966), 86.

[128] Cook, *Opera for a New Republic*, 78.

[129] Stewart says of the musical style of the opera in general that it 'entertains by mixing mildly provocative dissonance with ingratiating tonality' (*Ernst Krenek*, 71–2), while Cook comments that it 'combines his early dissonant, complex style with elements borrowed from American popular music' (*Opera for a New Republic*, 80). Rogge talks little about the jazz elements in the work beyond observing their presence; his analysis is mostly on the level of plot description, although he does see the jazz as operating parodistically. He also makes the interesting comment that 'the jump over the shadow' could be interpreted as 'a jump into the Republic' (*Ernst Kreneks Opern*, 23).

Sprung also turns towards the popular, *Zeitoper* style of the later opera in its lighter subject matter and 'up to date' references.[130] The concerns which Krenek addressed in *Der Sprung über den Schatten* are those which would resurface in *Jonny*; the use of American popular music to signify the 'free land of America' relies on 'the sociological symbolism of American dance'.[131] However, despite its popular elements, *Der Sprung* did not attain the wide-ranging success of *Jonny*.

With this career trajectory in mind, we can see the two artist characters in the opera as showing how Krenek is 'trying on' different personae, playing them off against each other, and actively constructing a different artistic identity through them. Max, at the beginning of *Jonny spielt auf*, is a persona for the young Krenek in his early life, both in his comparative isolation from society and in his musical style. 'Als ich damals' can be seen as signifying Krenek's earlier music, although it is not as atonal as much of the real composer's early style. Max continues to represent Krenek in the way he decides to adapt himself to the modern world, and may also suggest him through Max's possible change in compositional style, indicated through the inclusion of popular elements to accompany him as the opera progresses. Krenek underwent a parallel transformation to Max by writing *Jonny spielt auf*, as well as his previous works influenced by dance music; this integrated him with the society in which he lived. By the end of the opera, though, Max has become assimilated into Jonny's world, while it is Jonny who more thoroughly displays Krenek's own aesthetic; the jazz musician as well as Max may thus be read as functioning as Krenek's projection of himself at the time of the opera's composition. While Max stands in for Krenek's life up to the composition of *Jonny spielt auf*, Jonny represents Krenek's self-construction, and how he thought of himself and music, at the time of writing the work.

Krenek's attitude towards Jonny was expressed by him some time after the opera was written. He spoke of the jazz-band musician as representing:

> the fullness of life, optimistic affirmation, freedom from futile speculation, and devotion to the happiness of the moment. He was the fulfillment of a wish

---

[130] Stewart, *Ernst Krenek*, 71.

[131] Cook, *Opera for a New Republic*, 80. Also see Grosch, *Die Musik der Neuen Sachlichkeit*, 155–6.

dream, for I felt that all of these elements, which I admired so greatly and passionately desired to acquire for myself, were really foreign to my nature.[132]

But despite the composer's protestations, the wish-fulfilment not only takes place on a fictional level; by writing *Jonny spielt auf*, Krenek himself carries out those desires which are expressed through the figure of Jonny. He refashions his compositional identity, and, rather than remaining fictional speculation, his fantasies are acted out through the change in his compositional style; this style brought him the success he sought, and bridged the composer-audience gap which had proved problematic for many art composers. Jonny forms a wish-fulfilment for Krenek in a similar way to Palestrina's status for Pfitzner, the difference being that Krenek went some way towards achieving this goal in his life, while Pfitzner's goal remained largely fictitious.

Both Krenek's essays of the mid-1920s and his opera illustrate his position towards the kind of music he felt a modern composer should write, music comprehensible to many and able to create communities. His dualism in *Jonny spielt auf* of the traditional versus modern artists encapsulates many of the concerns held by composers in the early twentieth century about the function of art, while the opera's resolution in favour of the modern is an allegorisation of his own stance on music and its place in society at this time. In its concern with reaching a mass audience, this position would have been seen at the time as left wing: its appeal to the public, through its use of the paraphernalia of 'Americanism', taps into the contemporary discourse centred around the construction of a new, progressive identity for the Weimar Republic.[133] The contrast this made with the old order, embodied in such figures as Pfitzner, means that *Jonny spielt auf* may be seen both as the locus for the progressive political thought of its time and the opposition to it.

Jonny spielt auf's ability to signify the forces of 'modernity' in its many guises is encapsulated in the use of the image of Jonny, playing the saxophone and wearing the Star of David, to express the right wing's disgust at

---

[132] Krenek, 'Self-Analysis', 16. Also see *Horizons Circled*, 27.

[133] In later years, Krenek admitted his left-wing propensities: 'In my adolescence I had developed strong sympathies for left and far left causes, and I have retained them to this day'. Ibid., 39. Also see 'Self-Analysis', 26.

such 'degeneracy' in the 'Entartete Musik' exhibition of 1938.[134] Both Jonny the character and *Jonny* the opera became powerful symbols for modern society, and resistance to it. In the years after the opera's success, the Weimar Republic's validity came increasingly into question, and its political ideals, as well as the artistic movements associated with them, became more and more suspect. With this development, questions began to resurface about what a true German art should be, and many composers, such as Hindemith, became caught up in this debate.

---

[134] This picture is reproduced in Albrecht Dümling (ed.), *Banned by the Nazis: Entartete Musik* (Catalogue of 1988 exhibition of the same name) (Berlin: Department of Cultural Affairs, n.d.), 11.

4   Painting and Politics in Hindemith's *Mathis der Maler*

Hindemith's Symphony *Mathis der Maler*, an orchestral suite comprising music from the opera, was premiered in Berlin in 1934; the opera itself, however, did not receive its first performance until May 1938, in Switzerland, despite having been completed in 1935.[1] The National Socialists had given permission for the Symphony, but would not do so for the opera, a fact symptomatic of Hindemith's problems with the regime, which could not decide if his work fitted within their categorisation of 'valid' art. This points to an ambiguity within the opera itself: its political content can be read in differing ways, and the position of the central character, Mathis, towards his society is, at first glance, equivocal. As with the other artist-operas which have been examined, it is possible to read the artist character as a persona for the composer himself; critical assessments of the work to date have always taken this approach and have read the opera as autobiographical, even more so than is the case with Pfitzner's or Krenek's works.[2]

---

[1] Giselher Schubert, *Paul Hindemith: Mit Selbstzeugnissen und Bilddokumenten* (Reinbek bei Hamburg: Rowohlt, 1981), 85 and 93.

[2] See Tim Ashley, 'An Act of Necessity', in the programme book for the Royal Opera House production, Nov.–Dec. 1995 (London: Royal Opera House Publications, 1995), 22–7; Gudrun Breimann, *'Mathis der Maler' und der 'Fall Hindemith': Studien zu Hindemiths Opernlibretto im Kontext der kulturgeschichtlichen und politischen Bedingungen der dreißiger Jahre* (Frankfurt a.M.: Peter Lang, 1997); Andres Briner, *Paul Hindemith* (Mainz: Schott, 1971); Siglind Bruhn, *The Temptation of Paul Hindemith: Mathis der Maler as Spiritual Testimony* (Stuyvesant, NY: Pendragon Press, 1998); Ian Kemp, *Hindemith* (Oxford Studies of Composers no.6. London: Oxford University Press, 1970); James Paulding, *'Mathis der Maler*: The Politics of Music', *Hindemith Jahrbuch* 5 (1976), 102–22; Hans F. Redlich, 'Paul Hindemith: a Re-assessment', *Music Review* 25 (1964); Dieter Rexroth, 'Von der moralischen Verantwortung des Künstlers. Zu den großen Opern von Paul Hindemith', *Hindemith Jahrbuch* 3 (1973), 63–79; Giselher Schu-

The predominant interpretation of the opera has been based on Hindemith's political position during the Third Reich, in which he lived until the autumn of 1938, and his supposed reaction to the situation in which he found himself: according to most commentators, the composer remained in Germany in a state of 'inner emigration', and his opera's hero is read as retreating from the world around him in the same way. This chapter will examine Hindemith's political context in order to reconsider how Mathis may function as a persona for the composer. I will suggest that a reading of the opera which argues for Mathis's, and Hindemith's, retreat from politics and society is inaccurate, and will suggest that elements of the opera resonate strongly with contemporary political thought.

The Context of *Mathis der Maler*: Germany in the 1930s

The world economic crisis, precipitated by the Wall Street Crash of October 1929, put an end to the relatively prosperous years of the mid-twenties. The crisis hit Germany particularly hard, mainly due to the fact that American loans to the country, made following World War I, were recalled. The crash resulted in mass unemployment, while the hyperinflation of 1922–3 was still fresh in the memory.[3] Those who did not lose their jobs often had to accept salary cuts; as a result, a large number of people were directly affected. Detlev Peukert states that 'the depression, immiseration and loss of security penetrated virtually every area of German society'.[4] The poor economy was accompanied by an increasingly unstable political structure. Under the existing proportional representation system, the country had been governed by a series of ineffectual coalitions, which were perceived as having achieved little, and having done nothing to combat the harsh realities of everyday life. By the late twenties and early thirties,

---

bert, *Paul Hindemith*; Geoffrey Skelton, *Paul Hindemith: The Man Behind the Music* (London: Victor Gollancz, 1975); and Skelton, 'One Person's Response', in the programme book for the Royal Opera House production.

[3] For details of the economic situation, see Peukert, *The Weimar Republic*, 249 ff. and Carr, *A History of Germany*, 340 ff. For further discussion of the history of the late Weimar Republic, see Passant, *A Short History of Germany* and Simon Taylor, *Germany 1918–1933: Revolution, Counter-revolution and the Rise of Hitler* (London: Duckworth, 1983).

[4] Peukert, *The Weimar Republic*, 252.

people had become increasingly disillusioned with the mainstream centre parties, and support for them waned. The result was that a 'political vacuum' was created, with all options apparently eroded except for the radical solutions of either National Socialism or Communism.[5] Increasing numbers of voters turned to parties on the extreme left or extreme right in their disillusionment with the familiar politicians: at least two-fifths of all voters voted for either the NSDAP (*Nationalsozialistische Deutsche Arbeiterpartei* or National Socialist German Workers' Party) or the Communist Party in 1930, and almost 52% in July 1932.[6] The Communists' vote came predominantly from the working class, while the Nazis appealed to the disenchanted middle classes. The political crisis confirmed what the conservatives had been saying all along: that the democratic experiment was doomed to failure, and would bring nothing but hardship, crime and vice.[7]

The series of ineffective coalitions reached a crisis point in 1930, when the President, Hindenburg, appointed Brüning of the Centre Party as Chancellor, despite the fact that Brüning did not have a parliamentary majority. Hindenburg side-stepped this technicality by agreeing with the new Chancellor that they would invoke Article 48 of the Weimar constitution, whereby power would be wielded by the President and Chancellor without the support of the Reichstag. This moment is often seen as the end of the Weimar Republic, for presidential rule had become established and parliamentary democracy was no longer effectual.[8] In the course of the next three years, the chancellors (Brüning, later von Papen followed by von Schleicher) continued to force measures through parliament by decree, with

---

[5] Ibid., 240 and 258.

[6] Carr, *A History of Germany*, 343 and Laffan, *The Burden of German History*, x. There are some discrepancies amongst historians as to what percentage of the population voted for extremist parties in particular elections, but the figure appears to be somewhere around two-fifths to a half in these years. Laffan's statistics (although not Carr's) are ratified by the statistics given by Nico Passchier, which show the combined vote of the NSDAP and KPD in 1930 being 31.4%, 51.6% in July 1932, and 50% in November 1932 ('The Electoral Geography of the Nazi Landslide. The Need for Community Studies', in Stein Ugelvik Larsen et al. (eds), *Who were the Fascists: Social Roots of European Fascism* (Oslo: Universitetsforlaget, 1980), 285).

[7] Peukert, *The Weimar Republic*, 257.

[8] Ibid., 258 ff.

next to no backing. Eventually, as the Nazis became an ever stronger force in the Reichstag, Hitler was persuaded to join a coalition cabinet, to which Hitler agreed provided he was given the chancellorship. Hindenburg agreed to this plan and appointed Hitler as Chancellor on 30th January 1933.[9]

Aspects of National Socialist Ideology

The train of events which led up to Hitler assuming the chancellorship are more understandable when we remember the deeply engrained conservatism of many Germans which was explored in Chapter 2; the change of political attitude which characterised the ostensibly more liberal Weimar Republic was only temporary and partial. Rather than a simple switch from an earlier *Weltanschauung* taking place in 1919, the conservative forces within the country were still very much present during the 1920s. Hindenburg, the president of the Weimar Republic from 1925 until his death in 1934, had been one of the leading monarchists during World War I. The fact that it was possible for such a conservative to be elected in the middle of the republican years indicates the strength of those forces in the country. Similarly, while right-wing politicians now had to be democratically elected, the power structures of the country (such as the army, the judiciary, the police, and leading industrialists) were still comprised of the same people as before, who were mostly conservative, monarchist, and profoundly suspicious of, if not actively hostile to, the new democracy.[10] Wilfried van der Will writes that the 'long-standing traditions of authoritarianism in Germany, which through the administration of state power and education shaped the character of large sections of the population, culminated

---

[9] Ibid., 269.

[10] Ibid., 222 ff. The remaining ethos of the pre-War era had practical consequences which favoured the right wing. For instance, various civil uprisings succeeded the founding of the Republic and were quashed by the military; in disturbances by the left wing it was common for the perpetrators to be routinely assassinated or imprisoned (the murders of Karl Liebknecht and Rosa Luxembourg in 1919 being perhaps the most famous example). Conversely, leaders of right-wing coups were frequently let off or were given only light sentences. In the first of two attempted right-wing *Putsche*, the 'Kapp Putsch' of 1920, only one person was sentenced and 412 amnestied; after his attempted *Putsch* of 1923, Hitler was sentenced to five years' imprisonment but was released after less than nine months.

in the vote for National Socialism not because this was inevitable but because the economic, parliamentary, and ideological crisis became so acute that it allowed the most negative and anti-democratic characteristics of the nation to become dominant'.[11]

The success of the National Socialists in winning support from large sections of the population was due to their exploitation of conservative beliefs at the same time as they reformed and radicalised those ideas. The National Socialists harnessed the existing conservatism of many Germans with the discontent brought about by social conditions, and tied it to a particular characteristic ideology which drew upon, and reformulated, pre-existent prejudices.[12] The National Socialists played on the belief in the inherent superiority of the German people and the nostalgic wish to return to better times. They brought together the divergent groups which disliked the Republic 'under the banner of [their] demagogic, uncompromising struggle against "the system"'.[13] In particular, the NSDAP portrayed itself as against modernity, arguing that greater industrialisation and new-fangled concepts like capitalism and democracy had only led to misery. Paradoxically, the Nazis also managed to portray themselves as new, dynamic and forward-looking, an attractive attribute for any political party, and fulfilled the demand for strong leadership which had been heard to ever greater degrees through the years of the Republic, with its unstable coalitions and increasingly unpopular chancellors.

The rhetoric in which the Nazis dressed their politics drew on a number of significant themes, foremost amongst which was the idea of the *Volk*. The word *Volk* has various meanings, most literally of 'people', but as George L. Mosse explains, it is 'a much more comprehensive term than "people"', also encompassing concepts of 'nation' and 'race', and invoking the image of a mythical German past.[14] An appeal to the *Volk* was an appeal to the very roots of one's Germanness, drawing upon a deep-seated faith in the superiority of the German people, and often a concomitant scorn of the non-German.[15] *Volk* signified 'the union of a group of people

---

[11] van der Will, 'Culture and the Organization of National Socialist Ideology', 104.

[12] Peukert, *The Weimar Republic*, 231.

[13] Ibid., 232.

[14] George L. Mosse, *The Crisis of German Ideology: Intellectual Origins of the Third Reich* (London: Weidenfeld and Nicolson, 1964), 4.

[15] Instances of such rhetoric appear in Pfitzner's and Mann's writings; see Chapter 2.

with a transcendental "essence"'; this essence was connected to the individual's inner nature, representing 'the source of his creativity, his depth of feeling, his individuality, and his unity with other members of the *Volk*'.[16] A contemporary writer, and later Nazi Minister of Agriculture, R. Walther Darré stated that 'Once we understand by "people" [*Volk*] not the purely quantitative total of all individuals whom chance has brought together within the present borders of the Reich, but only those within this mass who profess loyalty to their German blood and to a duty to their Germanness [*Deutschtum*], we thereby create a concept of people which by its nature relates to what is meant by Germanic'.[17] The long-standing concept of the *Volk* bound together by blood and destiny, upon which the National Socialists drew, was accompanied in the late nineteenth century by the rise of 'biological' racism. This 'proved' the inherent superiority of certain races, and gave rise to the belief in the pre-eminence of the Aryan race, thus ratifying the anti-Semitism already in existence.[18] Edgar Jung, a contemporary right-wing journalist, stated that 'biologically, the most powerful people in Europe are the Germans'.[19] Such beliefs were supported by a pre-existent mythical history, in which the German race was the founder of civilisation, and joined with a quasi-religious mysticism.[20]

Völkisch thought deemed that all members of the *Volk* were a unity, interconnected by race and history, and therefore should all work together as a whole. This concern inherent in National Socialism for the well-being of all of the *Volk* explains why it deemed itself a 'socialist' party, albeit of a very particular kind. Like the socialism which is associated with the left of the political spectrum, National Socialism was concerned with the emancipation of the majority of the population from its purported enemies. In the case of the left, this was the liberation of the 'masses' from capitalism: on the right, the *Volk* had to be freed from the enemies of capitalism and Judaism (the two being synonymous in Nazi understanding). The NSDAP

---

[16] Ibid.

[17] *Neuadel aus Blut und Boden* (1930), quoted in Roger Griffin (ed.), *Fascism* (Oxford Readers Series. Oxford and New York: Oxford University Press, 1995), 126.

[18] Berghahn, *Imperial Germany*, 102 ff. and 218.

[19] Jung, 'Deutschland und die Konservative [sic] Revolution', in Kaes et al. (eds), *The Weimar Republic Sourcebook*, 352.

[20] A.J. Nicholls, 'Germany', in S.J. Woolf (ed.), *Fascism in Europe* (London and New York: Methuen, 1981), 71–2.

called for the overthrow of the existing order of the capitalist elite, were hostile towards parliamentary democracy, and argued for the nationalisation of industries, the fair distribution of wealth, and the abolition of money not earned by labour. They also argued that the state should assist ordinary people by means of pensions, education, health provision and so on. These revolutionary demands were held in common with the Communists, but in contrast to the Communists' inclusive definition of the 'masses', the National Socialists' generosity was limited to those of 'German blood'.[21]

The *völkisch* world-view propagated by the fascists was sufficiently vague to be able to function as the expression of different, even conflicting, interests. The NSDAP was 'programmatically both anti-capitalist and anti-proletarian, conservative and revolutionary' and appealed to the middle classes which felt threatened by modern capitalism, and which could take refuge 'in a mixture of restorational and revolutionary daydreams which transcended the prosaic republican everyday existence'.[22] The Nazis combined a nostalgia for a pleasant rural past with vague, ill-defined policies advocating a 'third way' between capitalism and communism; these indulged the dreams of the patriotic industrialist while not immediately threatening his livelihood in the short term.[23] Conveniently, the National Socialist ideal did not require a significant economic reorganisation, as Communism did, merely a reinterpretation of the existing capitalist structure in language more suited to the new Germany. The workers would receive recognition, but this was only a promotion of status, and the structure of industrial society did not need to be radically changed.[24]

The 'socialist' elements of National Socialism means that the customary modern practice of thinking about political positions is unhelpful, with its image of a straight line, and the terminology of 'far-right' and 'far-left' which suggests an insurmountable distance between the two. A more useful model in discussion of German fascism of the early twentieth century,

---

[21] See the 1920 programme of the *Deutsche Arbeiterpartei* (the forerunner of the NSDAP), in Kaes et al. (eds), *The Weimar Republic Sourcebook*, 124–6, and Hermand and Trommler, *Die Kultur der Weimarer Republik*, 106.

[22] Karl Dietrich Bracher, *The German Dictatorship: The Origins, Structure and Consequences of National Socialism* (Harmondsworth: Penguin, 1973), 187.

[23] See the 1932 NSDAP campaign leaflet, in Kaes et al. (eds), *The Weimar Republic Sourcebook*, 142.

[24] Nicholls, 'Germany', 67.

according to Hugh Ridley, is that of a horseshoe where 'the extremes are closest to each other and the rest of the parameter (the centre) is out of touch with the extremes'.[25] After all, the spatial metaphors of an 'extreme right' and an 'extreme left' are merely reifications, and disguise what is often a more complex situation.[26] A further way of explaining the 'social-ist' element of National Socialism is to posit a 'grey area' between the two apparent extremes of left and right, in which the movement embraces the ideals of both the right (nationalism) and the left (socialism).

The socialist aspects of Nazism had been in evidence since the early history of the movement. One of the founders of the party, Anton Drexler, wrote in an early NSDAP leaflet from 1920, addressed to his 'Dear Colleagues', that 'I am a socialist like yourselves, and want manual work-ers to gain equality with all other creative groups... . I still hope for a true and just form of socialism, the salvation of the working masses, and the freeing of creative mankind from the chains of exploitative capitalism'.[27] (He goes on to show that the exploitative capitalists are the Jews.) In 1927, a Nazi leaflet pronounced: 'Help us build a new Germany that will be NATIONALIST AND SOCIALIST. Nationalist because it is free and held in respect; Socialist because any German who works and creates will be guar-anteed not just a slave's ration of bread, but an honourable life, decent earnings and the sanctity of his hard-earned property'.[28] Such an important Nazi as Goebbels embraced a socialist stance; in 1925 he wrote to a 'dear friend from the Left' that both his own party and that of his 'friend' are 'fighting honestly and resolutely for freedom and only for freedom'. The only difference between them is that the bolshevist wants this freedom for the whole world, the National Socialist just for his nation.[29] In 1930, Goebbels characterised the National Socialist movement as even more socialist than the Marxists:

---

[25] Ridley, 'The Culture of Weimar: Models of Decline', 23.

[26] See Andreski, 'Fascists as Moderates', in Larsen, *Who were the Fascists*, 52.

[27] Reprinted in Taylor, *Germany 1918–1933*, 63. See Bracher, *The German Dictatorship*. 73 ff., for more detail on the historical background to National Socialism and the socialist aspects of this early movement.

[28] Reprinted in Taylor, *Germany 1918–1933*, 84.

[29] 'Nationalsozialismus oder Bolschewismus?', in Kaes et al. (eds), *The Weimar Republic Sourcebook*, 127–9. It is not specified in this edition whether the letter was to a real person or a fictional one.

We are SOCIALISTS because we see in SOCIALISM the only possibility for maintaining our racial existence and through it the reconquest of our political freedom and the rebirth of the German state. SOCIALISM has its peculiar form first of all through its comradeship in arms with the forward-driving energy of a newly awakened nationalism. Without nationalism it is nothing, a phantom, a theory, a vision of air, a book. With it, it is everything, THE FUTURE, FREEDOM, FATHERLAND! It was a sin of the liberal bourgeoisie to overlook THE STATE-BUILDING POWER OF SOCIALISM. It was the sin of MARXISM to degrade SOCIALISM to a system of MONEY AND STOMACH. We are SOCIAL-ISTS because for us THE SOCIAL QUESTION IS A MATTER OF NECESSITY AND JUSTICE, and even beyond that A MATTER FOR THE VERY EXISTENCE OF OUR PEOPLE. ...DOWN WITH MARXISM: FOR TRUE SOCIALISM![30]

As time went by, the Nazis reviewed their stance towards socialism. Hitler in particular was less comfortable with the socialist dimension than were other members of his party, and did not wish to antagonise the industrialists on whose support and money he depended heavily. According to Hitler, anyone who was genuinely concerned about the people was a socialist; he allegedly exclaimed 'Why need we trouble to socialize banks and factories? We socialize human beings'.[31] Nevertheless, the concept continued to be used, as it served a useful propagandistic purpose and provided a rallying cry, even if the details of how precisely the Nazis would turn Germany into a socialist state were avoided.

For the National Socialists, 'socialism' meant above all a sense of a nationally and racially defined community, termed the *Volksgemeinschaft*. *Gemeinschaft*, or community, was contrasted with *Gesellschaft*, or society, a contrast which was already part of conservative ideology before fascism had gained ground.[32] *Gesellschaft* epitomised the modern, the materialistic and the 'un-German'; it suggested an urban and capitalistic way of life typical of the corrupt modern world. The idea of *Gemeinschaft*, in contrast, comprised everything that was denied in modern, *gesellschaftlich* life: Rex-roth writes that it consisted of 'a warm, close bond between people, a living

---

[30] 'Warum sind wir Judengegner?', in ibid., 137–8.

[31] Bracher, *The German Dictatorship*, 231; Nicholls, 'Germany', 67.

[32] The dualism *Gemeinschaft-Gesellschaft* had been used by Ferdinand Tönnies in 1887, in his book of that name. See Peter Gay, *Weimar Culture: The Outsider as Insider* (London: Secker and Warburg, 1968), 80, and Otto Friedrich, *Before the Deluge: A Portrait of Berlin in the 1920s* (London: Michael Joseph, 1974), 228.

and strong feeling of belonging and identification with one's fellow humans'.[33] The ideological split between *Gemeinschaft* and *Gesellschaft* betrayed a hostile attitude towards the alienating modernity of *Gesellschaft* and an embracing of the rural, 'rooted' community of *Gemeinschaft*.[34] National Socialism contrasted its vision of the *Volksgemeinschaft* with the ideal of society found in communism; in their view, the problem with Bolshevism was that it set the strata of society against each other. In contrast, National Socialist thought deemed that 'man can live only as a member of a nation, and therefore the nation transcends group interests. It is strong only as a cohesive unit, and therefore true "socialism" welds the classes together rather than dividing them'.[35] The contrast between 'false', divisive socialism and the 'true' socialism of the *Volksgemeinschaft* was continually played upon by the Nazis, who stressed the negative aspects of left-wing socialism, and contrasted them with the more noble aims of their own party. 'Socialism?', asked one party leaflet, 'That is the terrifying word that sends shivers down the back of every peaceful citizen. ...*Socialism*, that means to him *class-struggle*'. In reality, according to the NSDAP, '*Socialism* means nothing other than *community: A people's community. ...* [Man] should not be valued according to his money, rather according to his accomplishments for the community. ...THE COMMON GOOD BEFORE INDIVIDUAL GREED. THAT IS SOCIALISM'.[36]

The ideal of community within the concept of the *Volksgemeinschaft* frequently expressed the idea that the individual must give way to the common good in terms of being a part of a living whole. Metaphors of the organic were therefore frequently used. National Socialist rhetoric 'derived from a *Weltanschauung* anchored in an organic concept of society';[37] the nation was an organically united collection of the *Volk*, an 'organism of a people bound by destiny and blood', rather than the pejoratively viewed 'Western' nation, a 'mass of people formed into a State'.[38] The ideal of the

---

[33] Rexroth, 'Einige Voraussetzungen der "Gebrauchsmusik" bei Hindemith', *Musica* 34/6 (1980), 547.

[34] Mosse, *The Crisis of German Ideology*, 6.

[35] Bracher, *The German Dictatorship*, 316.

[36] Reprinted in Taylor, *Germany 1918–1933*, 90 (n.d.).

[37] van der Will, 'Culture and the Organization of National Socialist Ideology', 109. Also see Mosse, *The Crisis of German Ideology*, 4.

[38] Edgar Jung, *Die Herrschaft der Minderwertigen: Ihr Zerfall und ihre Ablösung durch ein*

Volk as an organism was expressed through images such as that of the tree, used to symbolise the strength of the rural *Volk*, its roots anchored in the past and a crown which reached up towards the cosmos.[39] Another slogan linked to the same metaphorical nexus which gained particular popularity was the appeal to *Blut und Boden*, or 'blood and soil', which encapsulated the combination of race and rural life.[40]

The vision of the *Volksgemeinschaft*, situated in an idyllic rural past, was a form of Utopianism, like Americanism. Amidst the tribulations of the late Weimar Republic, a sizeable portion of the German public sought to redefine themselves through an appeal to their 'roots'. Americanism was mostly limited to the big cities, and could be overtaken by the rise of Nazism because the latter tapped into the inherent beliefs of those people opposed to the Republic. The inhabitants of many areas of the country, especially outside the cities, tended to be more conservative; they were not impressed by Americanism, and did not espouse the ideal of society which it held up. The conservatives of Pfitzner's generation, along with a younger generation brought up on nationalist ideals and still smarting from the defeat of their country in the war and the imposition of a 'foreign' democracy, saw no need for a new, 'Americanised' society. They were happy with the old one, whether they saw this as the late Wilhelmine years which they may have experienced at first hand, or the more distant Utopia located in a rural Germanic past advocated by the Nazis.

Hindemith's Aesthetics

Just as the National Socialists at this time located themselves ideologically through their use of a particular rhetoric, artists positioned themselves in relation to their environment through their work and their aesthetic writings.

---

neues Reich (1927), quoted in Griffin *Fascism*, 107. Such language is reminiscent of Thomas Mann's *Betrachtungen eines Unpolitischen*, while Pfitzner described art in the same terms: 'National art is the noblest part in the organism of the body of the people (*im Organismus des Volkskörpers*)' ('Die neue Ästhetik', 245).

[39] Mosse, *The Crisis in German Ideology*, 26.

[40] The phrase was coined by R. Walther Darré in his book *Neuadel aus Blut und Boden* ('New Nobility from Blood and Soil'); part of this can be found in Kaes et al. (eds), *The Weimar Republic Sourcebook*, 133–7, and in Griffin, *Fascism*, 125–7.

Hindemith, who drew heavily on his German cultural heritage when formulating his theories about music, presents a complex picture which is politically ambiguous given his context: elements of his beliefs seem conservative, even reactionary, while others have been aligned with left-wing ideologies. Hindemith believed in a realm of music beyond the worldly, a philosophy which draws on the Romantic heritage of musical aesthetics in which music is transcendent and mystical. He argued in his book *A Composer's World* (published in 1952) that music has values which are above the ordinary realm, unchangeable, and 'not subject to instability'; they are not human-made, but 'are domiciled in the more esoteric realms of our musical nature. We have to turn to the immaterial, the spiritual aspects of music in order to find them'.[41] The 'veiled secrets of art dwell' in a 'region of visionary irrationality'. The composer cannot enter this region but can only 'be elected one of its messengers'.[42] This book, as well as his earlier composition manual of 1937 called *Unterweisung im Tonsatz*, also draws upon the historically more distant theory of the 'harmony of the spheres', which, although part of the aesthetic of an earlier era than Romanticism, places music in a similar otherworldly realm. In the *Unterweisung*, Hindemith writes that 'we shall observe in the tiniest building unit of music the play of the same forces that rule the movements of the most distant nebulae. This world harmony...exists not only for the seeking and calculating knower of the stars; for the naive believer, too, it is a fact as real as it is inconceivable'.[43]

Such a view of music originating on a divine level, above worldly concerns, is parallel to the aesthetic of Pfitzner, as exemplified in *Palestrina*. Hindemith's ideas are particularly reminiscent of the Schopenhauer quote used by Pfitzner for the preface of his score, which refers to the 'purely intellectual life of mankind' as 'like an ethereal adjunct,...[which] hovers

---

[41] Hindemith, *A Composer's World: Horizons and Limitations* (Cambridge, Mass.: Harvard University Press, 1952), 2.

[42] Ibid., 221. Also see Stephen Hinton, *The Idea of Gebrauchsmusik: A Study of Musical Aesthetics in the Weimar Republic (1919–1933) with Particular Reference to the Works of Paul Hindemith* (New York: Garland, 1989), 111–12.

[43] Entitled in translation *The Craft of Musical Composition. Book 1: Theoretical Part*, trans. Arthur Mendel (Fourth Edition. New York: Associated Music Publishers and London: Schott and Co., Ltd., 1945), 53–4. The 'harmony of the spheres' idea would later appear again in Hindemith's opera *Die Harmonie der Welt* of 1957.

above the bustle of the world, above the real life of the nations'. Other points of contact exist between Hindemith and Pfitzner; for example, in his *A Composer's World*, the younger composer discusses *Einfälle* as providing inspiration for the artist.[44] However, Hindemith also differs from Pfitzner's conception of music: while both have in common the idea of music being transcendent and above worldly concerns, Pfitzner believes that the artist should remain on a transcendent level, undistracted by worldly concerns. Hindemith, in contrast, thinks that this transcendent level should be actively put to use for the moral benefit of listeners. According to Hindemith, the composer should not merely entertain his audience, but should use music to transform the listener's soul. Music can be 'converted into moral power. ...its sounds and forms...remain meaningless unless we include them in our own mental activity and use their fermenting quality to turn our soul towards everything noble, superhuman, and ideal'.[45] The composer's objective should be to 'lift the consumer to a higher level', becoming his or her 'helper' or even 'spiritual leader'.[46] Composers who ignore the fact that music is a form of communication between composer and listener are criticised by Hindemith. Their attitude neglects 'one of the main reasons for artistic communication: the altruistic desire to present something of one's own to one's fellow men'.[47]

The book *Unterweisung im Tonsatz* is an interesting document given the context in which it was written, particularly because of the way in which the author is at pains to prove the 'natural' credentials of his music. The

---

[44] Hindemith differs from Pfitzner in that he believes that *Einfälle* are common to everyone, although the artist knows how to make use of them. He makes a further distinction between the artist and the non-artist by saying that the artist, especially of genius, has 'vision', a hazily defined term which in fact seems to serve the same purpose as *Einfälle* do for Pfitzner (*A Composer's World*, 57 ff.).

[45] Ibid, 5. Hindemith tries to combine this ideal, which he takes from a mediaeval treatise by St. Augustine, with that of Boethius, in which music 'impress[es] us with its ethic [sic] power' (ibid., 41). Thus, according to Augustine, music must be transformed into moral power by the listener, whereas for Boethius, music already inherently possesses this power. Hindemith argues that either may be at work when someone listens to music, depending on how they listen, although it is apparent from his text that he favours the Augustinian model.

[46] Ibid., 219.

[47] Ibid., 65.

book contains numerous references to the 'naturalness' of tonality; for instance, Hindemith writes that the major triad is 'one of the most impressive phenomena of nature, simple and elemental as rain, snow, and wind. ... The musician cannot escape it any more than the painter his primary colours, or the architect his three dimensions. ...the triad corresponds to the force of gravity'.[48] This insistence on nature forms the basis for his theory of composition: 'tonal relations are founded in Nature, in the characteristics of sounding materials and of the ear, as well as in the pure relations of abstract numerical groups. We cannot escape the relationship of tones. ... Tonality is a natural force'.[49] Compared to diatonicism, though, Hindemith's concept of 'tonality' is an expanded one. He sets forth a theory in which 'tonality' is based on the 'natural' overtone series, saying that the intervals of the overtone series are 'embedded in the tonal raw material which Nature has made ready for musical use'; but, he continues, this order 'is not arbitrary: it is determined by a strict law, and is as immutable as the color series of the rainbow'.[50] This leads him to the conclusion that the twelve-note chromatic scale, as he constructs it, is 'even more natural' than the major and minor scales. He nevertheless has some qualifiers: not all twelve-note music is valid, only that which returns to the anchor of more conventional tonality based on the triad, as his does:

> The adoption of the chromatic scale as the basis of music does not mean that harmony and melody must consist of an uninterrupted series of whining half-tone slides, or that according to some arbitrarily conceived plan the tones of this scale must be scattered broadcast through our music, reappearing aimlessly in a thousand different forms... . The advantages of tonal connection and of chordal and melodic interrelation are as much ours as they ever were. But we

---

[48] Hindemith, *The Craft of Musical Composition*, 22.

[49] Ibid., 152. This same image of tonality and gravity also appears in *A Composer's World*, as do further references to tonality as natural.

[50] Hindemith, *The Craft of Musical Composition*, 15–16. As well as using the overtone series ('Series 1'), 'the significant order in which the twelve tones of the chromatic scale made their appearance, in diminishing degree of relationship to the given tone', Hindemith also has a 'Series 2, a 'natural order' of different intervals, which the composer explains in depth to attempt to justify acoustically its 'naturalness' (ibid., 56–7). According to Kemp, Hindemith believed his Series 1 and 2 'to embrace discoveries of almost divine provenance. Until the end of his life he considered music which failed to take account of them to be little short of a betrayal' (*Hindemith*, 39).

have thrown off chains that hampered our movement; we have discarded the tinted lenses that transformed the many-colored world around us into a dull and monotonous image.[51]

While composition 'can never disregard the conditions laid down by the facts of the existence of pure intervals and the desire of the ear to perceive them wherever possible in tonal combinations', this does not mean 'that we must return to a more primitive level of harmonic and melodic practice'.[52] Hindemith therefore argues that his post-tonal music, with its 'dissonances', is actually tonal after all, and most importantly, completely 'natural'.

The *Unterweisung* can be seen as Hindemith's attempt to integrate himself into a cultural heritage which at this time was also being used politically, as a symbol of nationhood. Hindemith's language positions him both as aesthetically conservative, in his adherence to a musical system of the past, and links him to a politically reactionary discourse. His use of language invoking the 'natural' reminds us of the arch-conservative Pfitzner's rhetoric in 'Die neue Ästhetik', as well as other contemporaries such as Schenker.[53] The attempt to link oneself to the past was a recurrent strategy amongst many composers of the early twentieth century. Schoenberg and Webern, for instance, both continually sought to clarify the connections between twelve-tone technique and their musical heritage, although at the same time acknowledging the importance of moving on.[54] Yet when seen against the context of 1930s Germany, any claim for the political neutrality

---

[51] *The Craft of Musical Composition*, 48.

[52] Ibid., 45.

[53] Hindemith wrote to Schenker in 1926 expressing his interest in the theorist's work: 'I can say to you that I am an enthusiastic and delighted reader of your books. Delighted because...in them the foundations of musical creation are revealed, which...have always been and will always be valid. And for our present-day music they are just as important as for any in the past' (Hindemith, *Briefe*, ed. Dieter Rexroth (Frankfurt a.M.: Fischer Taschenbuch Verlag, 1982), 122–3 (25th October 1926). Translation as in Neumeyer, *The Music of Paul Hindemith*, 11). On Schenker's own right-wing politics, particularly his antipathy to 'bolshevism' in music and his praise of Hitler, see John, *Musikbolschewismus*, 355.

[54] See for instance, Webern's *The Path to the New Music*, ed. Willi Reich (London: Universal Edition, 1963); also see John, *Musikbolschewismus*, 113.

of Hindemith's book must surely be brought into question, even given the long history of the connection between music and nature.[55] The composer's attempt to assert his relationship to his past is not only part of a general tendency amongst composers to situate themselves within a larger context, but carries with it distinct ideological implications, and points to a conservative tendency especially significant within an environment that demanded conservatism. At the same time, though, Hindemith tries to show his progressiveness: his music and theory are not simply reactionary, but a new, modern form of an eternal truth. Hindemith recasts his aesthetic views to argue that he is facing towards the future, just as National Socialism attempted to portray itself as a forward-looking and modern movement.[56]

A further important aspect of Hindemith's aesthetics, and one which may at first glance seem to contradict his conservatism regarding tonality, is his belief in the importance of 'music for use', or *Gebrauchsmusik*. Hindemith produced a great deal of *Gebrauchsmusik*, for instance, the *Sing- und Spielmusik für Liebhaber und Musikfreunde*, and the children's opera, *Wir bauen eine Stadt*. The genre carried with it an ideal of fostering a sense of community, destined as the music is for amateurs to play together. A

---

[55] On this history, see Suzannah Clarke and Alexander Rehding (eds), *Music Theory and Natural Order from the Renaissance to the Early Twentieth Century* (Cambridge: Cambridge University Press, 2001).

[56] Hans Redlich has seen Hindemith's composition treatise as an apologia by the composer in the face of the accusations against him by the Nazis as musically 'degenerate' (*entartet*); according to Nazi artistic ideology, one of the main indications of musical 'degeneracy' was atonality. Redlich posits that Hindemith's move towards a more tempered musical style in these years, in comparison to his early works, was an attempt to distance himself from the Second Viennese School; he suggests that the composer perhaps did this 'in the hope of endearing himself to Dr. Göbbels', and in response to his 'increasingly precarious personal situation' ('Paul Hindemith: a Re-assessment', 245). It is interesting to note that Hindemith spends some time in the *Unterweisung* criticising 'atonal' composers and serialism because their music is 'contrary to nature'; see 152–6. Claudia Maurer Zenck comments that Hindemith's tonal system is presented by the composer as 'natural and lifted above time; the hierarchy is unchangeable. It forms the strong fortress (*die feste Burg*), the dam against the flood of products of an "arbitrarily changing spirit" (*Geist*), which has led to "confusion". This is the mode of expression and argument of the art-politicians of the Third Reich' ('Zwischen Boykott und Anpassung an den Charakter der Zeit. Über die Schwierigkeiten eines deutschen Komponisten mit dem Dritten Reich', *Hindemith Jahrbuch* 9 (1980), 128).

banner at the first performance of the Brecht-Hindemith collaboration *Lehrstück* declared the aesthetic of *Gebrauchsmusik*, stating 'Musik machen ist besser als Musik hören' ('Making music is better than listening to it').[57] With this stress on the importance of involving the members of one's audience themselves in music-making, Hindemith took a step away from the aesthetics of Romanticism, in contrast to his continuing belief in the timeless and eternal values of music. In his 1932 essay 'Forderungen an den Laien' ('Admonition to the Amateur'), he stated: 'The musical layman, who concerns himself earnestly with musical matters, is just as important a member of our musical life as the serious working musician'. Both professional and amateur music-making 'are equally important for the development of music'.[58] For its writers and practitioners, *Gebrauchsmusik* was preferable to the 'bourgeois' and exclusionary practice of listening reverently to professionals in a concert hall.

The *Gebrauchsmusik* ideal of music being integrated into everyday life became one of the main tenets of the *Jugendbewegung*, or Youth Movement, in 1930s Germany; Hindemith was involved for some years with the musical wing, the *Jugendmusikbewegung* (Youth Music Movement; both of these are blanket terms for a host of smaller organisations), and believed the movement to be central to 'the most important question of today's musical life, the bringing together of people and art'.[59] Prior to 1933, the *Jugendmusikbewegung* was part of an attempt, by both left- and right-wing parties, to bring art to the masses. The NSDAP on the right and the SPD and KPD on the left all implemented programmes to educate the populace in similar ways, although, as discussed above, there was a significant ideological difference in who exactly these masses were deemed to be.[60] For

---

[57] For discussion of *Gebrauchsmusik*, see Hinton, *The Idea of Gebrauchsmusik*, and '"Musik nach Maß": Zum Begriff der Gebrauchsmusik bei Paul Hindemith', *Musica* 39/2 (1985), 146–50; Bruhn, *The Temptation of Paul Hindemith*, 48–50; Donald Mitchell, 'Hindemith and the History of a Term', *Musical Opinion*, 79 (Dec. 1955), 163; and Rexroth, 'Einige Voraussetzungen', 546–9.

[58] Hindemith, 'Forderungen an den Laien', *Auftakt* 12 (1932), 137.

[59] Hindemith, *Briefe*, 131 (5th January 1927).

[60] For details of left-wing movements, see Hermand and Trommler, *Die Kultur der Weimarer Republik*, 123 ff.; Guttsmann, *Worker's Culture*; and John Rockwell, 'Kurt Weill's Operatic Reform and Its Context', in Kowalke (ed.), *A New Orpheus*, 53–4. For a comparison of *Gebrauchsmusik*'s use by the left and right, see Hanns Eisler,

both political wings of the *Jugendbewegung*, music was intended to help bring about a sense of community, or *Gemeinschaft*, and an understanding of one's place in the social order.[61] Folk music found particular favour for its ideological resonances, on both the left and the right.[62] The *Jugendbewegung* saw itself as tapping into the spirit of the people, expressed as the '*Volk*' or the 'mass', and offering a meaningful alternative to the shallowness of modernity, therefore showing clear allegiance to ideologies which portrayed themselves as 'socialist', whether on the 'left' or the 'right'.[63] The movement demonstrated a nostalgia for a mythical, Utopian past which was balanced by a rejection of nineteenth-century aesthetics. This worked in tandem with 'socialist' aims in the economic sphere: the rejection of the virtuoso and of professional musical life in general, in favour of collective music making, was consistent with the rejection of capitalist society of both left-wing and right-wing socialism.[64] While both the left- and right-wing versions of the *Jugendmusikbewegung* existed during the Weimar Republic, left-wing groups, such as the *Musikanten-gilde*, never gained as much popularity as those on the right, such as the *Wandervogel* and the *Bündische Jugend*. The *Jugendmusikbewegung* was later assimilated into the Nazis' propagandistic aims in groups such as the *Hitlerjugend*, which expounded a belief in music for the *Volk*.[65]

'Contemporary Music and Fascism' (1942), in his *Musik und Politik: Schriften 1924–1948*, ed. Günter Mayer (Munich: Rogner und Bernhard, 1973), 492. Also on Eisler and the *Jugendmusikbewegung*, see Hermand and Trommler, *Die Kultur der Weimarer Republik*, 340.

[61] The idea that music had the power to form communities is reminiscent of the thought of Paul Bekker, examined in the last chapter.

[62] Hermand and Trommler, *Die Kultur der Weimarer Republik*, 337.

[63] Mosse, *The Crisis of German Ideology*, 6; Hermand and Trommler, *Die Kultur der Weimarer Republik*, 334; Skelton, *Paul Hindemith*, 86. Briner maintains that the *Jugendmusikbewegung* was apolitical before the Nazis' appropriation of it, although this may be disputed ('Ich und Wir – Zur Entwicklung des jungen Paul Hindemith', in Dieter Rexroth (ed.), *Erprobungen und Erfahrungen: Zu Paul Hindemith's Schaffen in den Zwanziger Jahren* (Mainz: B. Schott's Söhne, 1978), 27 and 31).

[64] See Eric Levi, *Music in the Third Reich*, xiii; Neumeyer, *The Music of Paul Hindemith*, 14; and Potter, *Most German of the Arts*, 8.

[65] On the *Jugendmusikbewegung* before and during the Third Reich, see ibid., 7–9 and 13–16. On music in the Hitler Youth, see Kater, *The Twisted Muse*, 135 ff.

While Hindemith's involvement with the *Jugendmusikbewegung* and his composition of *Gebrauchsmusik* have generally been taken to show his left-wing leanings,[66] these activities are in fact more ambiguous. While the composer was involved with the left-wing *Musikantengilde* for a time, for which he earned praise from Kurt Weill,[67] he also came to prefer the term *Gemeinschaftsmusik* to *Gebrauchsmusik*, while Rexroth comments that the composer believed that 'through collective (*gemeinsames*) music-making the feeling of community (*Gemeinschaftsgefühl*) [would be] increased'.[68] This rhetorical shift to *Gemeinschaftsmusik* alludes to the rhetoric of socialism, of both the conventional, left-wing kind, and of National Socialism; indeed, his *Gebrauchsmusik* compositions were said to have impressed leaders of the Hitler Youth.[69] In a concomitant move, Hindemith began to employ folk songs within his music, either quoting actual folk songs, such as in *Der Schwanendreher*, or alluding to the style of folk song, such as in the *Konzertmusik* works.[70] Ernst Krenek, in later years, saw this style as tied to the right wing: 'An unbroken line leads from the activist *Wandervogel*..., by way of Hindemith's concerto grosso style, to the Hitler youth, of whom it is told that they give vent to their indomitable spirit of independence by secretly performing Hindemith's *Spielmusik*'.[71] To say that Hindemith, with his ideal

---

[66] See, for instance, Rexroth, 'Einige Voraussetzungen'.

[67] Weill, 'Shifts in Musical Composition', 479. On Weill and *Gebrauchsmusik*, see Hinton, *The Idea of Gebrauchsmusik*, 83 ff.

[68] Hindemith, *Briefe*, 131 (5th January 1927); Rexroth, 'Einige Voraussetzungen', 547.

[69] Lamb and Phelan, 'Weimar Culture', 76; Kater, *Composers of the Nazi Era*, 35.

[70] Kemp, *Hindemith*, 25. Jürgen Mainka comments that Hindemith's use of folk songs could be related to fascism, but goes on to argue that the composer rejected political involvement in favour of 'inner emigration', and used such sources to indicate his 'humanism' ('Von innerer zu äußerer Emigration. Eine Szene in Paul Hindemiths Oper *Mathis der Maler*', in Hanns-Werner Heister and Hans-Günter Klein (eds), *Musik und Musikpolitik im faschistischen Deutschland* (Frankfurt a.M.: Fischer Taschenbuch Verlag, 1984), 265 and 269).

[71] He continues by saying that these phenomena have characteristics in common, 'an activist trait, a tendency to whittle down, a reduction of music from a spiritual art to a professional craft. And so it is not accidental, either, that these movements look to the precapitalistic period, when the guild system prevailed, for their historical ideal of music' (*Music Here and Now*, 75). This would seem to contradict Hindemith's transcendental understanding of music; in fact, Krenek's implication that Hindemith 'reduced' music to a 'professional craft' by writing *Gebrauchsmusik* overlooks Hindemith's own motivations

of *Gebrauchsmusik*, was therefore right wing, however, is just as limiting as confining him to the left. A more balanced picture of the composer's politics can be discerned by considering the nature of his context; he may be seen as occupying a position in the 'grey area', the point where the ideologies of left and right overlapped.

Artist and Society in *Mathis der Maler*

Mathis der Maler tells the story of a painter who abandons his art to go and fight with a group of peasants trying to free themselves from the tyranny of their rulers. Mathis becomes disillusioned with war, however; he sees visions of angels and of St. Paul, who tells him how his art may be socially useful. He then decides to return to painting. The character of Mathis is based on the artist known as Matthias Grünewald (1455?-1528), painter of the Isenheim Altarpiece; Hindemith, who wrote his own libretto, bases much of Tableau 6, the vision scene, on parts of the Altarpiece. He also incorporates other contemporary figures into the opera: the historical Grünewald was court painter to the Archbishop of Mainz, Cardinal Albrecht, as Mathis is in the opera, while most of the other characters are also based on historical models.[72] Little is known of Grünewald's life, and therefore Hindemith's portrayal of him is largely fictional, including his sojourn in the Peasants' War. Although this lasted from 1524-26, and was therefore contemporary with the painter's life, the Isenheim Alterpiece was probably completed in 1515, whereas in the opera it is painted subsequent to Mathis's involvement in the conflict.

With its subject matter about war and oppression, *Mathis der Maler* seems to lend itself readily to a political reading, while Mathis's consideration of the role of his art in his society makes it a quintessential *Künstleroper*. Indeed, the work has frequently been viewed in these terms: interpretations have seen Mathis as representing Hindemith, and the plot as portraying the latter's position in, and towards, the Third Reich. Such a reading rests on one crucial moment in the drama, Mathis's vision scene; here, Mathis makes the decision to give up his involvement in the Peasants'

---

for doing so.

[72] For an outline of Grünewald's life, see Anne Tennant, 'Painter as Healer', in the programme book for the Royal Opera House production of *Mathis der Maler*, 31–7.

War and to return to art. The common – almost exclusive – understanding of this resolution is that the painter gives up his involvement with society and retreats into an artistic ivory tower: Rexroth, for instance, says that 'the close of *Mathis* is resignation', while Kemp writes that 'one of the lessons of *Mathis* is that the artist is *not* competent to dabble in politics'.[73] Breimann similarly states that the hero of the opera is characterised as an 'outsider, whose attempts to come into contact with the people fail'; the only solution left to him, therefore, is to renounce the world altogether.[74] However, while it is undoubtedly true that Mathis ceases to fight and returns to his art, it may be argued that a more nuanced interpretation of the work must consider Mathis's motivation for this move.

Unlike other artist-operas, *Mathis der Maler* has no straightforward opposition between artist and society. Instead, different elements within society are portrayed: the ruling class, comprising the Church and the merchants in the city of Mainz, and the peasants. These two groups are in conflict with each other, and Mathis himself comes into conflict with both. At the beginning of the opera, Mathis works for the Cardinal Albrecht, but is becoming disillusioned with art and the bourgeois world which supports it; in the first scene, he asks himself, 'Have you fulfilled the task that God ordered? It is enough that you create and paint? Or are you only being full of self-interest?'.[75] This feeling is intensified after he meets the leader of the peasants, Schwalb, who pours scorn on his profession: on seeing Mathis's painting, he asks disbelievingly, 'No, is that possible? People still paint!'.[76] When Mathis tries to defend himself, Schwalb counters that art has no meaning for the average person, and throws back at Mathis the

---

[73] Rexroth, 'Von der moralischen Verantwortung', 76; Kemp, *Hindemith*, 30.

[74] Breimann, *'Mathis der Maler'*, 173. For similar interpretations, also see Ashley, 'An Act of Necessity'; Friederike Becker, 'Des Künstlers Entsagung. Die "Dichtung" *Mathis der Maler*, ihre Entstehungsgeschichte und einige kritische Anmerkungen zur Legendenbildung um Paul Hindemiths Libretto', in Giselher Schubert (ed.), *Biographische Konstellation und künstlerisches Handeln* (Frankfurter Studien. Veröffentlichungen des Paul-Hindemith-Instituts Frankfurt/Main, Bd. 6. Mainz: Schott, 1997, 128–57); Bokina, 'Resignation, Retreat and Impotence'; Bruhn, *The Temptation of Paul Hindemith*; Paulding, *'Mathis der Maler'*; and Skelton, *Paul Hindemith*.

[75] 'Hast du erfüllt, was Gott dir auftrug? Ist, daß du schaffst und bildest, genug? Bist nicht nur eignen Nutzens voll?'.

[76] 'Nein, ist das möglich? Man malt, das gibt es noch!'.

questions that he has already asked himself. This prompts the artist to demand his release from Albrecht's service; he goes to help the peasants in their struggle. Mathis later becomes similarly disenchanted with fighting, however: on experiencing the peasants' violent and boorish behaviour, his dreams of justice and a fair society are shattered as he realises that they are as selfish and corrupt as the people they are fighting: 'Brothers, aren't you fighting for justice? You want to overthrow power, prevent self-interested activities, but are yourselves full of self-interest!'.[77]

In the vision scene of Tableau 6, which takes place after the peasants have just lost a crucial battle, Mathis imagines himself as St. Anthony, while his former employer, Albrecht, appears as St. Paul and persuades Mathis to return to art.[78] Despite his position within a suspect society, Albrecht is still portrayed as sympathetic towards the painter throughout the opera: he prides himself as a man who appreciates art, declaring 'What wouldn't I undertake to honour [art]!'.[79] Nevertheless, at the beginning of the opera, art functions for him as a symbol of wealth, and his purchase of art works has merely added to his financial problems. Albrecht's understanding position towards Mathis forms the basis of the events of the vision scene, which occurs after Albrecht has been converted to a life of simplicity and has renewed his religious piety. Of course, the conversation between Albrecht and Mathis is wholly imaginary – it is not the real Albrecht who is appearing to the artist, but only Mathis's own psychological projection of him.[80] Nevertheless, we may read the scene as providing important

---

[77] 'Brüder, kämpft ihr nicht für das Recht? Ihr wollt die Macht stürzen, eigennützige Tat verhindern und seid selbst voll Eigennutz!'.

[78] The two characters are designated in the score as St. Anthony and St. Paul. However, I shall use their normal names to refer to the characters in the following discussion, rather than their vision-names, as we tend to hear their voices as their real-life characters, and associate them accordingly.

[79] 'Was unternähme ich nicht, [die Kunst] zu ehren!'. In a further demonstration of his relationship to culture, Albrecht is appalled by the idea of burning the Lutheran books; he nonetheless eventually agrees to it when his advisers point out that he may not disobey Rome.

[80] In the final scene of the opera, Mathis tells Albrecht that 'only you understood my error' ('Ihr selbst mein Unrecht verstandet'). Whether Mathis is referring to his vision scene, unaware that this was not the real Albrecht, or whether it refers to elsewhere in his life, or even that Albrecht in some way really was present in the vision scene, is open to inter-

indications of Mathis's relationship to his art, mediated through this projection.

Albrecht persuades Mathis to return to painting, convincing him that combat is misguided when one is 'superhumanly talented' as he is.[81] The archbishop helps him to find renewed joy in his art, and encourages him to believe once more in his ability to create. Albrecht achieves this conversion through reconciling what have been two opposing positions in Mathis up until this point – his wish to help his 'brothers', and the fact that he is an artist. Crucially, Albrecht shows Mathis that he can accomplish his wish to help his fellows *through* his art; it is not a pointless solitary activity, producing only status symbols for the wealthy, but can be a way of reaching the people. By joining the peasants' fight, Mathis 'deprived' them, but if he returned to his art, he would become a part of them once more:

> When you humbly bow before your brother, and selflessly risk offering all that is holy in your inner creativity, then you will stand bound and free, a strong tree in your native soil. Mute, great, a part of the people (*Volk*), the people itself.[82]

Art can therefore be a way for Mathis to serve his people, and be at one with them. The true place of art in society is indicated by the fact that Albrecht has now renounced wealth as Mathis has, showing that art's true place is with the people, and that its position in Mainz society, where it functions as a symbol of wealth and privilege, is false. By relinquishing his art, Albrecht says, Mathis was 'unfaithful and ungrateful' to God;[83] God will be in Mathis's work if he sacrifices what he creates to him. Mathis can show his brothers a glimpse of a higher spiritual ideal with his works, which will be of more use to them than taking up arms.

By going back to painting, Mathis is not retreating from society but seeking to engage with it, albeit in a different way. Albrecht says that the painter will become 'a part of the people, the people itself' by serving his 'brothers' through his art; his work must be directed towards both heaven

---

pretation. Also see Weisstein, 'Die letzte Häutung', 218.

81 'übermenschlich begabt'.

82 'Wenn du demütig dem Bruder dich bogst, ihm selbstlos dein Heiligstes zu bieten wagtest im eigensten Können, wirst du gebunden und frei, ein starker Baum im Mutterboden stehen. Stumm, groß, ein Teil des Volkes, Volk selbst'.

83 'Undankbar warst du, untreu'.

and earth. We may contrast Mathis's decision to resume painting with Palestrina's lack of engagement with the world. Mathis's return to art is a ·withdrawal from literal political involvement, that is, fighting. However, he is still trying to serve political ends, because he is trying to do something for the ordinary people which will help them. If their thoughts are turned towards God because of his art, this will have implications for how they lead their lives and order their society. Palestrina, in contrast, distances himself from the world both literally, in that he has nothing to do with the Council, and because he does not attempt to make any comment upon society and its organisation. Palestrina tries to be autonomous from the world, whereas Mathis does not; Mathis is only manifesting his political actions in a different, and more unconventional, way.

The duet which Albrecht and Mathis sing at the end of the Tableau states how art should not exist in isolation: 'We cannot escape the circle where we were born... . Over us appears a wider circle: the power which holds us upright. If all that we begin is to be worthwhile, our deeds must be directed towards both centres'.[84] The reconciliation of Mathis with his art is demonstrated musically in this scene, which begins with Mathis trying to withstand Albrecht's endeavours to change his mind; when Albrecht reproaches him for leaving his calling, he is resistant and defensive. Eventually, though, he is persuaded and the two men join together to praise heaven and earth. This course of events is constructed musically through the use of contrasting tonal centres. (The tonal plan of this scene is shown in Table 4.1.) The main tonal centre of the scene is D, and is associated with Albrecht. The scene begins in this centre, when Albrecht first appears to Mathis; he persistently returns to a D centre as he talks to the painter (in the first section of the scene also employing the same musical material), for instance, Albrecht's speech beginning at fig.84+6 ('In der Hut deiner

---

[84] 'Dem Kreis, der uns geboren hat, können wir nicht entrinnen... . Über uns zeigt sich ein weiterer Kreis: Die Kraft, die uns aufrecht erhält. Was wir auch beginnen: Sollen wir uns echt bewähren, muß unser Tun nach beiden Mitten weisen'. The same sentiment is expressed by Mathis and Schwalb at the end of Tableau 1: 'Whatever deeds should blossom in you, they only flourish in God's sunlight if your absorbing roots reach deeply into the ground of your people' ('Was an Taten in dir aufblühen soll, gedeiht an der Sonne Gottes allein, wenn deine saugenden Wurzeln tief hinein in den Urgrund deines Volkes greifen').

Table 4.1: *Mathis der Maler* – **tonal plan of meeting of Mathis and Albrecht**

form	figure	tonal centre	character	words
A	81-5	D	Albrecht	Mein Bruder, entreiße dich
B	82+6	$D^\#$	Mathis	Die heiligen Männer fand der Tod
A	85-6	D	Albrecht	In der Hut deiner Arbeit
C	86+7	F	Albrecht	Dich berührte in Welschland
A	89-1	D	Albrecht	Der Zeit Gebrechen mahnten dich
D	90-2	$F^\#$	Mathis	Ja, meinem Gott mich darzubieten
A	91-1	D	Albrecht	Dem Volke entzogst du dich
E	92+6	D^b	Albrecht	Wenn du demütig dem Bruder dich bogst
F	98-3	D	both	Der Kreis, der uns geboren hat

Arbeit') is principally on D, also moving to the pitch a minor third higher, F at the subsection beginning at fig.86+7, as well as passing briefly through other centres. The final peroration is similarly based on D. In contrast, Mathis's initial resistance to Albrecht's statements are organised around a continual pulling away from this central D: his first statement (from 'Die heilgen Männer') is in a $D^\#$ centre. After Albrecht's move to an F centre, Mathis returns singing in a centre of $F^\#$ ('Ja, meinem Gott mich darzubieten'). Both his words and his music therefore contradict the D-F dyad set up by Albrecht. Although Albrecht later moves away from the D centre himself, this is in a section which is based around D^b with hints of E, which themselves together enclose D, in contrast to Mathis's $D^\#$-$F^\#$ which moves away from it.[85] At the end of Albrecht's excursion into the area of D^b,

---

[85] Both Mathis and Albrecht occasionally touch on tonal areas primarily associated with the other. Some of these seem insignificant, for instance, the section of Albrecht's speech in D^b and E ('Wenn du demütig dem Bruder dich bogst') uses music passing through a $D^\#$, and later an $F^\#$, centre in two places (fig.93+1 and 95+2), but both of these are part of a

Mathis is finally convinced, and the music endorses this shift in perspective. Albrecht's passage finishes resolutely in D^b (at fig.97), and for the first time, Mathis does not attempt to shift the music into a different key but remains in this D^b tonality. The two men then both move together into D for the passage which ends the scene, both singing together, and moving between homophony and canonic imitation. Both this texture and the unanimous move to the same tonal area shows Mathis's 'conversion', as Albrecht wins him over to his point of view, and signifies his reconciliation to the world of art.

Both the language used in this scene and elsewhere, and the artist's relationship towards the 'ordinary people', the peasants, throughout the opera, are central to understanding *Mathis der Maler* within its wider political context. Mathis's relationship to the people, whom he calls his 'brothers', is expressed in the first Tableau, when he says to Schwalb that 'All I want to do is help'.[86] Mathis does not produce esoteric art which only a few can understand, but tries to communicate with ordinary people: he paints his characters in the guise of contemporary Germans to whom his audience can relate. We are told that he represents Christ as 'a sick beggar', saints as 'peasants' and Mary as a 'cowgirl from Weisenau'.[87] While he becomes disillusioned when he goes to experience the peasants' struggle at first hand, it is important to note that he becomes estranged only from the peasants' methods, not from their cause: when the peasants turn against Mathis, he is forgiving of them, and recognises their plight: 'The poorest have to suffer death and misery so that the rich become richer'.[88]

---

downward progression, moving first diatonically and then chromatically, to D^b in the first instance and to E in the second. Albrecht also passes through $F^{\#}$ when referring to Mathis's art, for example at the words 'Meisterschaft' (fig.85), 'Kunst' (fig.89-2), and in the passage beginning 'Du bist zum Bilden übermenschlich begabt' (fig.90+2). Other excursions may be taken again as indicative of Mathis's resistance to Albrecht, or as Albrecht's attempts to persuade Mathis.

[86] 'Ich will ja nichts andres als helfen'.

[87] 'einen kranken Bettelmann'; 'Bauer[n]'; 'Weisenauer Kuhmagd'. See Weisstein, 'Die letzte Häutung', 206.

[88] 'Tod und Jammer müssen die Ärmsten leiden, damit die Reichen reicher werden'. Schwalb similarly pardons them: 'Despair lasting decades has worn them down' ('Die Verzweiflung Jahrzehnte lang hat sie mürbe gemacht'). He also tells Mathis: '[The peasant] labours in slavery day and night. His fields are trampled under foot, his cattle are

Schwalb's young daughter, Regina, may be read as showing the true nature of the ordinary people; she is untarnished by the peasants' oppression and consequent barbarity which, according to Schwalb, has blemished their real nature. When Regina is taken as representative of the peasants, a different, more positive, light is shed on Mathis's relationship to them. Although Mathis becomes disenchanted with the peasants, he remains close to Regina. They are the only two survivors of the battle; they move on from the barbarity of the peasants, both literally and figuratively, leaving the scene together and thus illustrating how both are treading the same path. Mathis's relationship to Regina and to the common people is symbolised by a ribbon which was originally given to Mathis by his lover Ursula. Ursula is the merchant Riedinger's daughter, and is therefore part of the world of Mainz. She never leaves this environment; despite her wish to go with Mathis, he rejects her and her world by telling her she must stay behind. Ursula gave Mathis the ribbon before they had parted from each other, saying that 'Nothing will separate us, as long as you still have it'.[89] However, Mathis gives the ribbon to Regina as a present. The ribbon therefore functions as a symbol for Mathis's relationship to different kinds of society: while he was first metaphorically bound to Ursula and her middle-class world, he confirms his association with the people when he gives the ribbon to Regina.

Regina's music underscores her presentation as representing the true nature of the people. It is sometimes based on diegetic quasi-folk songs, the only appearances of such songs in the opera. The peasants, in contrast, never use such music. The spirit of the people is encapsulated in these folk songs; it is 'their' music, not fashioned by one individual but reaching into the roots of the society itself and becoming their 'natural' expression. While the peasants have become distanced from their true nature through their violence and corruption, Regina has remained true to it. The first song

---

taken from him, he's squeezed by taxes and duties, he is plagued terribly. Only the rich man has rights. All of them are allowed to drive us poor blokes down. And he only fills the knapsacks of the princes and clerics to the brim, again and again'. ('In Fron dient [der Bauer] Tag und Nacht. Man stampft sein Feld darnieder, sein Vieh nimmt man ihm, mit Steuern und Zoll wird er gepresst, geplagt ist er fürchterlich. Recht hat nur der Reiche. Den armen Hansen darf jeder schinden. Wenn er nur immer wieder den Fürsten und Pfaffen den Ranzen stopft, bis obenhin voll'.)

[89] 'Nichts soll uns trennen solange es bei dir ruht'.

Regina sings, 'Es wollt ein Maidlein waschen gehn', is about a maid who goes to do washing at a spring, and is the most representative of a folk-song idiom within *Mathis der Maler*. The text of the song plays out the relationship between Mathis and Regina on another level:

> A maiden went to wash by a cool spring. She wore a white blouse, all in the bright sunshine. ...A knight came riding up to the maiden at the spring. 'Won't you come with me, my love, all in the bright sunshine?'. ...The knight gave her a silk ribbon, embroidered with crimson roses.[90]

The song is related to the actions of the actual characters of Regina and Mathis. Firstly, Regina herself is next to a spring as she sings; when she arrives at the verse about the ribbon, she wishes that she herself had one, and Mathis gives her his.[91] These two facts invite us to align the characters in the song with those on stage, Regina herself as the 'Maiden' and Mathis the 'Knight'. The knight's invitation to the maiden to go with him points to the way Regina and Mathis will travel together later on, albeit in different circumstances to the one in the song.

Regina's other song, 'Es sungen drei Engeln ein süssen Gesang' is less clearly a folk song, as it has a religious text. Nevertheless, the song's mediaeval origin and its folk-song style removes it from a religious discourse and places it, like folk song, as part of an ancient, shared heritage. Hindemith's source for this song, as for 'Es wollt ein Maidlein waschen gehn', was a nineteenth-century collection of songs by Franz M. Böhme called the *Altdeutsches Liederbuch*.[92] Böhme himself says that while not many spiritual songs were freely sung by ordinary people, when a spiritual song did

---

[90] 'Es wollt ein Maidlein waschen gehn bei einem kühlen Brunnen. Ein weißes Hemdlein hatt' sie an, wohl in der hellen Sonne. ...Es kam ein Reuter hergeritten zum Maidlein an den Brunnen. "Willst du, mein Lieb, nicht mit mir ziehen wohl in der hellen Sonne?". ...Der Reuter gab ihr ein seiden Band, bestickt mit Purpurrosen'.

[91] It is interesting to note in this regard that the ribbon does not feature in the original folk song, on which Hindemith bases the music of Regina's song. The original contains the meeting between a maiden who has gone washing and a knight, but the story then goes in another direction. See Franz M. Böhme, *Altdeutsches Liederbuch: Volkslieder der Deutschen nach Wort und Weise aus dem 12. bis zum 17. Jahrhundert* (Hildesheim: Georg Olms, 1966. Original edition: Leipzig, 1877), no.60.

[92] Franz Wöhlke, Mathis der Maler *von Paul Hindemith* (Berlin: Robert Lienau, 1965), 16 ff.

have an existence 'in the mouth of the people', outside a church context, then 'one may accept it as a true spiritual folk song'.[93] Some writers, such as Kemp, say that 'Es sungen' *is* a folk song, illustrating its ambiguity.[94]

These diegetic folk songs, as well as the hymns within the opera (the monks' Gregorian chant in Tableau 1, and the Lutheran hymn tune in Tableau 3), function as *Gebrauchsmusik*, thus demonstrating Hindemith's belief in the importance of 'music for use'. All of these diegetic moments are comprised of music of indeterminate heritage, that is, it is music which does not have a specific composer and which belongs to a common repertoire to which everyone has access; it is all, broadly speaking, 'folk' music.[95] Like Regina's folk songs, the hymn tune 'Lobt Gott ihr frommen Christen' in Tableau 3 existed outside a liturgical discourse, according to Böhme, functioning as a political rallying-cry by early Lutherans; this therefore also renders it folk-like.[96] The plainchant is liturgical, but has the same clouded origins even if it is sung by a more closely defined group of people. Mathis himself never sings any of this music, and his relationship to this 'folk' music is no different from that of the other characters. For all of the characters, this music exists as a fact of life, to be used functionally, without being elevated to the status of autonomous art music.

Mathis's wish to help the peasants is expressed particularly through the use of the word *Volk* in the opera, which is used prominently throughout to indicate Mathis's 'brothers'. Mathis tells Albrecht in their meeting as Paul and Anthony in Tableau 6 that he fought in order 'to offer my blood and spirit to my *Volk*'.[97] Albrecht's argument to Mathis persuading him to return to art is phrased in parallel terms: 'You deprived the *Volk* when you went to them, and denied your calling'.[98] If he returns to art, Albrecht says, Mathis will be 'a part of the *Volk*, the *Volk* itself',[99] and Mathis replies that 'the voice of the *Volk* has spoken through you'.[100] As discussed earlier, the peasants are an incipient yet tainted form of the *Volk*, who have lost their

---

[93] Böhme, *Altdeutsches Liederbuch*, xliii.

[94] Kemp, *Hindemith*, 31.

[95] Also see Stephen Hinton, *The Idea of Gebrauchsmusik*, 35.

[96] Böhme, *Altdeutsches Liederbuch*, no.394.

[97] 'meinem Volke Blut und Geist zu opfern'.

[98] 'Dem Volke entzogst du dich, als du zu ihm gingst, deiner Sendung entsagtest'.

[99] 'ein Teil des Volkes, Volk selbst'.

[100] 'der Mund des Volkes sprach durch dich'.

true, pure identity because of their espousal of violence. Despite his mis-givings about their brutality, though, Mathis still supports the peasants' cause, and their fight is portrayed as a noble one even if their methods are criticised. The way in which Mathis's actions are motivated by his concern for the *Volk* resonates with the language used by the National Socialists in this era, as does his use of folk song. In a further echo, rhetorical devices of organicism also appear. For example, Mathis asks in Tableau 1 'Where is the soil of creation, where growth and ripening?', answered by Schwalb's 'Whatever deeds should blossom in you, they only flourish in God's sun-light if your absorbing roots reach deeply into the ground of your *Volk*'.[101] In Albrecht's speech to Mathis converting him back to art in Tableau 6, the archbishop uses the image of a tree to describe Mathis's purpose in life: 'When you humbly bow before your brother...then you will stand bound and free, a strong tree in your native soil. ...If everything is taken from you and you are forgotten: the tree does not know what happens to its fruit'.[102] Continuing this image at the end of the opera, Mathis says that 'As all the fruit has now gone from me, may the last leaf of ripe autumn fall to earth'.[103] Ideas of the organic are thus used to suggest the relationship which the artist should have to his people: his 'roots' must be within the 'soil' of the people, and he should be like a 'tree' to them. The artist must be organically bound to the *Volk*, a vision which has much in common with the Nazis' conception of an ideal society. Such language is used in the opera in connection with artistic creation, thereby tapping into a familiar pattern within language about music in the late nineteenth and early twen-tieth century; however, it gains an additional connotation given contempor-ary Nazi rhetoric.

Another contextual echo is the ideal of community, which is contrasted in the opera several times with 'self-interest'. When he is questioning the purpose of his art in Tableau 1, Mathis asks himself, 'Are you only being

---

[101] 'Wo ist des Schaffens Boden, wo Wachsen und Reifen?'; 'Was an Taten in dir auf-blühen soll, gedeiht an der Sonne Gottes allein, wenn deine saugenden Wurzeln tief hin-ein in den Urgrund deines Volkes greifen'.

[102] 'Wenn du demütig dem Bruder dich bogst...wirst du gebunden und frei, ein starker Baum im Mutterboden stehen. ...Wenn man dir alles nahm und dich darob vergaß: Der Baum weiß nicht um seine Frucht'.

[103] 'Wie sich alle Frucht von mir löste, sei auch das letzte Blatt aus reifem Herbst dem Boden übergeben'.

full of self-interest?'.[104] Later, he reproaches the peasants, saying 'You want to overthrow those in power, prevent self-interested activities, but are yourselves full of self-interest!'.[105] Such language is reminiscent of contemporary ideas of socialism, both of the left- and right-wings; for instance, one Nazi slogan stressed the idea of community before the individual with the phrase 'the common interest comes before self-interest'.[106] Mathis's move from the world of the middle classes to the *Volk* may also be seen in relation to National Socialist ideology, in which capitalism and the modern world is seen as suspect and the wholesome *Volk* in a rural setting is lauded, while the way in which art is distanced from money at the close of the opera is comparable to the Nazis' anti-capitalism.[107] In *Mathis*, though, the vision of community remains largely on the level of the ideal: the peasants have not, in reality, achieved a *Volksgemeinschaft*.

However, before Mathis's fictional meeting with Albrecht, he sees a vision of angels, designated by Hindemith an *Engelkonzert* ('Angelic Concert'); this scene does suggest a Utopian community, as well as illustrating Hindemith's views about the otherworldly provenance of music discussed above. In the *Engelkonzert*, Mathis tells Regina a fairy tale, metaphorically painting a picture of angels. As he continues, we begin to suspect that it is not just a story, but that, in a mystical vision, Mathis and Regina are really seeing the figures he describes. What is notable about the *Engelkonzert* is that Mathis, a painter, is so concerned with music and musicians. In an evocation of the 'harmony of the spheres', Mathis's vision suggests that heaven is filled with music, and seems not too distant from the encounter with angels which Palestrina experiences. At the beginning of the *Engelkonzert*, Mathis says that music bears 'the trace of heavenly origin',[108] and describes the angelic musicians as they play. (The painting on which the

---

104 'Bist nicht nur eignen Nutzens voll?'.

105 'Ihr wollt die Macht stürzen, eigennützige Tat verhindern, und seid selbst voll Eigennutz!'.

106 'Gemeinnutz geht vor Eigennutz'. Quoted in Carr, *A History of Germany*, 344.

107 Albrecht also states that Mathis was attracted by 'strange new arts' ('fremder, süsser Kunst') in a 'foreign land', using for the latter the word *Welschland*. This term, also used by Hans Sachs's famous 'Honour your German masters' speech in Wagner's *Meistersinger*, has a negative connotation in the German. (For the text of Sachs's speech, see Chapter 1.)

108 'die Spur himmlischer Herkunft'.

scene is based is shown in Fig.4.1, part of the Isenheim Altarpiece.) He then moves into a more metaphysical vein:

> In the harmony of many coloured circles of light, form becomes visible from the hardly-heard song, in a wonderful way...you do not know, do those who pray make music, or do you hear the musicians praying? When music thus becomes prayer, then nature listens closely. A remnant of the shimmer of such spheres could transfigure our dark deeds.[109]

This scene is reminiscent of Hindemith's belief in a 'region of visionary irrationality'; the composer uses the persona of Mathis in order to expound his own philosophy.

The portrayal of the angels as performing musicians creates a semantic affiliation between the text of the *Engelkonzert* and its music. The music itself becomes the music of the angels; it is no longer merely accompanying background, but becomes, as it were, diegetic.[110] As Mathis describes the angels making music, we hear what they play, the orchestral accompaniment sounding as the angels' instruments themselves. The orchestral voices here lead the musical argument, rather than being in a supporting, accompanimental role to the singers; the orchestra sets the tone for the scene, around which Mathis and Regina fit their own lines. The interaction of these musical voices is less a drama than a tableau: the music does not tell a story, but constructs a picture, as Mathis's words do.[111]

The tableau portrayed through the *Engelkonzert* functions as a metaphor for a Utopian society not yet realised on earth. If the orchestral voices are taken to be the angels' music, then the angels' harmonious music-making can be read, in a basic way, as symbolic of a well-functioning,

---

[109] 'im Zusammenklang viel bunter Lichterkreise wird aus kaum gehörtem Lied auf wunderbare Art sichtbares Formenleben...du weißt nicht: musizieren, die Gebete dichten, oder hörst du der Musikanten Beten. Ist so Musik Gebet geworden, hört lauschend zu Natur. Ein Rest des Schimmers solcher Sphären mög unser dunkles Tun verklären'.

[110] The fact that the angels are not real but imaginary does not make them conventionally 'diegetic'; they can nevertheless be understood as such as they are 'real' within the vision itself.

[111] The fact that the *Engelkonzert* is used as the prelude to the opera illustrates how it may be divorced from the plot and reinforces its status as a tableau.

Fig.4.1 Matthias Grünewald: Isenheim Altarpiece (section) (Photo: AKG London / Erich Lessing)

peaceful society through the consonant sounding-together of notes. The structural organisation of the scene constructs the same idea on a more subtle level. Formally, the structure of the *Engelkonzert* comprises an 'exposition' and a 'development'.[112] The exposition comprises three distinct themes; on one level, these themes do not tie up particularly closely with Mathis's words. Repetitions of a theme are not linked to words on precisely the same subject, and therefore they seem to have a primarily formal significance. However, on another level, we can extrapolate the three themes as musically characterising the three angels whom Mathis describes. (It is therefore relevant that the three themes only appear in the orchestra, and are never sung by Mathis or Regina.) The first angel is not described by Mathis until during the second theme, at the words 'Der eine geigt mit wundersam gesperrtem Arm' (fig.16-3). Nevertheless, the first and second angels are separated from each other through a change in tonal area as the description of the second begins; the tonal centre for the first angel begins based on $F^\#$, and moves to C, before modulating to a centre of A for the appearance of the second angel (at 'Ein andrer streicht gehobenen Blicks aus Saiten seine Freude', fig.17+1).[113] The third angel has both a separate tonal area (based on G) and a new theme ('Verhaftet scheint der dritte dem fernen Geläute seiner Seele', fig.18). The development section (from fig.20-3) of the *Engelkonzert* replaces this third theme with the 'Es sungen drei Engeln' theme; these themes are then combined polyphonically, the 'Es sungen' theme interacting with the first and second themes. This takes place as Mathis stops describing the individual angels and instead describes them collectively, moving into the metaphysical description noted above as he says how their sounds interact with each other:

> Even their clothes make music with them. In their shimmering feathers swirls the play of sounds. Their light armour of unearthly metal glows, touched by the waves of sound as if by the trembling of a suffering heart. In the harmony of

---

[112] I draw here on David Neumeyer's analysis of the *Engelkonzert*, in his *The Music of Paul Hindemith*. His analysis is of the *Engelkonzert* movement of the *Mathis der Maler* Symphony, which is the same as the Prelude to the opera and essentially the same as the *Engelkonzert* in Tableau 6 (*The Music of Paul Hindemith*, 85 ff.).

[113] The music for the second angel later moves through $F^\#$ again before modulating to a centre of E^b.

many coloured circles of light, form becomes visible from the hardly-heard song, in a wonderful way.[114]

In this way, the polyphony of the *Engelkonzert* both functions as the music of the angels, and portrays their interaction as individuals within society.

The position of Regina's song 'Es sungen drei Engeln' at the climaxes of the *Engelkonzert* adds a dimension to this scene which further illustrates Hindemith's aesthetic. The *Engelkonzert* is not only a vision of another reality, a Utopian society, but is linked to earth through the use of folk song. 'Es sungen' is always sung by Regina over what Mathis, who has a separate text, is singing; her text corresponds with what Mathis is describing. For instance, as he finishes describing the three angels, Regina summarises by singing 'Three angels sang a sweet song that sounded far and wide in heaven'.[115] With Mathis's last line, 'A vestige of the shimmer of these spheres could transfigure all our dark deeds',[116] Regina sings the similar, but more idealistic line, 'The world is filled with the sound of God, which echoes in the hearts of humankind'.[117] While Regina's line is in the present tense, the conditional tense of Mathis's line is more realistic and indicates that the vision of Regina's song is not yet realised in actuality. The *Engelkonzert* symbolically brings together art, the divine and the people: the angels indicate the spiritual but also descend to the level of the ordinary people thanks to the presence of Regina, and particularly because of her song about them, which links a religious text with the folk-song style of its music. Regina's name also suggests how she helps to bring together the worldly and the divine: 'Regina' (literally 'queen') is used liturgically to refer to Mary, the mother of Christ, who was human yet touched by God. The alignment of the spiritual with the folk positions God on the side of the people; consequently, it is suggested, both the people, and Mathis's return to painting, are 'right' and have God's blessing. The combination of heaven and earth suggests how Mathis, being close to both the angels and the real

---

114 'Ihr Kleid selbst musiziert mit ihnen. In schillernden Federn schwirrt der Töne Gegenspiel. Ein leichter Panzer unirdischen Metalls erglüht, berührt vom Wogen des Klanges wie vom Beben bewegten Herzens. Und im Zusammenklang viel bunter Lichterkreise wird aus kaum gehörtem Lied auf wunderbare Art sichtbares Formenleben'.

115 'Es sungen drei Engeln ein süßen Gesang, der weit in den hohen Himmel erklang'.

116 'Ein Rest des Schimmers solcher Sphären mög unser dunkles Tun verklären'.

117 'Die Welt ist erfüllt von göttlichem Schall, im Herzen der Menschen ein Widerhall'.

spirit of the people, can use his art to convey a message to the world; it echoes Hindemith's own aesthetic tenets, in which a mystical vision can be communicated to ordinary listeners through music.[118] Rather than the divine being located above the world, as is the case in *Palestrina*, here God is involved with society through art.

By returning to his painting, Mathis creates art for the people, through which God can work. At the same time, however, he seems to find a degree of rapprochement with middle-class society: in the last Tableau, he is in his studio in Mainz, and is reconciled with Ursula. He would therefore seem to join together the two spheres which were previously separate: he is still painting for his people, but is at least nominally within the context of middle-class life, where, it seems, it is possible for him to work to his best ability. It is notable, though, that he still rejects any bourgeois ostentation: while he is physically located in Mainz, he does not interact with this world, and refuses Albrecht's offer of a house. There are also continuing reminders of the world of the *Volk*, for instance when Regina recapitulates 'Es sungen drei Engeln' as she dies. Mathis's last act in the opera is to pack away his belongings: his painting is finished and he believes that he will soon die. He states that now, 'my spirit [is] too weary to serve art'.[119] This, then, would appear to be his final 'retreat' from the world, and as Mathis packs, the last thing he comes to is the ribbon, saying it is 'a breath...of what I loved'.[120] The opera thus ends with this symbol of his allegiance to the *Volk*.

---

[118] The relationship between the worldly and the divine is a theme which resurfaces at other points of the opera. It is often indicated that the only valid ruler of the peasants is God, rather than an earthly power; the peasants say in Tableau 4 that 'we want only to be Christ's, and not endure agony because of knights and priests' ('Wir wollen nur Christi eigen sein. Nicht Qual dulden von Rittern und clerics'). (They also say that they accept 'no other ruler than the Kaiser' ('Kein Herrscher gilt als der Kaiser'), but this is probably legitimised by the fact that the Kaiser's position is God-given.) The importance of God as the supreme source of power is hinted at near the beginning of the opera, as the monks' chorus sings to 'Rector potens, verax Deus, qui temperas rerum vices' ('Almighty ruler, true God, who governs the world's course'). Both of these groups, peasants and monks, are associated with Mathis.

[119] 'Mein Geist, zu matt, der Kunst zu dienen'.

[120] 'einen Hauch dessen...was ich liebte'.

Hindemith and the Third Reich

The way in which one reads Tableau 6, the vision scene, is critical for how one situates *Mathis der Maler* within the context of 1930s Germany. Many writers have seen Mathis's return to art in this scene as a rejection of, and retreat from fighting, and thus as an act of de-politicisation, yet it is possible to view Mathis as *remaining* political precisely through his return to painting. His art becomes politicised, in his wish to use it to help the people. This scene is central to understanding Hindemith's own position within Nazi Germany: because Mathis has been seen as representing the real composer, when Mathis is read as rejecting politics Hindemith is similarly viewed as retreating from the environment around him.[121] In this regard, the phrase 'inner emigration' is frequently encountered, a term often found in discussions of public figures who remained in Germany after 1933. Zenck writes that the term developed within literary history after World War II, to refer to a position 'which developed from political distance from the Hitler state, implied a claim of moral satisfactoriness, and understood the retreat inwards as an expression and consequence of opposition'.[122] Figures who stayed in Germany in a state of 'inner emigration' were, by this argument, opposed to the regime, and resisted it on a spiritual level if not on a practical one. The term functions as a way of making sense of a difficult situation, namely the reasons behind why a figure like Hindemith remained in Nazi Germany. How far the term is valid or not varies depending on the individual discussed; for instance, it seems particularly appropriate in the case of the composer Karl Amadeus Hartmann, who re-

---

[121] See for instance, Breimann, *'Mathis der Maler'*, 15: Hindemith 'insisted on the unrestricted sovereignty of artistic creation and the division of aesthetics from politics, and consequently refused as an artist to become politically active'. Breimann restricts her argument to how Hindemith himself allegedly withdrew from the world and does not consider aspects of either his political or his aesthetic views which could contradict her initial assumption that the work demonstrates a retreat. She does say that Hindemith believed 'that the artist, despite his basic sovereignty, is obliged towards society', and mentions Hindemith's concerns in the 1920s with music for amateurs, yet she continues that this position 'is not given any consideration in the final version of the opera libretto whatsoever' (172). Also see Briner, *Paul Hindemith*, 101 and 108.

[122] Zenck, 'Zwischen Boykott und Anpassung', 111. Zenck lists literature dealing with the 'inner emigration' idea with reference to writers.

mained in Germany throughout the war, but removed himself from musical life and withdrew his works from performance in the country.[123] Interpretations which are based on 'inner emigration', however, often do not consider the complexity of reasons around why someone may have stayed in Germany, and neglect the fact that our present-day understanding of Nazism is not that of the German citizens of the 1930s, but has been coloured by subsequent events.

Clearly, if one reads Mathis as remaining political despite his return to painting, this has ramifications for any interpretation of the opera in which the central character acts as a persona for Hindemith. We may ask, therefore, firstly how far the opera was in fact understood by the composer to be autobiographical, and secondly, which reading of the work – retreat or engagement – is more consistent with his stance towards his political environment. Hindemith himself gave little explicit indication as to whether he regarded Mathis as an autobiographical persona. The nearest clue we have about the composer's opinion is in a letter from his publisher and friend Willy Strecker, writing to his brother Ludwig in August 1933. Strecker writes that 'The figure of Grünewald, who went his own way in spite of being misunderstood, and resisted the foreign influence of the Italian Renaissance, is of course a reflection of [Hindemith] himself, and that is why it interests him so tremendously'. This may suggest that this is Hindemith's own view, but this is contradicted later on in the letter: 'it was so characteristic of Hindemith the way he constantly – and almost shyly – tried to conceal the human connections with his own personality, dragging in irrelevant historical happenings to hide the essential point'.[124] The autobiographical interpretation here would therefore seem to be Strecker's rather than Hindemith's; the composer was resisting any connection being made between himself and Mathis.[125]

---

[123] Guy Rickards, *Hindemith, Hartmann and Henze* (London: Phaidon Press, 1995), 90; Kater, *The Twisted Muse*, 233 ff.

[124] Quoted in Skelton, *Paul Hindemith*, 112–13. In a letter to the composer of 26th September 1933, Willy Strecker addresses him as 'Lieber Hindemathis' (Hindemith Institut, Schott Briefwechsel). The line that Grünewald resisted the influence of the Renaissance could betray a belief that Hindemith similarly resisted modernism.

[125] Later writers generally follow Strecker's lead: Skelton says that 'Hindemith...saw the predicament [of Mathis] as similar to his own'; Redlich says it is 'his greatest, confessionally conceived opera'; Schubert writes that it has 'autobiographical features', and

If Hindemith himself was guarded about how far he saw Mathis as auto-biographical, we may nevertheless view the fictional artist as consistent with many of Hindemith's expressed aesthetic and social ideals, for instance, his belief in the transcendent, spiritual power of music; the composer thus constructs a persona through the figure of Mathis. To place these views within their historical and political context, though, necessitates that we examine Hindemith's own position in the Third Reich, and ask what could be uncomfortable questions: did he 'retreat' from Nazism, as Mathis is seen by many to retreat from the world? Was Hindemith more sympathetic to the left wing or to the right? It has generally been asserted that the composer was nothing less than fully oppositional to the Nazis, and that he was, at heart, left wing. Skelton, for example, writes that Hindemith's teaching at an evening class in a workers' district of Berlin demonstrates the composer's 'lean[ing] towards social democracy',[126] while Schubert says that Hindemith is politically 'classified as "left-bourgeois"'. (He neglects to say who classifies him.)[127] Hindemith does, indeed, often express views which outwardly seem consistent with a conventionally socialist position, such as in *A Composer's World* where he states that 'one of the main reasons for artistic communication [is] the altruistic desire to present something of one's own to one's fellow men'.[128] He displays an idealistic view of community music-making, and says that an amateur music group is

---

Briner says that Mathis is a version of Hindemith himself (Skelton, 'One Person's Response', in the programme book for the Royal Opera House production, 11; Redlich, 'Paul Hindemith: a Re-assessment', 242; Schubert, *Paul Hindemith*, 84; Briner, *Paul Hindemith*, 128 and 270). Kemp points to the fact that the opera is set in the area from which Hindemith came (around Mainz), and says that 'by writing his own text he emphasized its autobiographical aspects. It is indeed a personal testament' (*Hindemith*, 30). Breimann attempts to explore the question of 'how far Hindemith's understanding of himself as an artist (*Künstlerverständnis*) is reflected' in *Mathis*, and concludes that the opera is 'very closely linked to Paul Hindemith's own artistic life both through the circumstances of its formation in fascist Germany and through its content' (*'Mathis der Maler'*, 15 and 183). Also see Bruhn, *The Temptation of Paul Hindemith, passim*.

[126] Skelton, *Paul Hindemith*, 101.

[127] Schubert, *Paul Hindemith*, 49. Kemp likewise denies that Hindemith was anything other than politically reputable, saying that Hindemith 'could scarcely believe' that Germany would remain 'hypnotized' by the Nazis for long (*Hindemith*, 28).

[128] Hindemith, *A Composer's World*, 65.

a 'great fraternity' whose purpose is 'to inspire one another and unite in building up a creation that is greater than one individual's deeds'.[129] Indeed, he goes so far as to advocate a peace movement through collective music-making, in which politicians would enjoy the pleasures of playing together, because 'people who make music together cannot be enemies, at least not while the music lasts'.[130] Hindemith's collaborations in 1929 with Bertolt Brecht on the works *Lehrstück* and *Der Lindberghflug* have also been seen as substantiating his left-wing tendencies.[131] The belief that Hindemith was politically towards the left supports the view of his 'inner emigration' in the Third Reich, as well as influencing – or being influenced by – how Mathis is read as retreating from the world in Tableau 6.

However, one should not forget the ambiguities of 'socialism' within the Germany of the 1920s and 1930s: the far-right, too, believed themselves to be socialists. While it is indisputable that Hindemith worked with the communist Brecht, one must also acknowledge that not only did Brecht and Hindemith part company acrimoniously a few years later, but that the composer worked with the writer Gottfried Benn in 1931 on *Das Unaufhörliche*; Benn was later involved with the Nazis.[132] This in itself suggests that Hindemith must have felt ideologically comfortable working with both writers, and the composer's apparent swing from working with a communist to a Nazi sympathiser may be explained by the 'grey area' model discussed above; in their wishes to bring art to the people, Hindemith, Brecht and Benn all resided within the same ideological field, their differences arising in who exactly they wished the recipients of their efforts to be.

Mathis der Maler, with its praise of the *Volk* and its use of rhetoric which echoes Nazi slogans, also raises problematic questions. Hindemith did not often voice his political opinions, although in 1934 he did refer to

---

129 Ibid., 217.

130 Ibid., 218.

131 Kemp, *Hindemith*, 22 and 24.

132 Hindemith and Benn later considered another collaboration, although this never materialised. In his letters to the composer, Benn suggests that a possible topic might be 'die W.R.' (Gottfried Benn, *Briefwechsel mit Paul Hindemith*, ed. Ann Clark Fehn (Wiesbaden: Limes Verlag, 1978), 44 and 52 (Aug.–Sept. 1931). According to Fehn's 'Afterword', Benn used this abbreviation to refer to 'die weiße Rasse' ('the white race') (ibid., 197).

himself as a 'passionate patriot'[133], but his actions within German political life at this time may nonetheless be examined. Hindemith emigrated from Germany in 1938, five years after Hitler came to power; one must therefore ask whether these years were really a period of 'inner emigration' for the composer. In fact, many leading Nazis saw Hindemith as potentially valuable to their cause; they believed his supposedly 'German' musical style might be harnessable to their own ends.[134] Others in the party were more hostile, though, and this ambivalence towards the composer continued for a number of years; some, but not all, of his works were banned in the early years of the Third Reich, and eventually all were. Hindemith himself exerted some effort trying to secure his position with Nazi Germany, and it could be argued that his frustration at his lack of success was a significant factor leading to his eventual emigration.[135]

From 1933, Hindemith was involved with a number of cultural organisations which were either part of the NSDAP party structure, such as the *Kraft durch Freude* (Strength through Joy) movement, or were originally independent far-right groups that were later affiliated with the Party, such as the *Kampfbund für deutsche Kultur* (Fighting League for German

---

[133] Letter of 15th November 1934, quoted in Skelton, *Hindemith*, 119. He also expressed admiration for a line of Wagner's, which reads 'I feel like the only German amongst this idiotic (*stumpfsinnigen*) population, which one calls the Germans!' (Willy Strecker to Paul Hindemith, 13th July 1936, and Gertrud Hindemith to Strecker, 14th July 1936. Hindemith Institut, Schott Briefwechsel).

[134] See Levi, *Music in the Third Reich*, 108 ff.; Karen Painter, 'Symphonic Ambitions, Operatic Redemption: *Mathis der Maler* and *Palestrina* in the Third Reich', *Musical Quarterly*, 85/1 (Spring 2001), 125 ff.; and Kater, *The Twisted Muse*, 179 ff.

[135] Hindemith's wife Gertrud was also Jewish, leading one, perhaps, to ask why the couple did not feel moved to emigrate earlier (Zenck, 'Zwischen Boykott und Anpassung', 104; Kater, *Composers of the Nazi Era*, 34 and 42). Gertrud's Jewishness is rarely mentioned by the composer in this era, and in fact, Paul left Germany before Gertrud did. Stein, the director of the Berlin Hochschule where Hindemith taught, reported on the composer's decision to resign from his post in a letter to Furtwängler of 22nd March 1937, and is clearly under the impression that Hindemith is planning to emigrate soon: 'While Hindemith has refused the most tempting offers from abroad for the last three years, he is now forced to go abroad, because of the fact that no authority in Germany will make a clear decision about his circumstances' (Hindemith Institut, Akte Paul Hindemith 1927–1937 Musikhochschule Berlin, doc.144–145). However, Hindemith did not leave Germany for Switzerland until a year and a half later.

Culture).[136] His letters from the early years of the Third Reich state his position towards the new scene. In April 1933, he wrote to Willy Strecker that 'I don't think we need worry too much about the musical future. ... Recently...I had a long talk with some of the higher-ups in the *Kampfbund*. It was only about educational matters, but I got the impression (after having satisfied them that I was neither a half nor any other fractional Jew) that they have a good opinion of me there'. He goes on to say that 'they have commissioned me (though not quite officially) to work out plans for a new system of teaching composition and musical theory'.[137] Hindemith also talks in this letter about his position within the new cultural order: 'One of these days I shall of course have to get the *Kampfbund* to support my things officially, but it is a bit too early yet for that'. He says that at present there is too much 'uncertainty'; however, Hindemith would seem to wish to keep on the right side of the Nazis, telling Strecker that he should continue with 'any kind of campaign or attempts at conversion amongst smaller cultural associations' that he may have planned. (The letter does not explain what these might be.)

The following year, in February 1934, Hindemith was approached by *Kraft durch Freude*; he wrote to Strecker that he would make suggestions to them 'for a very far-reaching musical education system for the German people and, if things continue to show goodwill towards me, I hope to provide the impetus for vast plans and to cooperate in putting them into effect'.[138] In a different letter of around the same time, he says that the

---

[136] Breimann, *'Mathis der Maler'*, 33. On the *Kampfbund für deutsche Kultur*, see Kater, *The Twisted Muse*, 14 ff.

[137] Hindemith, *Selected Letters of Paul Hindemith*, ed. and trans. Geoffrey Skelton (New Haven and London: Yale University Press, 1995), 69 (15th April 1933). Also in German in Breimann, *'Mathis der Maler'*, 34. That these discussions must have almost become official is indicated by the fact that Alban Berg was aware of them, as he reported to his wife in May 1933: 'the German government is about to give a mandate to Hindemith for the reorganization of the entire musical life' (reported in Kater, *Composers of the Nazi Era*, 297 n.33).

[138] Hindemith, *Letters*, 76 (5th February 1934); Kater, *Composers of the Nazi Era*, 35. Also see Strecker to Hindemith, 8th February 1934: 'Your official incorporation into the *Arbeitsfront* and youth education is undoubtedly a development as important as it is useful, even if it is associated with unavoidable irritations and disturbances to your own productive activities. You could achieve a lot of good and stop some stupidities' (Hin-

Kraft durch Freude suggestions would 'provide the basis for the most ambitious programme of popular musical education...the world has ever seen. One could literally have the musical enlightenment of millions in one's hand'.[139] Skelton says that Hindemith was 'tempted', although he did not become involved in an official capacity; the composer wrote that he 'trust[ed] to achieve all the more in the background'.[140]

These are not the only instances of Hindemith's involvement in the Nazi cultural scene. In February 1934, he accepted an official position on the council of the Composers' Section of the *Reichsmusikkammer* (the Reich Music Chamber), and conducted a performance of his *Concert Music for Brass and Strings* at a concert in Berlin to unveil the same organisation.[141] A few weeks before this, the composer had taken part in an official National Socialist concert in Lübeck, the first in which he had been involved; in a letter to Strecker he wrote that 'Lübeck was a big success, as first official concert in the III. [sic] Reich a good omen, anyway'.[142] In the summer of 1936, Hindemith accepted a commission to write a work for the *Luftwaffe* and wrote to Strecker that 'I want to give them something really good. ...I am quite certain that this piece, if reasonably successful, could mean *Mathis* in the Staatsoper'.[143] Perhaps most significantly, as a requirement of keeping his teaching position at the Berlin Hochschule, he signed an oath of loyalty to Hitler in January 1936.[144]

---

demith Institut, Schott Briefwechsel).

[139] Hindemith, *Letters*, 76 (9th February 1934).

[140] Ibid.; Skelton, *Paul Hindemith*, 115.

[141] Kater, *The Twisted Muse*, 179; Levi, *Music in the Third Reich*, 109.

[142] Hindemith, *Letters*, 77 (9th February 1934); Breimann, *'Mathis der Maler'*, 35.

[143] Quoted in Skelton, *Paul Hindemith*, 133 (8th July 1936). This piece was never written; Hindemith reported to Ludwig Strecker that it had been put off because of lack of time (23rd October 1936. Hindemith Institut, Schott Briefwechsel).

[144] Levi, *Music in the Third Reich*, 114–15; Kater, *Composers of the Nazi Era*, 41. The words of the oath can be found in Berndt Heller and Frieder Reininghaus, 'Hindemiths heikle Jahre. Eine Dokumentation', *Neue Zeitschrift für Musik* 145/5 (1984), 8. Also see Zenck, 'Zwischen Boykott und Anpassung', for details of these events. Breimann notes that Hindemith took the oath, but explains it by saying all state employees were required to do so (*'Mathis der Maler'*, 48). In 1935, and again in 1936 and 1937, Hindemith spent some months in Turkey, assisting in the foundation of a conservatoire. This trip was approved of by the National Socialists, who saw it as ambassadorial for German

Hindemith's comment about the *Luftwaffe* commission points to the situation in which he found himself regarding a first performance for *Mathis der Maler*. The authorities wavered for years about whether or not to allow a performance, having doubts about the 'Germanness' of his musical style, and being suspicious of his earlier Expressionist works. He was suspected of being '*entartet*' ('degenerate') because his music, particularly that of the early and mid-1920s, was often dissonant, and had used elements of popular music (for instance in the *Kammermusik* no.1). The plots of many of his earlier operas were seen as subversive or frivolous.[145] Hindemith and his colleagues struggled to assure the authorities that *Mathis* was a suitable work for performance in the National Socialist state. In late 1934 the composer planned a campaign with Wilhelm Furtwängler, who wished to conduct the first performance of the piece. Furtwängler would write an article about the opera, making sure Hitler saw it, and would then go and see the Führer with the libretto of the opera in an attempt to win him over and to bypass his subordinates who were objecting to a performance. Hindemith would simultaneously write to Hitler and invite him to visit his Hochschule class, and would have the *Plöner Musiktag* cantata performed for him there.[146] The plan backfired; the Nazis reacted strongly against Furtwängler's plea in the *Deutsche Allgemeine Zeitung* for art and politics to remain separate. Nevertheless, the article itself is revealing; it is not a refutation of Nazi cultural politics, but attempts to show Hindemith's suitability for the Nazis' aim of creating a German music. The conductor points out, for instance, how Hindemith works in the 'spirit of simple craftsmanship...like the old German tradesmen', and that his 'blood is purely Germanic'.[147] Furtwängler writes of Hindemith's affiliation to the Youth Movement and to the ordinary people:

---

culture; Hindemith also referred to it in these terms. Space does not allow a detailed discussion of this part of Hindemith's life here; for further information, see Heller and Reininghaus, 'Hindemiths heikle Jahre', and Kater, *Composers of the Nazi Era*, 39–40.

[145] For instance, his Expressionist *Sancta Susanna* dealt with the sexual frustrations of a young nun, while his *Neues vom Tage* famously appalled Hitler because of its scene in which the heroine sings the praises of hot water systems while in her bath.

[146] Skelton, *Paul Hindemith*, 120; Kater, *Composers of the Nazi Era*, 38.

[147] Quoted in Paulding, '*Mathis der Maler*', 106–7. Despite its title, Paulding's essay is an uncritical account of the Furtwängler-Hindemith campaign which attempts to maintain Hindemith's anti-Nazism. However, it does quote the text of Furtwängler's article in

no one in modern Germany has the youth behind him as does Hindemith...unceasingly he strives in his own way to productively close the gap between art music and the music of the people. In this instance his desire parallels the present tendencies of the new national socialistic Germany.[148]

The following year, Hindemith's publisher Strecker wrote to Gustav Havemann, an important figure within the *Reichsmusikkammer*, in a further attempt to win official approval.[149] With a similar tactic to Furtwängler, he pointed to the admirably National Socialist qualities in Hindemith's work, saying that Hindemith's aim in his music, as Skelton reports it, 'was to overcome post-Wagnerian influences and to return to the strict polyphony of the old German masters; his harmonic language was not atonal, but followed understandable laws of logic'.[150] (Hindemith's 1937 treatise *Unterweisung im Tonsatz*, with its justification of his music in terms of 'nature', should also be remembered in this regard.)[151] Strecker argued that Hindemith's positive, constructive music could not be compared with 'the decadent intellectual musical efforts of a Schönberg', to whose ideas Hindemith was sharply opposed. The composer had never written 'cheap successes' such as *Die Dreigroschenoper* or *Jonny spielt auf*, and he did not owe his success to Jewish cliques and critics; in fact, he had often had trouble with Jewish critics. Nor did he use 'fashionable instruments typical of a destructive age', such as vibraphones and wind-machines.[152] Through

---

full, in translation. Many accounts of the Furtwängler incident misrepresent it by not paying attention to the particularities of the conductor's language; a typical example is Meyer, *The Politics of Music in the Third Reich*, 352.

[148] Paulding, '*Mathis der Maler*', 106.

[149] Breimann, '*Mathis der Maler*', 38; Kater, *The Twisted Muse*, 17.

[150] Skelton, *Paul Hindemith*, 126.

[151] Hindemith wrote to Willy Strecker of the book that he had 'the feeling that the whole thing will make an impression of inspiring confidence'; Strecker believed that the book would 'open some eyes' (letter of Hindemith to Strecker, 1st April 1937, and of Strecker to Hindemith, 8th March 1937. Hindemith Institut, Schott Briefwechsel).

[152] Strecker quoted in Skelton, *Paul Hindemith*, 127. Part of this letter is also in Breimann, '*Mathis der Maler*', 46–7. Strecker's comments, particularly about Jewish critics and fashionable instruments, are not wholly accurate. Strecker sent a draft to Hindemith, who according to Skelton, 'surprisingly approved it. He even made a hand-written addition to Strecker's list of his musical aims: "A search for concise expression, for clarity of melody and harmony."' Skelton says that this 'was an uncharacteristic moment of

all the attacks he had suffered, according to Strecker, Hindemith had 'dedicated himself without wavering' to his art and was 'at pains to serve German music to his best'.[153]

Such attempts by Hindemith and his colleagues could, of course, explain his involvement with the Nazis as simple opportunism. This is no doubt possible, especially as the true nature of the regime would not have been apparent to those living under it at the time (although some dubious elements would have been known about).[154] However, whatever Hindemith's motivation, he cannot have been wholly antipathetic to the National Socialists, as is often held, and nor can he be said to have gone into 'inner emigration'. Furtwängler, Strecker and Hindemith himself obviously believed that such campaigning would have an effect, and that their rulers would come to see the merits of Hindemith's music. As has been demonstrated, *Mathis der Maler* played on may favourite Nazi tropes, its concern for the *Volk* being the most notable, as well as being based on a historical event, the Peasants' War, which was admired in National Socialist circles.[155]

---

weakness which can perhaps most charitably be explained as a symptom of his current anxiety' (*Paul Hindemith*, 127).

[153] Quoted in Breimann, *'Mathis der Maler'*, 47.

[154] Bokina and Zenck both interpret Hindemith's actions as opportunism; Bokina writes that 'the choice of Grünewald as an opera subject may have...been an instance where opportunism meets principle. Hindemith hoped for a work that would be both popular and acceptable to the Nazi regime' ('Resignation, Retreat and Impotence', 172). Zenck comments that Hindemith 'definitely wanted a public and to find recognition as a German composer. To this end he was ready to let himself by used for the benefit of the disliked state, until he learnt to realise that making pacts weighed on his conscience' ('Zwischen Boykott und Anpassung', 117).

[155] Ibid., 126; Kater, *Composers of the Nazi Era*, 34. Albrecht Dümling notes that the songs of the Peasants' War, along with the music of Heinrich Schütz, was a model for many composers of the Nazi era (*Entartete Musik*, 31). Hindemith sometimes commented at this time that his motivation was to help German art: for instance, writing to the Streckers, he said that 'naturally, I consider it necessary to take German culture and particularly music to the outside world (*nach aussen*)' (Hindemith Institut, Schott Briefwechsel, 5th September 1933), and in a letter to Gustav Havemann of the *Reichsmusikkammer* he said that 'I continue...to write the best possible music, and I hope thereby to accomplish a better service to German art' (Hindemith Institut, Schott Briefwechsel, 3rd February 1935).

How far *Mathis* did appeal to National Socialist sensibilities is illustrated by the prevarication about its fate. Various officials had conflicting views about Hindemith and his music. The young Hindemith's tendency to *épater les bourgeois* had not done him any favours, despite his later retreat from such a stance. The leader of the *Kampfbund für deutsche Kultur*, Alfred Rosenberg, in particular disliked Hindemith's music, much of which was placed on the *Kampfbund*'s blacklist in 1933.[156] Other Nazis though, such as the Reich Propaganda Minister Goebbels, initially took a more lenient line, believing that keeping Hindemith on side would be useful to their own aims.[157] The *Kampfbund* was assimilated into the *NS-Kultur-gemeinde* (National Socialist Cultural Community) in June 1934, and this organisation itself expressed its dislike for Hindemith in November of that year; this led to fewer of his works being performed, as concert arrangers were careful not to fall foul of the regime.[158] Hindemith himself was not allowed to perform within Germany. An official ban on his works, on the instruction of Goebbels, did not come, though, until October 1936 (two years before his emigration), as part of a new campaign to 'clean up' music, although it was fought against by Hindemith's colleagues.[159] However, despite these events, the Nazis still hesitated over the fate of *Mathis der Maler*. In June 1936, officials from the *Reichstheaterkammer* met with the Propaganda Ministry to talk about the opera, having ordered two vocal scores and two librettos, and finally gave their consent to it being performed.[160] Once Rosenberg himself read the libretto of the opera in 1937,

---

[156] Breimann, *'Mathis der Maler'*, 33.

[157] Ibid., 34. Breimann states that the developing antagonism between Rosenberg and Goebbels during the 1930s was less about Hindemith himself or his music than it was a power struggle between two individuals who both believed they had responsibility for the musical life of the Third Reich (ibid., 37). Willy Strecker reported to Gertrud Hindemith in September 1935 that Goebbels had given his permission for the opera's first performance, and that only Rosenberg remained to be convinced (18th September 1935; Hindemith Institut, Schott Briefwechsel). Also see Painter, 'Symphonic Ambitions, Operatic Redemption', 132; John, *Musikbolschewismus*, 350–51; and Kater, *Composers of the Nazi Era*, 35.

[158] Breimann, *'Mathis der Maler'*, 36 and 38.

[159] Ibid., 50; Zenck, 'Zwischen Boykott und Anpassung', 101–2.

[160] Breimann, *'Mathis der Maler'*, 49. Also see Painter, 'Symphonic Ambitions, Operatic Redemption', 125.

he was, according to Skelton, 'completely converted. At any rate, he was now anxious that Hitler should at last be told the truth about the work, and there was even the suggestion of a meeting between Rosenberg and the composer'.[161]

While the Nazis prevaricated about the opera, it is apparent from the efforts made on his behalf, and with his full support, by his publishers and other friends, that the composer felt strongly that the work should have its first performance in Germany. Hindemith received offers to stage the premiere from opera houses outside Germany, including the Metropolitan Opera in New York, all of which he initially refused.[162] Even when the composer had moved to Switzerland and the premiere had taken place in Zurich, efforts continued to secure a performance in Germany: letters to and from Willy Strecker dating from the summer of 1939 report that occasional discussions were still being held with Nazi officials such as Goebbels and Goering, and Strecker seemed to be optimistic as to their outcome.[163]

Although Hindemith did have explicit dealings with the National Socialists, there are also instances where he appears to have been more equivocal towards them. For instance he decided to remain in the 'background' of the *Kraft durch Freude* organisation's educational project, cited above, rather than taking an official position.[164] Similarly, in 1934, he refused a position on the Music Committee of the group organising the Olympic games.[165] There are also a few instances of hostile language about the National Socialists in Hindemith's letters, such as when he refers to 'the

---

[161] Skelton, *Paul Hindemith*, 157. It is not clear why this consent was later withdrawn.

[162] Ludwig Strecker wrote to Hindemith on 9th May 1935 that there had been 'about ten' enquiries from abroad about the premiere of the opera; by the 4th June 1936 this had increased to 'about twenty' (Hindemith Institut, Schott Briefwechsel). A letter from the director of the Berlin Hochschule, Stein, to a Herr Oberst Gossrau of the Ministry for Air Transport, of 22nd December 1936, reports that the Metropolitan Opera has offered Hindemith a 'really fabulous sum' ('eine geradezu märchenhafte Summe') (Hindemith Institut, Akte Paul Hindemith 1927–1937 Musikhochschule Berlin, document 130–133).

[163] See for instance Strecker's letter to Ernst Praetorius, 15th May 1939, and Johannes Petschull's letter to Strecker of 17th April 1939 (Hindemith Institut, Schott Briefwechsel), as well as others from this period. Also see Kater, *Composers of the Nazi Era*, 46.

[164] Breimann, *'Mathis der Maler'*, 35; Hindemith, *Letters*, 77 (9th February 1934).

[165] Breimann, *'Mathis der Maler'*, 37.

swamp of musical life' in 1936, or when in 1933 he wrote, after his meeting with *Kampfbund* officials, that he did not wish to 'curry favour' in these quarters.[166] He also expressed reservations about his previous collaborator Benn's conversion to Nazism in 1933, saying he seemed to 'have been completely dragged into things', and that 'he could have gone more slowly with offering the kiss of comradeship'. He thought that Benn would be 'disappointed' after a few months.[167] Given Hindemith's difficulties with the regime, his occasional reservations are, perhaps, not surprising; what is more surprising is that he went on trying to work with the Nazis for as long as he did. This fact points to his political naïveté, that he thought an accommodation with the regime might still be possible. Many writers have also held that the book-burning scene in Tableau 3 of *Mathis* is an anti-Nazi comment.[168] However, it may be suggested that the book-burning scene, the most overt reference to contemporary politics within the opera, is strangely equivocal. It seems inconceivable that anyone seeing the opera would have failed to notice the reference to the Nazis' burning of 'un-German' books, which took place in Berlin in May 1933, yet the presentation of the Catholics' burning of Protestant literature is not much more than background colour within the opera, albeit with condemnation of the event by the Lutherans which could, perhaps, be interpreted as Hindemith's own comment on the book-burning in Berlin. In general, though, this event has little relevance to either the main plot of the opera, Mathis's artistic dilemma, or the subsidiary plot of Albrecht's financial difficulties.

Hindemith's engagement with the political forces of the Third Reich casts a different light on *Mathis der Maler*, and supports the view of Mathis

---

[166] Ibid., 49; letter of Hindemith to Willy Strecker, 29th June 1936 (Hindemith Institut, Schott Briefwechsel); and Hindemith, *Letters*, 69 (15th April 1933). However, his comment about the 'swamp' appears in the same letter where he reports having accepted the commission from the *Luftwaffe*.

[167] Hindemith, *'Das private Logbuch': Briefe an seine Frau Gertrud*, ed. Friederike Becker and Giselher Schubert (Mainz: Schott/Munich: Piper, 1995), 101 (25th May 1933). According to Hindemith's erstwhile student Franz Reizenstein, Hindemith expressed his opposition to the Nazis during his Hochschule classes in the thirties; how far Reizenstein's report (written in 1965) can be trusted remains a matter for speculation; see Kater, *Composers of the Nazi Era*, 34.

[168] For instance, Kemp, *Hindemith*, 28 and 30, and Meyer, *The Politics of Music in the Third Reich*, 132.

as remaining political through his art. The figure of Mathis can, perhaps, be aligned with his creator, but only partially: the way in which Hindemith sought to use his art actively within the real world is different from how Mathis merely hopes his painting will speak to the people. Hindemith's engagement with society through art was altogether more active than Mathis's. Nevertheless, the composer and the fictional artist still have in common their wish to use art to help ordinary people, and in this, Mathis functions as a persona for Hindemith. Indeed, Hindemith's belief in art, and particularly in *Gebrauchsmusik*, as a means to combat the isolation of the contemporary composer from his or her audience and to bring the public spiritual succour, makes an interpretation of the opera in terms of 'retreat' unlikely: if Mathis is interpreted as removing himself from society, then the opera advocates a separation of the artist from the world which directly contradicts what Hindemith expressed elsewhere, and what he practised in his own life. Through Mathis, Hindemith constructs an artistic ideal who 'gives his best to his fellow men' in order to point them towards a higher, more spiritual plane, and which he sought to realise himself.[169]

This aesthetic idealism is political, and yet ambiguous: the opera reflects the complexities of the situation in which it was written, and the resultant difficulties in interpreting its composer's ideology. The Utopia presented in *Mathis* may be read as having elements in common with the Utopia advocated by National Socialism, and the rhetoric of the opera, with its accent on the *Volk*, may be seen as concordant with the ideas of the NSDAP. At the same time it is also more conventionally 'socialist', thanks to the ambiguity between the left-wing socialism to which we are accustomed and the exclusive 'socialism' of the right. The equivocal nature of Hindemith's political context helps to elucidate the opera itself, as well as going some way towards clarifying the composer's own activities during the Third Reich: Hindemith is shown as a man who at first thought the Nazis shared his own vision of an ideal society, and who was only later disabused of this belief.

---

[169] Hindemith, *A Composer's World*, 220.

5 Conclusion: Artistic Identity as Performative

As the previous three chapters have demonstrated, *Palestrina*, *Jonny spielt auf* and *Mathis der Maler* are succinct articulations of their era's concerns about the role of art and the artist in modern society. The three works have several common themes: the position of the artist towards his audience, the wish (or otherwise) for recognition, a reaction to modernity and Romanticism, and the creation of some kind of artistic Utopia. How far these characteristics are applicable to all operas which have a central artist figure is debatable: indeed, if one considers the diversity of works written in this period (as detailed in the Appendix), one can probably point to few common features which are present in all of the works, beyond the fact of them having an artist character. The 'traditional' definition of the *Künstleroper* (taken from studies of the *Künstlerroman*), which states that the artist is specifically dissatisfied with his relationship to society, is apparent in only a limited number of works, including those three considered here. But while not all works with a central artist character are, according to this strict definition, true artist-operas, the inclusion of such a figure nevertheless raises interesting questions, about the composer's understanding of himself, and about the way in which the fictional character might convey the artist's process of self-construction.

One way of interpreting an artist-opera might be to say that the artist figure 'expresses' what the real composer actually thought and felt; that it is 'autobiographical'. On one level, one could say that this is indeed the case – with Pfitzner's, Krenek's and Hindemith's operas, after all, there is some degree of consistency between what the composers say about art and the way in which their characters act. However, such an interpretation neglects one crucial point, namely, that we cannot know what the composer actually thought or felt; what he might say, in or about his art, does not possess any essential truth. Rather, any statements about art (through writings or, in the case of modern-day artists, broadcasts) are already themselves a kind of artistic creation: they configure an image of the artist for public consumption, and create a persona for that individual. Private documents, such as letters or diaries, are also co-opted, particularly in the twentieth century when artists became highly aware of the possibility that they might one day be the subject of biography, and were therefore acting 'publicly' even in these seemingly 'private' realms.[1] The recipients of these public statements may (and generally do) take them to articulate the real beliefs of the artist, but this is by no means a necessary move; public statements about art, just like the art works themselves, are fictive, possessing nothing which can really be said to *express* the artist, and his or her feelings, but which rather, like the art works themselves, articulate a persona. While the art works and the statements about art may be consistent with each other, neither possess an intrinsic 'truth'. The artist-opera is revealing because it makes this construction of a persona transparent, through its use of an actual (yet clearly fictional) artist character on stage.

Thus the artistic persona which is demonstrated to the world is not necessarily the 'real' person. While this assertion might be fairly readily accepted, we can go further, and suggest that, if one were to strip away the layers, to remove the public persona of the artist, one would find no intrinsic essence underneath, only more and more levels of personae. There is no 'genuine' person underneath who does not act himself out, but only a continual series of actings-out; the individual is constituted *through what he acts out*. (This could be said to be true for everyone, not just artists.) This idea is based on Judith Butler's theory of gender, which was mentioned in Chapter 1: for Butler, one 'becomes' one's gender through acting in the socially prescribed manner for that gender. This concept can be applied to other aspects of identity: so one 'becomes' an artist through acting in the socially prescribed manner for artists. Artistic creation is an act of self-construction, presenting a persona not only to an audience, but to oneself. According to Butler, there are usually two genders which one can act out, which need not correspond to one's biological sex;[2] similarly, there are various artistic identities from which one can choose – the populist, the

---

[1] Such formation of a persona happens for anyone who operates within the public realm, of course, not only artists.

[2] Butler in fact wishes to explode the idea that there are only two possible genders, seeing this as itself a social construction (*Gender Trouble, passim*).

aesthete, the modernist, etc. Thus, both gender and artistic identity are performative. One does not, usually, choose one's gender identity, rather it is imposed through enculturation; nevertheless, it is possible to choose to reject one's gendering. Similarly, it is debatable how far an artist consciously chooses his or her artistic identity, or whether this too is enculturated. But just as one can discard one's gendering, one can also choose to reject a particular way of 'being an artist'. This is what happens with many composers of the early twentieth century: those who refuse Romanticism, for instance, may refuse not only its musical style but also the trappings of the Romantic artist-ideal, and the associated beliefs concerning the alleged purpose of music.

Following this model, how one acts determines who one is; one is always creating, and performing, one's persona. For a composer, this acting-out encompasses one's behaviour, one's aesthetic and political ideology, and one's compositional style. So, for instance, there is usually a close link between the style of the work and the personal ideology of the artist: the former makes manifest the latter. An artist who espouses a modernist aesthetic, believing that art should be rigorous, autonomous, and should follow its own internal logic, will produce art works which are consistent with that aesthetic. The aesthetic ideal, and the way this is expressed artistically, must not necessarily be linked, but through their ideological association, the two reinforce each other, and give the artist the status of a 'modernist'.[3]

To look for the 'real' composer who expresses himself through the mechanism of the artist-figure is therefore to search in vain – there is no 'real' composer, and nothing intrinsic to express. The composer only becomes something like 'real' through acting himself out in various ways, of which making an artist-character might be one. Krenek's career is particularly pertinent in this respect; his change in musical style from his early modernist works to his popular *Jonny spielt auf* has already been discussed. After *Jonny* though, he moved to a 'neo-Romantic' tonal style, as in *Reisebuch aus den österreichischen Alpen*, and then to modernism, primarily using serial technique, which made its first appearance in the *Gesänge des späten Jahres* of 1931. His shifts in compositional style were accompanied

---

[3] This contrasts with Cone's use of 'persona' in *The Composer's Voice*: rather than the persona of the composer being expressed in the music, as Cone suggests, the musical style of the composer functions (along with other elements) to constitute the artistic persona.

by written justifications of his change of direction; in the case of his move to serialism, for example, this was expressed in terms of the necessity for the audience to 'come up' to his level, rather than him 'going down' to them.[4] The close relationship of musical style and aesthetic beliefs is evident here.

Krenek's changes in style point to the ideological basis of the belief that a composer must possess one single compositional identity, or 'voice', which is articulated through his works. The ideology of the artist demands that a genuine, mature composer (as opposed to a mere pasticher) possesses one single 'voice', which is identifiable, original and unique, and which does not essentially change over the artist's lifetime.[5] Krenek, though, unlike most canonic composers, was not stylistically consistent, and it is possible that it is his lack of these qualities that has resulted in him not generally being recognised as a composer of the first rank.[6] But while the ideology of the artist demands consistency, it nevertheless allows for some variation: one could argue, perhaps, that Mozart's Requiem presents a different 'voice' from his *Eine kleine Nachtmusik*, and that with these two works, Mozart constructs himself as two different kinds of artist. Krenek's more dramatic changes of style are only more extreme, and thereby illustrate

---

[4] His friendship with Adorno seemed to have been a crucial factor in his change of perspective. For instances of his revised aesthetic, see the essays 'The Freedom of the Human Spirit' (1932) and 'The Ivory Tower' (1944), both in *Exploring Music*, and 'Self-Analysis'.

[5] Any mention of voice must be placed within the context of the work of Cone (*The Composer's Voice*), and of Carolyn Abbate (*Unsung Voices: Opera and Musical Narrative in the Nineteenth Century* (Princeton: Princeton University Press, 1991)). Both Cone and Abbate take 'voice' to signify a presence within the music (in Cone's case, this voice expresses the persona of the composer; for Abbate, music creates independent, self-sufficient 'voices', irrespective of the intentions of the composer). Here, though, I use 'voice' more generally, to mean a composer's personal, individual style. For a critique of 'originality', see Lawrence Kramer: *Musical Meaning: Toward a Critical History* (Berkeley, Los Angeles and London: University of California Press, 2002), chapter 12.

[6] One of Krenek's last works, *The Dissembler*, reveals his own awareness of the self-constructedness of artistic identity: the text of the work tells of personae, acting, and masks, and interrogates the nature of 'truth'. The same phenomenon of a significant change in style can be found with other composers, for instance Weill, who made a clear shift when he moved from Germany to America. While he has arguably achieved more recognition than Krenek, the 'two Weills problem' has preoccupied many Weill scholars.

what degree of variation is 'permissible' for a composer. However, to search for a fundamental *essence* underlying these different works, whether by Mozart or Krenek, is to subscribe to an ideology which demands consistency and individuality from the artist.

The value of the artist-opera is that it demonstrates this process of artistic self-construction, and the composer's wish to position himself in relation to a particular ideal of what an artist is. The composer's stated beliefs about art and society, the plot of the opera and the musical style used all work together in order for the artist to act out his chosen identity. While the early twentieth-century examples of the genre are fascinating precisely because they come at a time when the notion of artistry was in dispute, they are representative of a much wider phenomenon. The artist-opera not only tells us something about a composer or his society, but about the nature of what it means to become an artist.

Appendix

German Operas Written Between 1912 and 1935 Featuring Artists or the Idea of Art

1912: Schreker: *Der ferne Klang* (Composer – Fritz)
 Strauss: *Ariadne auf Naxos* ('The Composer'. Also a Music Teacher, a Dancing Teacher, a Primadonna, and actors.)
1913: Schoenberg: *Die glückliche Hand* ('The Man' makes jewels.)
 Schreker: *Das Spielwerk und die Prinzessin* (Centres around the mechanical instrument created by Meister Florian, and the ability of the 'Wandering Youth' to make it sound when he plays his flute.)
1915: Pfitzner: *Palestrina* (Composer)
1917: Busoni: *Arlecchino* (Singer – Leandro)
1918: Schreker: *Die Gezeichneten* (Painter – Carlotta. Also Alviano, who has created a wonderful garden.)
1920: Schreker: *Der Schatzgräber* (Minstrel – Elis)
1923: Krenek: *Orpheus und Eurydike*
 Krenek: *Der Sprung über den Schatten* (Poet – Goldhaar)
 Schreker: *Irrelohe* (Musician – Christobald)
1924: Strauss: *Intermezzo* ('Kappellmeister' Robert Storch)
1925: Weill: *Der Protagonist* (A group of actors)
1926: Hindemith: *Cardillac* (Jeweller – Cardillac)
 Krenek: *Jonny spielt auf* (Composer – Max; Jazz musician – Jonny)
1927: Schreker: *Der singende Teufel* (Organist/Organ Builder – Amandus)
1929: Schreker: *Christophorus* (About a group of music students and their teacher.)
1935: Hindemith: *Mathis der Maler* (Painter – Mathis)
 Berg: *Lulu* (Composer – Alwa)

Bibliography

Abbate, Carolyn (1991), *Unsung Voices: Opera and Musical Narrative in the Nineteenth Century*, Princeton: Princeton University Press.

Abendroth, Walter and Danler, Karl-Robert (eds) (n.d. [1969]), *Festschrift aus Anlaß des 100. Geburtstags am 5. Mai 1969 und des 20. Todestags am 22. Mai 1969 von Hans Pfitzner*, Munich: Peter Winkler Verlag.

Adamy, Bernhard (1980), *Hans Pfitzner: Literatur, Philosophie und Zeitgeschehen in seinem Weltbild und Werk*, Tutzing: Hans Schneider.

——————— (1984), 'Das *Palestrina*-Textbuch als Dichtung', in Wolfgang Osthoff (ed.), *Symposium Hans Pfitzner, Berlin 1981*, Tutzing: Hans Schneider, pp.21–65.

Adorno, Theodor W. (1973), *Philosophy of Modern Music*, London: Sheed and Ward.

Adorno, Theodor W. and Krenek, Ernst (1974), *Briefwechsel*, ed. Wolfgang Rogge, Frankfurt a.M.: Suhrkamp.

Alter, Robert (1975), *Partial Magic: The Novel as a Self-Conscious Genre*, Berkeley, Los Angeles and London: University of California Press.

Amidon, Kevin Scott (2001), *'Nirgends brennen wir genauer': Institution, Experiment, and Crisis in the German* Zeitoper, *1924–31*, University of Princeton: Ph.D. dissertation.

Andreski, Stanislav (1980), 'Fascists as Moderates', in Stein Ugelvik Larsen et al. (eds), *Who Were the Fascists: Social Roots of European Fascism*, Oslo: Universitetsforlaget, pp.52–5.

Arblaster, Anthony (1992), *Viva la Libertà! Politics in Opera*, London and New York: Verso.

Ashley, Tim (1995), 'An Act of Necessity', in Royal Opera House Programme for *Mathis der Maler*, Nov.–Dec. 1995, London: Royal Opera House Publications, pp.22–7.

——————— (1997), 'In Sympathy with Death', *Opera* (January), pp.33–9.

Attinello, Paul (1995), 'Pfitzner, *Palestrina*, Nazis, Conservatives: Longing for Utopia', *Journal of Musicological Research*, Vol.15, pp.25–53.

Auner, Joseph Henry (2000), '"Soulless Machines" and Steppenwolves:

Renegotiating Masculinity in Krenek's *Jonny spielt auf*, in Mary Ann Smart (ed.), *Siren Songs: Representations of Gender and Sexuality in Opera*, Princeton: Princeton University Press, pp.222-36.

Bailey, Kathryn (ed.) (1996), *Webern Studies*, Cambridge: Cambridge University Press.

Baresel, Alfred (1926), 'Kunst, Technik und Publikum', *Anbruch*, Vol.8 no.2, pp.61–2.

Becker, Friederike (1997), 'Des Künstlers Entsagung. Die "Dichtung" *Mathis der Maler*, ihre Entstehungsgeschichte und einige kritische Anmerkungen zur Legendenbildung um Paul Hindemiths Libretto', in Giselher Schubert (ed.), *Biographische Konstellation und künstlerisches Handeln*, Mainz: Schott, pp.128–57.

Beebe, Maurice (1964), *Ivory Towers and Sacred Founts: The Artist as Hero in Fiction from Goethe to Joyce*, New York: New York University Press.

Bekker, Paul (1918), *Die Sinfonie von Beethoven bis Mahler*, Berlin: Schuster and Loeffler.

——————— (1919), *Das deutsche Musikleben*, Berlin: Schuster and Loeffler.

——————— (1921), *Kritische Zeitbilder*, Berlin: Schuster and Loeffler.

Benjamin, Walter (1970), 'The Work of Art in the Age of Mechanical Reproduction', in *Illuminations*, ed. and intro. Hannah Arendt, trans. Harry Zohn, n.p.: Fontana/Collins, pp.219–53.

Benn, Gottfried (1978), *Briefwechsel mit Paul Hindemith*, ed. Ann Clark Fehn, Wiesbaden: Limes Verlag.

Benvenuto, Bice and Kennedy, Roger (1986), *The Works of Jacques Lacan: An Introduction*, London: Free Association Books.

Berg, Alban and Schoenberg, Arnold (1987), *The Berg–Schoenberg Correspondence: Selected Letters*, ed. Juliane Brand, Christopher Hailey and Donald Harris, London: Macmillan.

Berghahn, Volker R. (1994), *Imperial Germany, 1871–1914: Economy, Society, Culture, and Politics*, Providence and Oxford: Berghahn Books.

Berlioz, Hector (1929), *Evenings in the Orchestra*, trans. Charles E. Roche, New York and London: Alfred A. Knopf.

Berman, Marshall (1982), *All That is Solid Melts Into Air: The Experience of Modernity*, New York: Simon and Schuster.

Blackbourn, David (1997), *The Fontana History of Germany, 1780–1918: The Long Nineteenth Century*, London: Fontana Press.

Böhme, Franz M. (1966), *Altdeutsches Liederbuch: Volkslieder der Deutschen nach Wort und Weise aus dem 12. bis zum 17. Jahrhundert*, Hildesheim: Georg Olms (Original edition: Leipzig, 1877).

Bokina, John (1988), 'Resignation, Retreat and Impotence: The Aesthetics and Politics of the Modern German Artist-Opera', *Cultural Critique*, Vol.9 (Spring), pp.157–95.

———— (1997), *Opera and Politics: From Monteverdi to Henze*, New Haven and London: Yale University Press.

Botstein, Leon (1985), *Music and its Public: Habits of Listening and the Crisis of Musical Modernism in Vienna, 1870–1914*, University of Harvard, Ph.D. dissertation.

———— (2001), 'Pfitzner and Musical Politics', *Musical Quarterly*, Vol.85 no.1 (Spring), pp.63–75.

Bracher, Karl Dietrich (1973), *The German Dictatorship: The Origins, Structure and Consequences of National Socialism*, Harmondsworth: Penguin.

Bradbury, Malcolm and McFarlane, James (1976), *Modernism 1890–1930*, Harmondsworth: Penguin.

Brand, Juliane and Hailey, Christopher (eds) (1997), *Constructive Dissonance: Arnold Schoenberg and the Transformations of Twentieth-Century Culture*, Berkeley, Los Angeles and London: University of California Press.

Brantner, Christina (1991), *Robert Schumann und das Tonkünstler-Bild der Romantiker*, New York: P. Lang.

Breimann, Gudrun (1997), *'Mathis der Maler' und der 'Fall Hindemith': Studien zu Hindemiths Opernlibretto im Kontext der kulturgeschichtlichen und politischen Bedingungen der dreißiger Jahre*, Frankfurt a.M.: Peter Lang.

Briner, Andres (1970), 'Entstehung und Aussage der Oper "Mathis der Maler"', *Melos*, Vol.37, pp.437–46.

———— (1971), *Paul Hindemith*, Mainz: Schott.

———— (1978), 'Ich und Wir – Zur Entwicklung des jungen Paul Hindemith', in Dieter Rexroth (ed.), *Erprobungen und Erfahrungen: Zu Paul Hindemith's Schaffen in den Zwanziger Jahren*, Mainz: B. Schott's Söhne, pp.27–34.

Brinkmann, Reinhold (1997), 'Schoenberg the Contemporary. A View from Behind', in Juliane Brand and Christopher Hailey (eds), *Constructive Dissonance: Arnold Schoenberg and the Transformations of Twentieth-*

Century Culture, Berkeley, Los Angeles and London: University of California Press, pp. 196–219.

Bruhn, Siglind (1998), *The Temptation of Paul Hindemith:* Mathis der Maler *as a Spiritual Testimony*, Stuyvesant, NY: Pendragon Press.

Budde, Elmar and Stephan, Rudolph (eds) (1980), *Franz-Schreker-Symposion*, Schriftenreihe der Hochschule der Künste Berlin, Berlin: Colloquium Verlag.

Bullivant, Keith (ed.) (1977), *Culture and Society in the Weimar Republic*, Manchester: Manchester University Press.

Bullmann, Franz, Rathert, Wolfgang and Schenk, Dietmar (eds) (1997), *Paul Hindemith in Berlin: Essays und Dokumente*, Berlin: Hochschule der Künste.

Burns, Rob (ed.) (1995), *German Cultural Studies: An Introduction*, Oxford: Oxford University Press.

Busoni, Ferruccio (1987), *Selected Letters*, trans., ed. and intro. Antony Beaumont, New York: Columbia University Press.

Butler, Christopher (1994), *Early Modernism: Literature, Music and Painting in Europe, 1900–1916*, Oxford: Clarendon Press.

Butler, Judith (1990), *Gender Trouble: Feminism and the Subversion of Identity*, New York and London: Routledge.

Carner, Mosco (1977), 'Pfitzner v. Berg, or Inspiration v. Analysis', *Musical Times*, Vol.118 (May), pp.379–80.

Carr, William (1979), *A History of Germany 1815–1945*, Second Edition, London: Edward Arnold.

Chanan, Michael (1995), *Repeated Takes: A Short History of Recording and its Effects on Music*, London: Verso.

Clarke, Suzannah and Rehding, Alexander (eds) (2001), *Music Theory and Natural Order from the Renaissance to the Early Twentieth Century*, Cambridge: Cambridge University Press.

Cone, Edward T. (1974), *The Composer's Voice*, Berkeley, Los Angeles and London: University of California Press.

Cook, Susan C. (1988), *Opera for a New Republic: The* Zeitopern *of Krenek, Weill and Hindemith*, Ann Arbor: UMI Research Press.

Csobádi, Peter et al. (eds) (1990), *Antike Mythen im Musiktheater des 20. Jahrhunderts: Gesammelte Vorträge des Salzburger Symposions 1989*, Anif/Salzburg: Verlag Ursula Müller-Speiser.

Dasatiel, Dr. Jos. A. [sic] (1921), 'Die musikalischen Krise der Gegenwart', *Anbruch*, Vol.3 no.17–18, pp.304–6.

Del Mar, Norman (1986), *Richard Strauss. A Critical Commentary on His Life and Works*, London and Boston: Faber and Faber.

Dennis, David B. (1996), *Beethoven in German Politics, 1870–1989*, New Haven and London: Yale University Press.

Diettrich, Eva (1982), 'Auf den Spuren zu Jonnys Erfolg', in Otto Kolleritsch (ed.), *Ernst Krenek*, Vienna: Universal Edition, pp.119–24.

Drew, David (1961–2), 'Musical Theatre in the Weimar Republic', *Proceedings of the Royal Musical Association*, Vol.88, pp.89–108.

———————— (1987), *Kurt Weill: A Handbook*, London and Boston: Faber and Faber.

Dümling, Albrecht (1977), 'Symbol des Fortschritts, der Dekadenz und der Unterdrückung. Zum Bedeutungswandel des Jazz in den zwanziger Jahren', in Dietrich Stern (ed.), *Angewandte Musik 20er Jahre: Exemplarische Versuche gesellschaftsbezogener musikalischer Arbeit für Theater, Film, Radio, Massenveranstaltung*, Berlin: Argument-Verlag, pp.81–100.

———————— (1981), '"Im Zeichen der Erkenntnis der socialen Verhältnisse": Der junge Schönberg und die Arbeitersängerbewegung in Österreich', *Österreichische Musikzeitschrift*, Vol.36 no.2 (February), pp.65–73.

———————— (ed.) (n.d. [1988]), *Banned by the Nazis: Entartete Musik* (catalogue of 1988 exhibition of the same name), Berlin: Department of Cultural Affairs.

———————— (ed.) (1988), *Entartete Musik: Zur Düsseldorfer Ausstellung von 1938* (catalogue of 1988 exhibition of the same name), Düsseldorf: n.p.

Dunsby, Jonathan (1992), *Schoenberg:* Pierrot Lunaire, Cambridge: Cambridge University Press.

Eichner, Hans (1978), 'Thomas Mann and Politics', in Hans H. Schulte and Gerald Chapple (eds), *Thomas Mann: Ein Kolloquium*, Bonn: Bouvier Verlag Herbert Grundmann, pp.5–19.

Einstein, Alfred (1947), *Music in the Romantic Era*, London: J.M. Dent and Sons Ltd.

Eisler, Hanns (1973), *Musik und Politik: Schriften 1924–1948*, ed. Günter Mayer, Munich: Rogner and Bernhard.

Eley, Geoff (1986), *From Unification to Nazism: Reinterpreting the German Past*, London and New York: Routledge.

Ellis, Katharine (2002), 'The Structures of Musical Life', in Jim Samson (ed.), *The Cambridge History of Nineteenth-Century Music*, Cambridge: Cambridge University Press, pp.343–70.

Ermen, Reinhard (1986), *Musik als Einfall: Hans Pfitzners Position im ästhetischen Diskurs nach Wagner*, Aachen: Rimbaud Presse.

———————— (ed.) (1984), *Franz Schreker (1878–1934) zum 50.Todestag*, Aachen: Rimbaud Presse.

Evans, Richard J. (1987), *Rethinking German History: Nineteenth-Century Germany and the Origins of the Third Reich*, London: Unwin Hyman.

Feuchtwanger, E.J. (1993), *From Weimar to Hitler: Germany, 1918–1933*, London: Macmillan.

Franklin, Peter (1982–3), 'Style, Structure and Taste: Three Aspects of the Problem of Franz Schreker', *Proceedings of the Royal Musical Association*, Vol.59, pp.134–46.

———————— (1984), '*Palestrina* and the Dangerous Futurists', *Musical Quarterly*, Vol.70 no.4, pp.499–514.

———————— (1985), *The Idea of Music: Schoenberg and Others*, London: Macmillan.

———————— (1989), 'Audiences, Critics and the Depurification of Music: Reflections on a 1920s Controversy', *Journal of the Royal Musical Association*, Vol.114, pp.80–91.

———————— (1997), 'A Musical Legend', in Royal Opera House Programme for *Palestrina*, Jan.–Feb. 1997, London: Royal Opera House Publications, pp.12–17.

Friedrich, Otto (1974), *Before the Deluge: A Portrait of Berlin in the 1920s*, London: Michael Joseph.

Frosh, Stephen (1991), *Identity Crisis: Modernity, Psychoanalysis and the Self*, London: Macmillan.

Gay, Peter (1968), *Weimar Culture: The Outsider as Insider*, London: Secker and Warburg.

Gieseler, Walter (1980), '"Was an der Zeit ist". Versuch einer Annäherung an Kreneks Musikdenken', *Musica* Vol.34 no.2, pp.127–31.

Gilliam, Bryan (1994), 'Stage and Screen: Kurt Weill and Operatic Reform in the 1920s', in Bryan Gilliam (ed.), *Music and Performance during the Weimar Republic*, Cambridge Studies in Performance Practice 3, Cambridge: Cambridge University Press, pp.1–12.

———————— (ed.) (1994), *Music and Performance during the Weimar Republic*, Cambridge Studies in Performance Practice 3, Cambridge: Cambridge University Press.

Goebbels, Josef (1925), 'Nationalsozialismus oder Bolschewismus?', *NS-Briefe*, 25th October 1925, trans. as 'National Socialism or Bolshevism?' in Anton Kaes, Martin Jay and Edward Dimendberg (eds) (1994), *The Weimar Republic Sourcebook*, Berkeley, Los Angeles and London: University of California Press, pp.127–9.

————— (1930), 'Warum sind wir Judengegner?', in *Die verfluchten Hakenkreuzler: Etwas zum Nachdenken*, Munich: Franz Eher Nachfolger, pp.1–28, trans. as 'Why are We Enemies of the Jews?' in Anton Kaes, Martin Jay and Edward Dimendberg (eds) (1994), *The Weimar Republic Sourcebook*, Berkeley, Los Angeles and London: University of California Press, pp.137–8.

Goehr, Lydia (1994), 'Political Music and the Politics of Music', *Journal of Aesthetics and Art Criticism*, Vol.52 no.1, pp.99–112.

Goldschmidt, Helene (1925), *Das deutsche Künstlerdrama von Goethe bis R. Wagner*, Weimar: Alexander Duncker Verlag.

Gregor-Dellin, Martin (1983), *Richard Wagner: His Life, His Work, His Century*, trans. J. Maxwell Brownjohn, London: Collins.

Grosch, Nils (1999), *Die Musik der Neuen Sachlichkeit*, Stuttgart and Weimar: Verlag J.B. Metzler.

Griffin, Roger (ed.) (1995), *Fascism*, Oxford Readers Series, Oxford and New York: Oxford University Press.

Griffiths, Paul (1980), 'Webern', in *The New Grove: Second Viennese School*, London: Macmillan.

Guttsmann, W.L. (1990), *Workers' Culture in Weimar Germany: Between Tradition and Commitment*, New York: Berg.

Hailey, Christopher (1986): 'Creating a Public, Addressing a Market: Kurt Weill and Universal Edition', in Kim H. Kowalke (ed.), *A New Orpheus: Essays on Kurt Weill*, New Haven and London: Yale University Press, pp.21–35.

————— (1993), *Franz Schreker, 1878–1934: A Cultural Biography*, Cambridge: Cambridge University Press.

————— (1994), 'Rethinking Sound: Music and Radio in Weimar Germany', in Bryan Gilliam (ed.), *Music and Performance during the Weimar Republic*, Cambridge Studies in Performance Practice 3, Cambridge: Cambridge University Press, pp.13–36.

Hausdörfer, Sabrina (1987), *Rebellion im Kunstschein: Die Funktion des fiktiven Künstlers in Roman und Kunsttheorie der deutschen Romantik*, Heidelberg: Carl Winter Universitätsverlag.

Heister, Hanns-Werner and Klein, Hans-Günter (eds) (1984), *Musik und Musikpolitik im faschistischen Deutschland*, Frankfurt a.M.: Taschenbuch Verlag.

Heller, Berndt and Reininghaus, Frieder (1984), 'Hindemiths heikle Jahre. Eine Dokumentation', *Neue Zeitschrift für Musik*, Vol.145 no.5, pp.4–10.

Heller, Erich (1958), *Thomas Mann: The Ironic German*, Cambridge: Cambridge University Press.

Henderson, Donald (1970), 'Hans Pfitzner's *Palestrina*: A Twentieth-Century Allegory', *Music Review*, pp.32–43.

Hermand, Jost and Trommler, Frank (1978), *Die Kultur der Weimarer Republik*, Munich: Nymphenburger Verlagshandlung.

Hindemith, Paul (1932), 'Forderungen an den Laien', *Auftakt*, Vol.12, pp.137–8.

———— (1945), *The Craft of Musical Composition. Book 1: Theoretical Part*, trans. Arthur Mendel, Fourth Edition, New York: Associated Music Publishers and London: Schott and Co.

———— (1952), *A Composer's World: Horizons and Limitations*, Cambridge, Mass.: Harvard University Press.

———— (1965), *Mathis der Maler. Oper in sieben Bildern*, Studien-Partitur, Mainz: B. Schott's Söhne.

———— (1982), *Briefe*, ed. Dieter Rexroth, Frankfurt a.M.: Fischer Taschenbuch Verlag.

———— (1995), *Selected Letters of Paul Hindemith*, ed. and trans. Geoffrey Skelton, New Haven and London: Yale University Press.

———— (1995), *'Das Private Logbuch': Briefe an seine Frau Gertrud*, ed. Friederike Becker and Giselher Schubert, Mainz: Schott and Munich: Piper.

Hinton, Stephen (1985), '"Musik nach Maß": Zum Begriff der Gebrauchsmusik bei Paul Hindemith', *Musica*, Vol.39 no.2, pp.146–50.

———— (1989), *The Idea of Gebrauchsmusik: A Study of Musical Aesthetics in the Weimar Republic (1919–1933) with Particular Reference to the Works of Paul Hindemith*, New York: Garland.

Hoffmann, Bernd (1995), 'Alptraum der Freiheit oder: Die Zeitfrage "Jazz"', in Helmut Rösing (ed.), *'Es liegt in der Luft was Idiotisches...': Populäre Musik zur Zeit der Weimarer Republik*, Baden-Baden: Coda, pp.69–81.

Hofmüller, Max (1927), 'Opernkrise und Stilpflege', *Anbruch*, Vol.9 no.1–

2, pp.29–34.

Jay, Martin (1984), *Adorno*, Cambridge, Mass.: Harvard University Press.

John, Eckhard (1994), *Musikbolschewismus: Die Politisierung der Musik in Deutschland 1918–1938*, Stuttgart and Weimar: Verlag J.B. Metzler.

Jung, Edgar J. (1932), 'Deutschland und die Konservative [sic] Revolution', in *Deutsche über Deutschland*, Munich: Albert Langen, pp.369–82, trans. as 'Germany and the Conservative Revolution' in Anton Kaes, Martin Jay and Edward Dimendberg (eds) (1994), *The Weimar Republic Sourcebook*, Berkeley, Los Angeles and London: University of California Press, pp.352–4.

Kaes, Anton, Jay, Martin and Dimendberg, Edward (eds) (1994), *The Weimar Republic Sourcebook*, Berkeley, Los Angeles and London: University of California Press.

Kater, Michael H. (1988), 'The Jazz Experience in Weimar Germany', *German History*, Vol.6, pp.145–58.

———— (1992), *Different Drummers: Jazz in the Culture of Nazi Germany*, New York and Oxford: Oxford University Press.

———— (1997), *The Twisted Muse: Musicians and Their Music in the Third Reich*, New York and Oxford: Oxford University Press.

———— (2000), *Composers of the Nazi Era: Eight Portraits*, New York and Oxford: Oxford University Press.

Kayser, Rudolf (1925), 'Amerikanismus', *Vössische Zeitung* no.458 (27th September 1925), trans. as 'Americanism' in Anton Kaes, Martin Jay and Edward Dimendberg (eds) (1994), *The Weimar Republic Sourcebook*, Berkeley, Los Angeles and London: University of California Press, pp.395–7.

Keller, Ernst (1965), *Der unpolitische Deutsche: Eine Studie zu den 'Betrachtungen eines Unpolitischen' von Thomas Mann*, Berlin: Francke Verlag.

Kemp, Ian (1970) *Hindemith*, Oxford Studies of Composers 6, London: Oxford University Press.

Kienzle, Ulrike (1998), *Das Trauma hinter dem Traum: Franz Schrekers Oper 'Der ferne Klang' und die Wiener Moderne*, Schliengen: Edition Argus.

Knessl, Lothar (1967), *Ernst Krenek*, Vienna: Elisabeth Lafite.

Koebner, Thomas (1978), 'Die Zeitoper in den zwaniger Jahren: Gedanken zu ihrer Geschichte und Theorie', in Dieter Rexroth (ed.), *Erprobungen und Erfahrungen: Zu Paul Hindemith's Schaffen in den Zwanziger*

Jahren, Mainz: Schott, pp.60–115.

Kolleritsch, Otto (ed.) (1978), *Franz Schreker: Am Beginn der Neuen Musik*, Graz: Universal Edition.

————— (ed.) (1982), *Ernst Krenek*, Vienna: Universal Edition.

Kowalke, Kim H. (1979), *Kurt Weill in Europe*, Ann Arbor: UMI Research Press.

————— (1995), 'Kurt Weill, Modernism and Popular Culture: Öffentlichkeit als Stil', *Modernism/Modernity*, Vol.2 no.1, pp.27–69.

————— (ed.) (1986), *A New Orpheus: Essays on Kurt Weill*, New Haven and London: Yale University Press.

Kracauer, Siegfried (1947), *From Caligari to Hitler: A Psychological History of the German Film*, Princeton: Princeton University Press.

Kramer, Lawrence (1990), *Music as Cultural Practice, 1800–1900*, Berkeley, Los Angeles and London: University of California Press.

————— (2002), *Musical Meaning: Toward a Critical History*, Berkeley, Los Angeles and London: University of California Press.

Kravitt, Edward F. (1992), 'Romanticism Today', *Musical Quarterly*, Vol.76 no.1 (Spring), pp.93–109.

Krenek, Ernst (1925), 'Musik in der Gegenwart', in *25 Jahre neue Musik*, Vienna: Universal Edition, trans. as 'Music of Today', in Susan C. Cook (1988), *Opera for a New Republic: The* Zeitopern *of Krenek, Weill and Hindemith*, Ann Arbor: UMI Research Press, pp.193–203.

————— (1927), 'Ernst Krenek über sich und sein Werk', *Blätter der Staatsoper und der Städtischen Oper*, Vol.8 no.4 (October), pp.2–4.

————— (1927), *Jonny spielt auf: Oper in zwei Teilen*, Vienna: Universal Edition.

————— (1953), 'Self-Analysis', *New Mexico Quarterly*, Vol.23, pp.5–57.

————— (1958), *Zur sprache gebracht: Essays über Musik*, Munich: Albert Langen – Georg Müller Verlag.

————— (1964), 'A Composer's Influences', *Perspectives of New Music*, Vol.3 no.1 (Fall–Winter), pp.36–41.

————— (1965), *Prosa, Dramen, Verse*, Munich and Vienna: Albert Langen – Georg Müller Verlag.

————— (1966), *Exploring Music*, trans. Margaret Shenfield and Geoffrey Skelton, London: Calder and Boyars.

————— (1966), *Music Here and Now*, trans. Barthold Fles, New York: Russell and Russell.

—————— (1980), 'Jonny erinnert sich', *Österreichische Musikzeit-schrift*, Vol.4 no.5, pp.187–9.

—————— (1984), *Im Zweifelsfalle: Aufsätze zur Musik*, Vienna: Europa.

—————— (1998), *Im Atem der Zeit: Erinnerungen an die Moderne*, trans. Friedrich Saathen and Sabine Schulte, Hamburg: Hoffmann und Campe Verlag.

Krenek, Ernst with Will Ogdon and John L. Stewart (1974), *Horizons Circled: Reflections on My Music*, Berkeley, Los Angeles and London: University of California Press.

Kurth, Ulrich (1987), '"Ich pfeif' auf Tugend und Moral": Zum Foxtrott in den zwanziger Jahren', in Sabine Schutte (ed.), *Ich will aber gerade vom Leben singen...: Über populäre Musik vom ausgehenden 19. Jahrhundert bis zum Ende der Weimarer Republik*, Reinbek bei Hamburg: Rowohlt, pp.365–84.

Kytzler, Bernhard (1990), 'Moses und Mathis, Aaron und Palestrina. Zur Krise des kreativen Künstler [sic] im mythischen Spiegel der Moderne', in Peter Csobádi et al. (eds), *Antike Mythen im Musiktheater des 20. Jahrhunderts: Gesammelte Vorträge des Salzburger Symposions 1989*, Anif/Salzburg: Verlag Ursula Müller-Speiser, pp.195–207.

Lacan, Jacques (1977), *Écrits: A Selection*, trans. Alan Sheridan, London: Tavistock.

Laffan, Michael (ed.) (1988), *The Burden of German History 1919–1945: Essays for the Goethe Institute*, London: Methuen.

Lamb, Stephen and Phelan, Anthony (1995), 'Weimar Culture: The Birth of Modernism', in Rob Burns (ed.), *German Cultural Studies: An Introduction*, Oxford: Oxford University Press, pp.53–99.

Lange, Horst H. (1966), *Jazz in Deutschland: Die deutsche Jazz-Chronik 1900–1960*, Berlin: Colloquium Verlag.

Laqueur, Walter (1974), *Weimar: A Cultural History 1918–1933*, London: Weidenfeld and Nicolson.

Large, David C. and Weber, William (eds) (1984), *Wagnerism in European Culture and Politics*, Ithaca and London: Cornell University Press.

Larsen, Stein Ugelvik et al. (eds) (1980), *Who Were the Fascists: Social Roots of European Fascism*, Oslo: Universitetsforlaget.

Lee, M. Owen (1986), 'Pfitzner's *Palestrina*: A Musical Legend', *Opera Quarterly*, Vol.4 no.1, pp.54–60.

Le Huray, Peter and Day, James (eds) (1988), *Music and Aesthetics in the Eighteenth and Early-Nineteenth Centuries*, abridged edition, Cambridge: Cambridge University Press.

Leichtentritt, Hugo (1926), 'Die deutsche Opernbühne und der künstlerische Nachwuchs', *Anbruch*, Vol.8 no.5, pp.217–20.

—————— (1926), 'Konzertierende Künstler und zeitgenössische Musik',
Anbruch, Vol.8 no.6, pp.277–9.

Lenman, Robin, Osborne, John and Sagarra, Eda (1995), 'Imperial Ger-
many: Towards the Commercialization of Culture', in Rob Burns (ed.),
German Cultural Studies: An Introduction, Oxford: Oxford University
Press, pp.9–52.

Le Rider, Jacques (1993), *Modernity and Crises of Identity: Culture and
Society in Fin-de-Siècle Vienna*, trans. Rosemary Morris, Cambridge:
Polity Press.

Levi, Erik (1994), *Music in the Third Reich*, London: Macmillan.

Levin, David J. (2001), '"Father Knows Best": Paternity and Mise-en-
Scène in Hans Pfitzner's *Palestrina*', *Musical Quarterly*, Vol.85 no.1
(Spring), pp.168–82.

Longyear, Rey M. (1988), *Nineteenth-century Romanticism in Music*,
Englewood Cliffs, NJ.: Prentice Hall.

Mainka, Jürgen (1984): 'Von innerer zu äußerer Emigration. Eine Szene in
Paul Hindemiths Oper *Mathis der Maler*', in Hanns-Werner Heister and
Hans-Günter Klein (eds), *Musik und Musikpolitik im faschistischen
Deutschland*, Frankfurt a.M.: Taschenbuch Verlag, pp.265–72.

Malmgren, C.D. (1987), '"From Work to Text". The Modernist and Postmodernist Künstlerroman', *Novel – A Forum on Fiction*, Vol.21 no.1,
pp.5–28.

Mann, Thomas (1956), *Betrachtungen eines Unpolitischen*, Frankfurt a.M.:
S. Fischer Verlag.

Mann, Thomas (1983), *Reflections of a Nonpolitical Man*, trans. and intro.
Walter D. Morris, New York: Frederick Ungar Publishing.

Marcuse, Herbert (1978), 'Der deutsche Künstlerroman', in *Schriften*,
Vol.1, Frankfurt a.M.: Suhrkamp Verlag, pp.7–344.

Mattl, Siegfried (2001), 'Metapolitics and the Avant-Garde', *Musical
Quarterly*, Vol.85 no.1 (Spring), pp.184–93.

McClary, Susan (1991), *Feminine Endings: Music, Gender and Sexuality*,
Minneapolis: University of Minnesota Press.

Metzger, Heinz-Klaus and Riehn, Rainer (eds) (1984), *Ernst Krenek*,
Munich: edition text + kritik.

Meyer, Michael (1991), *The Politics of Music in the Third Reich*, New

York: Peter Lang.

Miller, Daniel (1987), *Material Culture and Mass Consumption*, Oxford: Basil Blackwell.

Mitchell, Donald (1955), 'Hindemith and the History of a Term', *Musical Opinion*, Vol.79 (Dec.), p.163.

Molkow, Wolfgang (1980), 'Der Sprung über den Schatten. Zum Opern-schaffen Ernst Kreneks in den 20er und 30er Jahren', *Musica*, Vol.34 no.2, pp.132–5.

———— (1989), 'Die Rolle der Kunst in den frühen Opern Franz Schrekers', *Österreichische Musikzeitschrift*, Vol.44 no.5, pp.219–28.

Mosse, George L. (1964), *The Crisis of German Ideology: Intellectual Origins of the Third Reich*, London: Weidenfeld and Nicolson.

Müller-Blattau, Joseph (1969), *Hans Pfitzner: Lebensweg und Schaffens-ernte*, Frankfurt a.M.: Waldemar Kramer.

Neumeyer, David (1986), *The Music of Paul Hindemith*, New Haven: Yale University Press.

Newsom, Jon (1974), 'Hans Pfitzner, Thomas Mann and "The Magic Mountain"', *Music and Letters*, Vol.55 no.2, pp.136–50.

Nicholls, A.J. (1981), 'Germany', in S.J. Woolf (ed.), *Fascism in Europe*, London and New York: Methuen, pp.65–91.

Osthoff, Wolfgang (ed.) (1984), *Symposium Hans Pfitzner, Berlin 1981*, Tutzing: Hans Schneider.

Painter, Karen (2001), 'Symphonic Ambitions, Operatic Redemption: *Mathis der Maler* and *Palestrina* in the Third Reich', *Musical Quarterly*, Vol.85 no.1 (Spring), pp.117–66.

Passant, E.J., with Henderson, W.O., Child, C.J., and Watt, D.C. (1962), *A Short History of Germany 1815–1945*, Cambridge: Cambridge University Press.

Passchier, Nico (1980), 'The Electoral Geography of the Nazi Landslide. The Need for Community Studies', in Stein Ugelvik Larsen et al. (eds), *Who Were the Fascists: Social Roots of European Fascism*, Oslo: Universitetsforlaget, pp. 283–300.

Paulding, James E. (1976), '*Mathis der Maler*: The Politics of Music', *Hindemith Jahrbuch*, Vol.5, pp.102–22.

Perle, George (1993), 'Standortbestimmung', *Österreichische Musikzeit-schrift*, Vol.48 no.3–4, pp.152–60.

Peukert, Detlev J.K. (1991), *The Weimar Republic: The Crisis of Classical Modernity*, trans. Richard Deveson, London: Penguin.

Pfitzner, Hans (1926), 'Futuristengefahr', in *Gesammelte Schriften*, Vol.1, Augsburg: Dr. Benno Filser-Verlag, pp.185–223.

————— (1926), *Gesammelte Schriften*, Vol.1, Augsburg: Dr. Benno Filser-Verlag.

————— (1926), 'Die neue Ästhetik der musikalischen Impotenz', in *Gesammelte Schriften*, Vol.2, Augsburg: Dr. Benno Filser-Verlag, pp.101–252.

————— (1926), 'Zur Grundfrage der Operndichtung', in *Gesammelte Schriften*, Vol.2, Augsburg: Dr. Benno Filser-Verlag, pp.7–97.

————— (1926), *Gesammelte Schriften*, Vol.2, Augsburg: Dr. Benno Filser-Verlag.

————— (1951), *Palestrina: Musical Legend in 3 Acts*, London: Ernst Eulenberg Ltd.

————— (1955), 'Palestrina. Ein Vortrag über das Werk und seine Geschichte', in *Reden, Schriften, Briefe*, ed. Walter Abendroth, Berlin: Hermann Luchterhand, pp.23–34.

————— (1955), *Reden, Schriften, Briefe*, ed. Walter Abendroth, Berlin: Hermann Luchterhand.

————— (1987), 'Eindrücke und Bilder meines Lebens', in *Sämtliche Schriften*, Vol.4, ed. Bernhard Adamy, Tutzing: Hans Schneider, pp.556–692.

————— (1987), 'Über musikalische Inspiration', in *Sämtliche Schriften*, Vol.4, ed. Bernhard Adamy, Tutzing: Hans Schneider, pp.269–307.

————— (1987), *Sämtliche Schriften*, Vol.4, ed. Bernhard Adamy, Tutzing: Hans Schneider.

————— (1991), *Briefe*, Vol.1, ed. Bernhard Adamy, Tutzing: Hans Schneider.

Pisk, Paul A. (1927), 'Das neue Publikum', *Anbruch*, Vol.9 no.1–2, p.94.

Potter, Pamela M. (1996), 'Musicology under Hitler: New Sources in Context', *Journal of the American Musicological Society*, Vol.49 no.1 (Spring), pp.70–113.

————— (1998), *Most German of the Arts: Musicology and Society from the Weimar Republic to the End of Hitler's Reich*, New Haven and London: Yale University Press.

Ragland-Sullivan, Ellie (1986), *Jacques Lacan and the Philosophy of Psychoanalysis*, London and Canberra: Croom Helm.

Raynor, Henry (1976), *Music and Society since 1815*, London: Barrie and

Jenkins.

Rectanus, Hans (1967), *Leitmotivik und Form in den musikdramatischen Werken Hans Pfitzners*, Würzburg: Konrad Triltsch Verlag.

Redlich, Hans F. (1964), 'Paul Hindemith: a Re-assessment', *Music Review*, Vol.25, pp.241–53.

Reschke, Claus and Pollack, Howard (eds) (1992), *German Literature and Music: An Aesthetic Fusion, 1890–1989*, Houston German Studies, Munich: Wilhelm Fink Verlag.

Rexroth, Dieter (1973), 'Von der moralischen Verantwortung des Künstlers: Zu den großen Opern von Paul Hindemith', *Hindemith Jahrbuch*, Vol.3, pp.63–79.

————— (1980), 'Einige Voraussetzungen der "Gebrauchsmusik" bei Hindemith', *Musica*, Vol.34 no.6, pp.546–9.

————— (ed.) (1978), *Erprobungen und Erfahrungen: Zu Paul Hindemith's Schaffen in den Zwanziger Jahren*, Mainz: Schott.

Rickards, Guy (1995), *Hindemith, Hartmann and Henze*, London: Phaidon Press.

Ridley, Hugh (1988), 'The Culture of Weimar: Models of Decline', in Michael Laffan (ed.), *The Burden of German History 1919–1945: Essays for the Goethe Institute*, London: Methuen, pp.11–30.

Ringer, Alexander L. (1975), 'Dance on a Volcano: Notes on Musical Satire and Parody in Weimar Germany', *Comparative Literature Studies*, Vol.13 no.3, pp.248–59.

Rink, John (2002) 'The Profession of Music', in Jim Samson (ed.), *The Cambridge History of Nineteenth-Century Music*, Cambridge: Cambridge University Press, pp.55–86.

Ritzel, Fred (1987), '"Hätte der Kaiser Jazz getanzt...". US-Tanzmusik in Deutschland vor und nach dem Ersten Weltkrieg', in Sabine Schutte (ed.), *Ich will aber gerade vom Leben singen...: Über populäre Musik vom ausgehenden 19. Jahrhundert bis zum Ende der Weimarer Republik*, Reinbek bei Hamburg: Rowohlt, pp.265–93.

Robinson, J. Bradford (1994), 'Jazz Reception in Weimar Germany: In Search of a Shimmy Figure', in Bryan Gilliam (ed.), *Music and Performance during the Weimar Republic*, Cambridge Studies in Performance Practice 3, Cambridge: Cambridge University Press, pp.107–34.

Rockwell, John (1986), 'Kurt Weill's Operatic Reform and Its Context', in Kim H. Kowalke (ed.), *A New Orpheus: Essays on Kurt Weill*, New Haven and London: Yale University Press, pp.51–9.

Rogge, Wolfgang (1970), *Ernst Kreneks Opern: Spiegel der zwanziger Jahre*, Wolfenbüttel and Zürich: Möseler Verlag.

————— (1980), 'Oper als Quadratur des Kreises: zum Opernschaffen Ernst Kreneks', *Österreichische Musikzeitschrift*, Vol.34 (September), pp.453–7.

Röhl, J.C.G. (1970), *From Bismarck to Hitler: The Problem of Continuity in German History*, London: Longman.

Rösing, Helmut (ed.) (1995), *'Es liegt in der Luft was Idiotisches...': Populäre Musik zur Zeit der Weimarer Republik*, Baden-Baden: Coda.

Royal Opera House (1995): Programme for *Mathis der Maler*, Nov.–Dec. 1995, London: Royal Opera House Publications.

Royal Opera House (1997): Programme for *Palestrina*, Jan.–Feb. 1997, London: Royal Opera House Publications.

Sachs, Joel (1970), 'Some Aspects of Musical Politics in pre-Nazi Germany', *Perspectives of New Music*, Vol.9 no.1 (Fall–Winter), pp.74–95.

Sadie, Stanley (ed.) (1980), *The New Grove Dictionary of Music and Musicians*, London: Macmillan.

Samson, Jim (2002), 'The Great Composer', in Jim Samson (ed.), *The Cambridge History of Nineteenth-Century Music*, Cambridge: Cambridge University Press, pp.259–84.

————— (ed.) (1991), *The Late Romantic Era: From the mid-19th Century to World War I*, London: Macmillan.

————— (ed.) (2002), *The Cambridge History of Nineteenth-Century Music*, Cambridge: Cambridge University Press.

Sanders, Ronald (1980), *The Days grew Short: The Life and Music of Kurt Weill*, New York: Holt, Rinehart and Winston.

Schaal, Susanne and Schader, Luitgard (eds) (1996), *Über Hindemith: Aufsätze zu Werk, Ästhetik und Interpretation*, Mainz: Schott.

Schmidt, Jochen (1988), *Die Geschichte des Genie-Gedankens in der deutschen Literatur, Philosophie und Politik, 1750–1945*, Darmstadt: Wissenschaftliche Buchgesellschaft.

Schmidt, Matthias (ed.) (2000), *Ernst Krenek: Zeitgenosse des 20. Jahrhunderts / Companion of the Twentieth Century*, Vienna: Wiener Stadt- und Landesbibliothek.

Schoenberg, Arnold (1964), *Letters*, ed. Erwin Stein, trans. Eithne Wilkins and Ernst Kaiser, London: Faber and Faber.

————— (1975), *Style and Idea: Selected Writings of Arnold Schoenberg*, ed. Leonard Stein, trans. Leo Black, London: Faber and Faber.

Scholz, Gottfried (2001), 'The Image of Giovanni Pierluigi da Palestrina in Pfitzner's *Palestrina*', *Musical Quarterly*, Vol.85 no.1 (Spring), pp.76–83.

Schopenhauer, Arthur (1909), *The World as Will and Idea*, Vol.3, trans. R.B. Haldane and J. Kemp, Sixth Edition, London: Kegan Paul, Trench, Trübner and Co. Ltd.

——— (1974), *Parerga and Paralipomena: Short Philosophical Essays*, Vol.1, trans. E.F.J. Payne, Oxford: Clarendon Press.

Schreker-Bures, H., Stuckenschmidt, H.H. and Oehlmann, W. (1970), *Franz Schreker*, Vienna: Verlag Elisabeth Lafite.

Schubert, Bernhard (1983), 'Wagners "Sachs" und die Tradition des romantischen Künstlerselbstverständnisses', *Archiv für Musikwissenschaft*, Vol.40 no.3, pp.212–53.

——— (1986), *Der Künstler als Handwerker: zur Literaturgeschichte einer romantischen Utopie*, Königstein: Athenäum Verlag.

Schubert, Giselher (1970), 'Aspekte der Bekkerschen Musiksoziologie', *International Review of Music Aesthetics and Sociology*, Vol.1 no.2, pp.179–86.

——— (1981), *Paul Hindemith: Mit Selbstzeugnissen und Bilddokumenten*, Reinbek bei Hamburg: Rowohlt.

——— (ed.) (1997), *Biographische Konstellation und künstlerisches Handeln*, Frankfurter Studien: Veröffentlichungen des Paul-Hindemith-Instituts Frankfurt/Main, Vol. 6, Mainz: Schott.

Schulte, Hans H. and Chapple, Gerald (eds) (1978), *Thomas Mann: Ein Kolloquium*, Bonn: Bouvier Verlag Herbert Grundmann.

Schutte, Sabine (ed.) (1987), *Ich will aber gerade vom Leben singen...: Über populäre Musik vom ausgehenden 19. Jahrhundert bis zum Ende der Weimarer Republik*, Reinbek bei Hamburg: Rowohlt.

Seebohm, Reinhard (1974), 'Triumph und Tragik des Künstlertums: die Stellung von Pfitzners "Palestrina" in der Geschichte des deutschen Künstlerdramas', *Pfitzner*, Vol.32 (April), pp.10–35.

Skelton, Geoffrey (1975), *Paul Hindemith: The Man Behind the Music*, London: Victor Gollancz.

——— (1995): 'One Person's Response', in Royal Opera House Programme for *Mathis der Maler*, Nov.–Dec. 1995, London: Royal Opera House Publications, pp.11–15.

Smart, Mary Ann (ed.) (2000), *Siren Songs: Representations of Gender and Sexuality in Opera*, Princeton: Princeton University Press.

Solie, Ruth A. (1988), 'Beethoven as Secular Humanist: Ideology and the Ninth Symphony in Nineteenth-Century Criticism', in Eugene Narmour and Ruth A. Solie (eds), *Explorations in Music, the Arts and Ideas*, New York: Pendragon Press, pp.1-42.

Specht, R. John (1987), 'Schoenberg Among the Workers: Choral Conducting in pre-1900 Vienna', *Journal of the Arnold Schoenberg Institute*, Vol.10 no.1, pp.28–37.

Spitta, Phillip (1894), 'Palestrina im sechzehnten und neunzehnten Jahrhundert', *Deutsche Rundschau*, Vol.79, pp.74–95.

Steinberg, Michael P. (2001), 'Opera and Cultural Analysis: The Case of Hans Pfitzner's *Palestrina*', *Musical Quarterly*, Vol.85 no.1 (Spring), pp.53–62.

Stern, Dietrich (ed.) (1977), *Angewandte Musik 20er Jahre: Exemplarische Versuche gesellschaftsbezogener musikalischer Arbeit für Theater, Film, Radio, Massenveranstaltung*, Berlin: Argument-Verlag.

Stewart, John L. (1991), *Ernst Krenek: The Man and His Music*, Berkeley, Los Angeles and Oxford: University of California Press.

Sullivan, Jack (1999), *New World Symphonies: How American Culture Changed European Music*, New Haven: Yale University Press.

Tambling, Jeremy (1996), *Opera and the Culture of Fascism*, Oxford: Clarendon Press.

Tanner, Michael (1996), *Wagner*, London: HarperCollins.

Taylor, Simon (1983), *Germany 1918–1933: Revolution, Counter-revolution and the Rise of Hitler*, London: Duckworth.

Tennant, Anne (1995), 'Painter as Healer', in Royal Opera House Programme for *Mathis der Maler*, Nov.–Dec. 1995, London: Royal Opera House Publications, pp. 31–7.

Theilacker, Jörg (1988), *Der erzählende Musiker: Untersuchung von Musikererzählungen des 19. Jahrhunderts und ihrer Bezüge zur Entstehung der deutscher Nationalmusik, mit einer Bibliografie der Musikererzählungen des Zeitraums 1797 bis 1884*, Frankfurt a.M.: Verlag Peter Lang.

Tregear, Peter John (1999), *Ernst Krenek and the Politics of Musical Style*, University of Cambridge, Ph.D. dissertation.

Toller, Owen (1997), *Pfitzner's* Palestrina: *The 'Musical Legend' and its Background*, Exeter: Toccata Press.

Ursprung, Otto (1926), *Palestrina und Deutschland*, in Karl Weinmann, (ed.), *Festschrift Peter Wagner zum 60. Geburtstag*, Leipzig: Breitkopf und Härtel.

Vogel, Johann Peter (1989), *Hans Pfitzner: Mit Selbstzeugnissen und Bild-dokumenten*, Reinbek bei Hamburg: Rowohlt.

Wagner, Gottfried (1977), *Weill und Brecht: Das musikalische Zeittheater*, Munich: Kindler Verlag.

Wallace, Robin (1986), *Beethoven's Critics: Aesthetic Dilemmas and Resolutions during the Composer's Lifetime*, Cambridge: Cambridge University Press.

Walter, Michael (1995), *Hitler in der Oper: Deutsches Musikleben 1919–1945*, Stuttgart and Weimar: Verlag J.B. Metzler.

Waugh, Patricia (1984), *Metafiction: The Theory and Practice of Self-Conscious Fiction*, London and New York: Methuen.

Weber, William (1984), 'Wagner, Wagnerism, and Musical Idealism', in David C. Large and William Weber (eds), *Wagnerism in European Culture and Politics*, Ithaca and London: Cornell University Press, pp.28–71.

Webern, Anton (1963), *The Path to the New Music*, ed. Willi Reich, London: Universal Edition.

Wehler, Hans-Ulrich (1985), *The German Empire 1871–1918*, trans. Kim Traynor, Providence and Oxford: Berg.

Weill, Kurt (1979), 'Tanzmusik', *Der deutsche Rundfunk*, 14th March 1926, trans. as 'Dance Music' in Kim H. Kowalke, *Kurt Weill in Europe*, Ann Arbor: UMI Research Press, pp.473–5.

——————— (1979), 'Verschiebungen in der musikalischen Produktion', *Berliner Tageblatt*, 1st October 1927, trans. as 'Shifts in Musical Composition' in Kim H. Kowalke, *Kurt Weill in Europe*, Ann Arbor: UMI Research Press, pp.478–81.

——————— (1979), 'Gesellschaftsbildende Oper', *Berliner Börsen-Courier*, 19th February 1929, trans. as 'Socially-Creative Opera' in Kim H. Kowalke, *Kurt Weill in Europe*, Ann Arbor: UMI Research Press, pp.489–90.

——————— (1990): 'Die Stellung des Rundfunks innerhalb des Musiklebens', *Der deutsche Rundfunk*, 21st June 1925, in *Musik und Theater: Gesammelte Schriften. Mit einer Auswahl von Gesprächen und Interviews*, ed. Stephen Hinton and Jürgen Schebera, Berlin: Henschelverlag Kunst und Gesellschaft, pp.190–91.

——————— (1990), 'Fort vom Durchschnitt! Zur Krise der musikalischen Interpretation', *Berliner Börsen-Courier*, 29th August 1925, in *Musik und Theater: Gesammelte Schriften. Mit einer Auswahl von Gesprächen und Interviews*, ed. Stephen Hinton and Jürgen Schebera, Berlin: Henschelverlag Kunst und Gesellschaft, pp.22–5.

————— (1990), 'Der Rundfunk und die Umschichtung des Musik-lebens', *Der deutsche Rundfunk*, 13th June 1926, in *Musik und Theater: Gesammelte Schriften. Mit einer Auswahl von Gesprächen und Inter-views*, ed. Stephen Hinton and Jürgen Schebera, Berlin: Henschelverlag Kunst und Gesellschaft, pp.221–3.

————— (1990), 'Musikalische Illustration oder Filmmusik?', *Film-Kurier*, 13th October 1927, in *Musik und Theater: Gesammelte Schriften. Mit einer Auswahl von Gesprächen und Interviews*, ed. Stephen Hinton and Jürgen Schebera, Berlin: Henschelverlag Kunst und Gesellschaft, pp.297–9.

————— (1990), *Musik und Theater: Gesammelte Schriften. Mit einer Auswahl von Gesprächen und Interviews*, ed. Stephen Hinton and Jürgen Schebera, Berlin: Henschelverlag Kunst und Gesellschaft.

Weiner, Marc A. (1993), *Undertones of Insurrection: Music, Politics and the Social Sphere in the Modern German Narrative*, Lincoln: University of Nebraska Press.

Weinmann, Karl (ed.) (1926), *Festschrift Peter Wagner zum 60. Geburts-tag*, Leipzig: Breitkopf und Härtel.

Weisstein, Ulrich (1992), 'Die letzte Häutung. Two German *Künstleropern* of the Twentieth Century: Hans Pfitzner's *Palestrina* and Paul Hinde-mith's *Mathis der Maler*' in Claus Reschke and Howard Pollack (eds), *German Literature and Music: An Aesthetic Fusion, 1890–1989*, Hous-ton German Studies, Munich: Wilhelm Fink Verlag, pp.193–236.

Wellesz, Egon (1922), 'Der Musiker und diese Zeit', *Anbruch*, Vol.4 no.1–2, pp.3–4.

————— (1924), 'Probleme der modernen Musik', *Anbruch*, Vol.6 no.10, pp.392–402.

Will, Wilfried van der (1995), 'Culture and the Organization of National Socialist Ideology 1933 to 1945', in Rob Burns (ed.), *German Cultural Studies: An Introduction*, Oxford: Oxford University Press, pp.104–45.

Willett, John (1978), *The New Sobriety 1917–1933: Art and Politics in the Weimar Period*, London: Thames and Hudson.

Williamson, John (1992), *The Music of Hans Pfitzner*, Oxford: Clarendon Press.

————— (2002), 'Progress, Modernity and the Concept of an Avant-

Garde', in Jim Samson (ed.), *The Cambridge History of Nineteenth-Century Music*, Cambridge: Cambridge University Press, pp.287–317.

Witkin, Robert W. (1998), *Adorno on Music*, London and New York: Routledge.

Wöhlke, Franz (1965), Mathis der Maler *von Paul Hindemith*, Berlin: Robert Lienau.

Woltmann, Ludwig (1905), *Die Germanen und die Renaissance in Italien*, Leipzig: Thüringische Verlagsanstalt.

Woolf, S.J. (ed.) (1981), *Fascism in Europe*, London and New York: Methuen.

Wulf, Joseph (1983), *Musik im Dritten Reich: Eine Dokumentation*, Frankfurt a.M.: Ullstein.

Zenck, Claudia Maurer (1980), 'Zwischen Boykott und Anpassung an den Charakter der Zeit. Über die Schwierigkeiten eines deutschen Komponisten mit dem Dritten Reich', *Hindemith Jahrbuch*, Vol.9, pp.65–129.

———————— (1980), *Ernst Krenek: Ein Komponist im Exil,* Vienna: Lafite.

———————— (1985), 'The Ship Loaded with Faith and Hope: Krenek's "Karl V" and the Viennese Politics of the Thirties', *Musical Quarterly*, Vol.71 no.2, pp.116–34.

Zwink, Eberhard (1974), *Paul Hindemiths 'Unterweisung im Tonsatz' als Konsequenz der Entwicklung seiner Kompositionstechnik*, Göppingen: Kümmerle.

Index